Advance Praise for

The Internet Audience

"Fernando Bermejo's book makes an impressive and much-needed contribution to the development of institutionalist analyses of information media. His focus on the self-interested construction of Internet audiences through an extremely limited system of measurement and assessment helps us to understand how the development of this medium has been constrained by a concern with commoditization, rather than enablement. His is an informed analysis. Readers will benefit from the great detail and extensive documentation that Bermejo provides to support his conclusions about the nature of this deeply flawed process of social construction."

Oscar H. Gandy Jr., Emeritus Professor of Communication, Annenberg School for Communication, University of Pennsylvania

"*The Internet Audience* helps fill not just a gap, but a gaping hole, in audience research literature. Fernando Bermejo's analysis of the development of the Internet audience is exceptionally well contextualized within the broader institutional and technological development of the Internet, as well as within the broader literature on media institutions and audiences. This book expertly depicts the intertwining of the medium and its measurement at the theoretical, economic, and institutional levels."

Philip Napoli, Associate Professor, Graduate School of Business; Director, Donald McGannon Communication Research Center, Fordham University

The Internet Audience

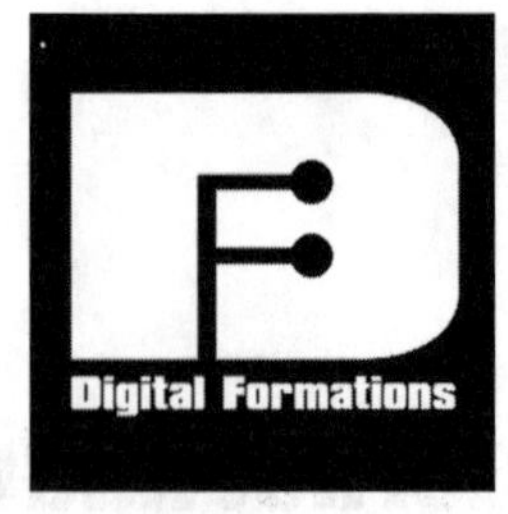

Steve Jones
General Editor

Vol. 35

PETER LANG
New York • Washington, D.C./Baltimore • Bern
Frankfurt am Main • Berlin • Brussels • Vienna • Oxford

Fernando Bermejo

The Internet Audience

Constitution & Measurement

PETER LANG
New York • Washington, D.C./Baltimore • Bern
Frankfurt am Main • Berlin • Brussels • Vienna • Oxford

Library of Congress Cataloging-in-Publication Data

Bermejo, Fernando.
The Internet audience: constitution and measurement / Fernando Bermejo.
p. cm. — (Digital formations; v. 35)
Includes bibliographical references.
1. Internet users—Statistics. 2. Mass media—Audiences—Statistics. I. Title.
ZA4235.B47   302.23'1—dc22   2006022450
ISBN 978-0-8204-7932-3
ISSN 1526-3169

Bibliographic information published by **Die Deutsche Bibliothek**.
Die Deutsche Bibliothek lists this publication in the "Deutsche
Nationalbibliografie"; detailed bibliographic data is available
on the Internet at http://dnb.ddb.de/.

Cover design by Lisa Barfield

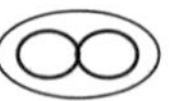

To Smriti and Nil

Table of Contents

Section IV: The Audience Measurement Industry **173**

Conclusions **219**

Acknowledgments

After finishing a book, one realizes that it is the crystallization of a long series of experiences, teachings, conversations, readings, encounters, and discussions. It would be impossible for me to recount all those who have helped me along the way, but I would like at least to mention some of the people most directly involved in the process that led to the completion of this book.

Years ago, when I had just moved from the United States to Spain and was considering returning to academia, Angel Badillo invited me to participate in a conference he was organizing on audience research. He knew I had been doing market research for Internet companies for several years, and he asked me to prepare a presentation on Internet audience measurement. That presentation made me realize that the topic deserved a thorough investigation, and it became the starting point for this book. I have to thank Angel for that invitation and, especially, for many years of friendship and support.

When I decided to go back to academia, the Universidad Rey Juan Carlos offered me the space to develop my work. It was Enric Saperas who created the right environment for that work to flourish. I am particularly thankful for his encouragement and his appreciation of true scholarship.

My first attempt at carrying out a full-scale investigation of the Internet audience and its measurement was my dissertation. Amparo Huertas, at the Universitat Autònoma de Barcelona, skillfully supervised that dissertation and made me rethink what I wanted to accomplish. The final structure of my work owes much to her advice.

While I was writing my dissertation I had the privilege of meeting Carlos Lamas, and he became a constant source of ideas, readings, and updates on the Internet audience measurement industry and on the methods it uses. His generosity, his passion for the issues I was studying, and his quick intelligence inspired me to pursue my goal.

Once my dissertation was complete, I thought I had something that could be of interest to a wider audience. No one in Spain, however, seemed ready to consider it. I was at a loss for a way forward, and David Park came to the rescue and pointed me in the right direction. He also read parts of my work and made invaluable comments to help me turn a dissertation in Spanish into a book in English. I am immensely thankful for this, but it is his friendship which I treasure as one of the most valuable gifts I received during my years in America.

Oscar Gandy also read parts of my then manuscript, and he pointed out some mistakes and omissions, while reassuring me I was on the right track. That reassurance meant a lot to me, since he had introduced me years before to many of the ideas that shape this book.

When Steve Jones, editor of this series, learned about my work he was so enthusiastic and supportive that I still find it hard to express how grateful I am. He has encouraged me, he has been there all the way through, he has generously corresponded with me, all with a smile and while attending a million other duties. People like Steve make academia a wonderful place to be.

At Peter Lang, Damon Zucca was what I had always dreamt an editor would be, helpful, patient, knowledgeable, and kind. Brittany Schwartz skillfully helped me navigate the production process, and she made it easier and more enjoyable than I could have ever imagined.

All along I have been privileged with the companionship of a wonderful network of friends and family. They all know how much they mean to me. Still, I would like to mention what an immense source of love and support my parents have always been. And I would like to especially thank Smriti and Nil, not just for her constant help and his healthy distractions, but for filling my life with joy.

Introduction

Communication research needs constantly to examine the evolution of the media world and the theories and concepts it uses to describe that world. This is the case because its field of study is constantly changing and, therefore, its theories and concepts have to adjust to those changes. But it is also because of the reflexive nature of any discipline that deals with social and human issues. The theories and concepts used to describe society and communication re-enter their object of study and contribute to changing it. It could be said that they have both a descriptive and a transformative facet. This transformative power means that the very description of the media world can contribute to changing that world, requiring further description of this new state. Also, for researchers, it means that they need to be extremely vigilant with the tools they apply, the theories they formulate, and the concepts they use.

If communication researchers need to pay attention to the transformations of the media, then it seems impossible to avoid studying the Internet. The popularization of the Internet and the advent of the World Wide Web are perhaps the most far reaching transformation that the media world has undergone in decades. The impact of the Internet and of the tools associated with it, their capacity to transform communication processes at all levels, from the global to the local, and from the personal to the massive, make it necessary for communication researchers to carefully examine this complex and constantly evolving phenomenon. Furthermore, it is not only necessary to pay attention to it because of what it is today or what it has meant in recent years—which is plenty—but also because of what it might become, since to a certain extent the Internet seems to embody the defining characteristics of the media of the future.

The Internet is an extremely rich and complex phenomenon, and it can, therefore, be studied in many different ways and in many of its multiple facets. In this book, the idea of the audience has been chosen as the point of entry. The concept of the audience has been from the start of communication research a fundamental pillar that has guided a significant amount of inquiry. It is a concept that emerged from face-to-face communication and referred to the individual activity of hearing. By extension, it was applied to groups of people who gather to listen. That speech situation, in turn, became the model for mediated communication and the word 'audience' was then applied to the people who pay attention to any communication medium. Applying a concept from the field of speech communication to the field of media means stretching its meaning to include new phenomena within it. However, this stretching has become naturalized, and there seems to be no problem when we apply the word 'audience' to situations other than those covered by its original meaning. It is possible to wonder whether we can extend the meaning of the word 'audience' even further in order to include within it the individuals who use the Internet. Does it make sense to use the concept of the audience to refer to the new media environment or should we rather discard it and use other concepts to talk about the people who inhabit it?

To a great extent, I think the decision is arbitrary. We can choose to restrict its meaning to refer only to those communication media that existed before the advent of the Internet. Or we can make its meaning a little more complex and use it to refer to the people who access any communication media, including the Internet. I will not argue here one way or the other. My goal is to contribute to the understanding of the Internet by using the idea of the audience as a lens through which to examine it and in the process, contribute to examine the field of application of the term 'audience.' Thus, through the course of this book I hope to offer new insights about the nature of the Internet as a communication medium and offer new arguments for the discussions regarding the applicability and usefulness of the 'audience' concept.

Even though the decision to examine the Internet through the concept of the audience already means a certain reduction of such a complex phenomenon as the Internet, it is still necessary to choose a perspective to examine our object of study. Audiences can be studied in many different ways, although most current work on media audiences deals with issues of uses and interpretation. For the purpose of this book, however, I have chosen an institutional perspective, in which the focus is not on what the audience does with the media, but rather on what the media as institutions do with the audience.

The audience is an intangible and elusive entity. However, it is clear the media depend on the existence of an audience for their own existence, both in ontological terms (there is no medium without an audience) and in economic terms (the audience is an essential commodity for the functioning of the media system). In order for the audience to become an institutional reality certain conditions need to be present. But the process of constitution of the audience is only culminated, from an institutional point of view, through its study and its measurement. That is why the media have developed a system for the observation, the measurement, and the cataloguing of the audiences. It is a system that has been consolidated throughout, at the least, eight decades of practice. Over the past decade, procedures similar to the ones developed for previous mass media have been developed for measuring the Internet audience. The process of developing these procedures, their variety and quantity, the involvement of advertisers, media companies and professionals in the process, and the efforts and resources devoted to it, all point to a significant interest in measuring the Internet audience, in giving that audience an institutional reality.

Since measurement confers reality to such an elusive phenomenon as the audience, and since the audience constitutes an essential element for the definition of any communication medium, the analysis of audience measurement leads in the end to a study of the Internet itself as a communication medium. The truth is that the status of the Internet as a communication medium is still rather undefined, perhaps due to the youth of the medium, but most probably due to its very complexity. I hope that the analysis of Internet audience measurement will help us illuminate some of the characteristics of the medium and some of the issues surrounding the appropriateness of the application of the 'audience' concept to the Internet, its meaning, its limits, and its heuristic capacity.

Therefore, the goal of this book is to examine the procedures for measuring the Internet audience, to define the institutional environment in which they appear, to analyze their possibilities and limitations, and to mark their main evolutionary lines. I will be presenting a short history of the Internet, but this is not a history book. I will be describing in detail the different methods used for measuring the Internet audience, but this is not a book about how to measure the audience. I will be analyzing the evolution of the Internet audience measurement industry, but this is not a report on industry dynamics. All these will serve as a way of carrying out an analysis of the Internet as a communication medium, of its place within the media system, of its peculiarities and similarities compared to other mass media, and, at the same time, this analysis will help us evaluate the appropriateness of some of the tools and some of the concepts we use to define and study the communication media.

With such a complex and dynamic topic as the Internet, it is impossible to exhaust all information sources, since they are too numerous and they change very rapidly. In that respect, I have tried to use the most up-to-date sources on the issues being examined, but obviously I have been selective regarding the sources, and I have privileged some specific ones, which I describe at the end of Section I. In addition, the Internet is a markedly global phenomenon. When studying the audience of other media, it is relatively simple, and even sensible, to restrict the reach of the research to a single country. In the case of the Internet, however, that restriction becomes much more difficult, and it might only be performed at the expense of generating a highly artificial and limited object of study, abstracted from its context and its history. On the other hand, trying to study a phenomenon as complex as the Internet on a global scale is a futile task. That is why I have chosen to focus on the United States, since it is there that the economic, technological, and cultural epicentre of the Internet lies. However, and whenever possible, I have also paid attention to developments regarding the Internet audience taking place in Europe.

In order to structure the analysis of the Internet audience, this book has been divided into four sections. Section I sets the context, perspective, and structure of the book. In particular, Chapter 1 presents a review of the literature on the Internet audience in order to place the book in context. This chapter also introduces the general perspective that will inform the rest of the book, that is the institutional perspective. Chapter 2 presents and explains the three axes that, taken from the institutional perspective on the study of audiences, structure the remainder of the book. The first of these axes deals with the issue of the audience as a commodity and of its constitution through measurement. The second axis revolves around the methods used for measuring the audience. And the third axis deals with the logics, dynamics, and strategies of the audience measurement industry. Each of the three remaining sections of the book examines one of these axes and applies it to the study of the Internet audience. Section I ends with some specifics regarding the information sources and the structure of the book.

Section II analyzes the constitution of the Internet audience and its final transformation, through measurement, into a commodity. Chapter 3 tries to put that process in context by sketching a brief history of the Internet. Chapter 4 examines the conditions that enable the constitution of the audience. In particular, the issue of asymmetry in online communication and the processes of popularization and commercialization of the Internet are analyzed in detail as necessary elements for the manufacturing of the Internet audience. The birth of Internet audience measurement, and its functions, is then examined as the fourth element leading to the constitution of the Internet audience.

Section III centers on the methods used to measure the audience of the World Wide Web, since, as it will be shown in Section II, it is in the web where the constitution of the Internet audience takes place. Chapter 5 discusses some of the general traits of the World Wide Web that might have an impact on the methods used to measure its audience and analyzes some peculiarities of web advertising. The chapter finishes with a classification of the methods used to measure the web audience. The subsequent three chapters analyze in detail each of the three types of methods: Chapter 6 deals with passive methods, Chapter 7 centers on active methods, and Chapter 8 examines mixed methods. Section III ends with a summary of the limits and possibilities of each of the three types of methods and with a discussion of the latest trends in this area.

Section IV analyzes the evolution of the Internet audience measurement industry. Chapter 9 reviews the logic and dynamics of the audience measurement industry and examines the role of media, advertisers, and agencies in the evolution of the Internet audience measurement industry toward a standardized measurement source. Chapter 10 reviews the role and the strategies followed by those organizations in charge of embodying the measurement standard, that is, the measuring organizations.

The book ends with some final conclusions that try to go beyond what has been discussed in the previous chapters. All in all, the book aims at presenting a comprehensive picture of the Internet audience, of its constitution, and of its measurement.

The Internet Audience

The goal of this first section is to lay the foundation for the rest of the book. In order to accomplish this, it examines three different but related issues: namely, the context in which the book should be placed, the perspective from which the object of study will be addressed, and the structure of the remaining sections.

Scholarship does not grow in a vacuum. Rather, it is always related to previous work, if even just tangentially or in opposition to it. Since the audience has traditionally been a central element in the study of communication media, and because the Internet has led the most relevant transformation of the media system in decades, there exists a huge body of literature on both subjects. It is not my intention, however, to delve into all aspects of this immense corpus. Rather, I will focus on those pieces that specifically address the idea of the audience in relation to the Internet, or the Internet in relation to its audience.

Obviously, the choice of the literature to be reviewed is to a certain extent influenced by the point of view from which the topic is to be examined. No matter how ambitious or wide-ranging the intended examination of the topic might be, it is impossible to write about it from every possible perspective and to cover every possible nuance. It is necessary to narrow and focus one's approach. In that respect, the perspective chosen here is the institutional perspective. The first chapter of this section is thus devoted to a review of the available literature on the Internet audience and to an introduction of the institutional perspective on the study of audiences.

The institutional perspective allows for various ways to structure the book. My approach is to examine the Internet audience through three different paths—a first path that deals with the process of constitution of the audience, a second path that centers on the methods used to measure that audience, and a third path that examines the audience measurement industry. The second chapter of this section introduces these three paths and sets the structure for the remainder of the book.

Context and Perspective

The Internet Audience: A Review of the Literature

The Internet audience[1] occupies an ambiguous space in communication research. This ambiguity arises because the advent of the Internet is a recent phenomenon and also because of the complexity and flexibility of this new medium. Though there are relevant works that address the idea of 'community' and the Internet (Jones, 1995; 1998; Rheingold, 1993), few authors within the academy have delved into the question of the audience of the new medium. Given the newfound prominence of this audience in recent years—as demonstrated by the interest shown by the media, advertisers, and research companies—communication research cannot afford to ignore the issue of the Internet audience.

In 1996, in a special issue of the *Journal of Communication* devoted to the Internet, Morris and Ogan (1996: 39) assert that:

> If mass communication researchers continue to largely disregard the research potential of the Internet, their theories about communication will become less useful. Not only will the discipline be left behind, it will also miss an opportunity to explore and rethink answers to some of the central questions of mass communications research, questions that go to the heart of the model of source–message–receiver with which the field has struggled.

Morris and Ogan go on to conduct an analysis of the possibilities for studying the Internet as a mass medium and mention some of the fundamental questions that emerge when communication researchers are confronted with the new medium. For example, the traditional division of communication into interpersonal, group, and mass communication seems to lose meaning in the face of a medium capable of generating communicative dynamics at all of these levels. Similarly, the fragmentation generated by this new medium seems to challenge the definition of the mass audience. For this reason, Morris and Ogan (1996: 43) argue that:

> reconceptualizing the audience of the communication that takes place on the Internet is a major problem, one that becomes increasingly important as commercial information providers enter the Internet in greater numbers.

However, academic attempts to 'reconceptualize' the Internet audience have not been easy to find. Let us now briefly review these attempts in an effort to understand the context that prompts this book.

The ways in which researchers and others have constructed the audience of the World Wide Web is the focus of Timothy Roscoe's work (1999). He calls our attention to changes in the perception of the Internet which manifest in the journalistic treatment of the medium. Once conceived mostly as a technology that allows computers and people to communicate and exchange information, the World Wide Web is now often conceived as a mass medium similar to television. Roscoe (1999: 677) defines a medium of mass communication as:

> one whose dominant model is that of a small number of centralized sites of production, which disseminate content to a large number of receivers: media like television, radio, print, the record industry, etc.

He cites technological reasons as the cause for this change. He argues that the scarcity of Internet Protocol (IP) addresses[2] establishes an asymmetry between content providers and content consumers. This brings the Internet closer to the traditional model of mass communications media. All connections to the Internet are realized and identified via an IP address. Such IP addresses may be either static or dynamic. Static addresses are those permanently assigned to a computer with an Internet connection. Dynamic addresses are used as a system for saving addresses: when someone connects to the Internet through an Internet Service Provider (ISP), the number of IP addresses owned by the provider is usually less than the total number of clients, who are randomly assigned one of these addresses each time they connect to the network, as it is assumed that not all clients will connect to the network at the same time. According to Roscoe, this situation divides Internet users into those who possess a fixed number from which they can make and receive calls (i.e., people using static IP addresses) and those who only have a temporary number from which to call, but who cannot be located (i.e., people using dynamic IP addresses). A small technical limitation such as this, Roscoe argues, generates an asymmetry which has made the Internet more similar to a traditional mass medium than it was before. However, Roscoe's argument seems to have been outdated by later events, given the development of the *Classless Inter-Domain Router* (CIDR) system and of the new generation of IP addresses (IPv6), which can do away with the scarcity of IP addresses described by Roscoe.

Roscoe reviews other technical considerations which could allow the Internet to be described as an asymmetrical medium. More specifically, he speaks of the technical knowledge required to become a content provider on the web and of the existing types of Internet connections. It is obvious that those who possess greater technical knowledge and better Internet connections will experience greater ease in becoming active agents or senders on the net. However, one also cannot ignore the constant improvement in connection speeds and the user-friendliness of many of the tools for posting information on the net. The obstacles to becoming an online content provider do not seem to have increased in recent years. Despite Roscoe's point, the issues of technical knowledge and connection speeds cannot explain the supposed transformation of the web into a traditional mass medium. Neither does it seem to be the case for the appearance, and failure, of *push* technology, also mentioned by Roscoe. *Push* technology allows for the reception, through a web browser, of content personalized according to the preferences of the user, without the user having to make an explicit request for specific content each time. In other words, the user, instead of actively seeking the content on the web (or *pulling*), receives the content that is *pushed* by the provider to her personal computer following interest criteria specified by the user in a more or less precise way. Even though at one time it was thought that *push* technology would transform the web and its use, the truth is that it has been practically forgotten and is only used in very restricted circles, such as, for example, some corporate intranets.

Other factors which seem to have contributed to the change in the perception of the Internet, according to Roscoe, are the commercialization of the Internet, the role of advertising, and the role played by net users themselves, who, taking the traditional media—and especially television—as the model, limit the medium's own development by using it only as a passive form of entertainment. Roscoe (1999: 678) concludes:

> The idea of an audience presupposes a binary opposition between producers and consumers, between the creators, providers and purveyors of content, and the 'audience' itself, which views, browses and 'consumes' the content. Internet users have come to be positioned as subjects who view the World Wide Web as a source of information (most often entertainment) and, recently, a place to make purchases, rather than a means of expressing their own creativity and ideas. The production of 'content' is increasingly seen to be a job for large commercial interests who can do this kind of thing 'properly.'

In sum, the term 'audience' when used in reference to the web has become, according to Roscoe, innocuous because in the popular imagination the web has been constructed as an asymmetrical medium.

The Internet audience can be conceptualized in different forms, however, and Daniel Downes (2000) focuses on three possible conceptualizations: the audience as a market, the audience as a public, and the audience as a relationship. For Downes, the vision of the Internet audience moves between the image of television and that of a shopping center, between the conception of the Internet as a traditional mass medium—with organizations that create messages directed at a large number of individuals—and the vision of the Internet as a place in which fragmentation and interactivity generate dynamics very different from those generated by the traditional mass media. Downes uses McQuail's (2000) approach to analyze the idea of the Internet audience as a market and then applies this to how large Internet companies, such as AOL or Microsoft, share the view of the audience as market, but conceptualize it simultaneously and confusingly in two different ways: (1) as an aggregate of consumer-users, individuals who pay for Internet access and make purchases on the web and (2) as an audience of content, in an advertising model similar to that of commercial television. He also analyzes another alternative conception of the Internet, that of the audience as a public, which emerges when the emphasis is placed on the community ties generated by the Internet. Finally, Downes notes how it is possible to conceptualize the Internet audience as a relationship. In this last view, the emphasis is placed on the capacity of the audience to become a co-participant in the communicative processes, where the agency of the audience is more apparent. In other words, according to Downes, the Internet audience, depending on the communicative level in which we move—mass, group, or interpersonal communication—can be variously understood as a market, similar to the mass media audience although with certain peculiarities; as a public or community; or as an interpersonal linkage.

But given that a good part of interactions on the Internet focuses on the creation of content or on the production of meaning through the consumption of content produced by other individuals, especially in IRC (chat) and MUD (games), Lelia Green (2001) raises the question of whether it is adequate to speak of an audience when referring to the Internet. It is her belief that, in spite of the commercial research aiming to depict Internet use as homogeneous, the medium is so diverse and complex that it does not allow for comparison with previous media.

This view seems to be contradicted by Christine Hine (2001). A series of interviews with the staff in charge of the webpages of the various departments of a British university is the point of departure for her analysis of the World Wide Web audience. She considers the conceptions of the audience revealed by these interviews to demonstrate that the World Wide Web presents more continuity with the existing mass media than what would be expected. Hine highlights two essential characteristics that are attributed to the web audience: it is global and it can be known. On the one hand, web content can be accessed from anywhere in the world, and, as such, to introduce web content means that the author is communicating, at least potentially, with the whole world. On the other hand, the development of tools for the control and analysis of web traffic creates a situation in which the web audience is considered an audience that can be known, segmented, and thus introduced into the commercial process of buying and selling advertising. However, Hine believes that, although it may seem that the web does away with many of the problems encountered in the measurement of television audiences, the data on web audience are open to debate, and "both on grounds of unpredictable technological behavior and unpredictable user behavior, statistics are contestable and contested" (Hine, 2001: 185). Nonetheless, these statistics can also be used to conceptualize the web audience, as is the case with Webster and Lin's (2002) work.

Webster and Lin use panel data from Nielsen NetRatings to assess the degree to which the audience of the World Wide Web shows the characteristics of a mass audience. In particular, their study focuses on audience size and on indices of audience duplication between different websites. They consider that web use can be thought of as a mass behavior, similar to selecting a television program or a newspaper, and that the web can be understood as a mass medium, and its users as a mass audience. They use the concept of a 'mass' to refer to a wide and heterogeneous collection of individuals who act autonomously and are, for the most part, anonymous. Their work examines the question of whether the behavior of the Internet audience follows two laws that characterize the mass audience of television:

1. *Pareto's law*: whose application to communication media asserts that the majority of the mass media audience tends to concentrate on a limited percentage of the offerings.
2. *The law of the duplication of the audience*: according to which the audience common to any pair of television programs is a function of the rating of the first program multiplied by the rating of the second, multiplied by a constant.

Although they consider their conclusions to be preliminary, as the data used for the analysis refer only to home Internet use and do not offer information on important details such as the amount of time spent on websites or the repetition of visits, they see the web audience as responding to the characteristics typical of a mass audience. Webster and Lin (2002: 9) conclude their study by asserting:

> With its millions of sites and services, it is easy to think of the World Wide Web as a thoroughly demassified medium. It is not. Even the smallest sites we examined had 175,000 different visitors in the course of a month. Such large groups have the essential characteristics of a 'mass.' The people using sites are largely anonymous to one another and almost certainly act autonomously.

The panels used to gather the data on which Webster and Lin's piece is based are the focus of Karen Buzzard's (2003) account of the web audience measurement industry. In a previous work, Buzzard (2002) analyzed the competitive strategies of measurement firms in television audience measurement. In her more recent piece, she uses a similar approach to sketch a history of web audience measurement panels. She points to the development of an Internet business model transferred from television in which a key part "was the rise of a system of audience measurement to identify and track its users" (Buzzard, 2003: 198), and goes on to describe some of the dynamics generated in the competition between different panels to measure the audience of the web. She stresses the similarities between the measurement of web and television audiences, in particular the strategy of 'fast second' followed by Nielsen in both markets. Instead of seeking the first-mover advantage, Nielsen opted to wait for competitors to innovate and then tried to overpower them. However, next to these similarities, Buzzard also mentions some of the specific problems faced by web audience measurement, such as the difficulty of recruiting large enough samples for such a fragmented medium or the complexity of the different possible metrics to be developed: measurement of web properties, websites, domains, measurement of visits, unique visitors, etc.

Besides these specific works, the Internet audience has also become part of the most recent generic examinations of audience measurement and audience economics. In their book, *Ratings Analysis: The Theory and Practice of Audience Research*, Webster et al. (2000) include references to the Internet audience. In particular, they assert that "the Internet audience research business is developing along the same lines as broadcast audience measurement" (2000: 25), and refer to the advertising interests behind Internet audience measurement as a fundamental element, since "for any new media technology to attract the sustained attention of advertisers, a system of audience measurement must be in place" (2000: 154). They mention some of the methodological problems that this new measurement faces: the blocking and deletion of cookies, the use of cache memory, the possible bias in the recruited samples, a definition of 'viewership" not in terms of exposure but in terms of 'clicking,' the use of multiple computers by a single user and the use of a single computer by multiple users, and the difficulty of knowing who exactly is using the Internet.

But it is in Philip Napoli's (2003) *Audience Economics: Media Institutions and the Audience Marketplace* that the Internet audience has been most clearly integrated within the study of other media audiences. In his thorough analysis of the audience as a product, Napoli pays attention to the new medium and to its audience measurement in order to situate it within the broader field of audience economics. In particular, Napoli draws distinctions between the "predicted audience," the "measured audience," and the "actual audience," and asserts that "the measured audience represents the primary coin of exchange among buyers and sellers of audiences and thus represents the central component of the audience product" (2003: 31). In this sense, measurement issues become central to any understanding of the audience product. He analyzes these issues in detail and, referring specifically to the Internet audience, reminds us of the sampling problems involved in measuring that audience—"measuring audiences for a medium such as the Internet, with its hundreds of thousands of advertiser-supported Web sites, requires a larger sample than does measuring audiences for radio or television, where the number of available content options is much smaller" (2003: 67)—of the low response rates achieved by measurement operations, of the evolution in measurement methods from the analysis of server records to user-based panels, and of some of the weaknesses of these methods.

Napoli also mentions the monopolistic tendency in the audience measurement industry and how that tendency is also present in Internet audience measurement. However, he reminds us (2003: 85),

> the continued lack of an accepted standard for Internet audience measurement, along with evidence of severe disparities among the different measurement techniques, has contributed to severe advertiser suspicion regarding the reliability and accuracy of these data and a consequent hesitancy to invest in Internet advertising.

Two other important issues pointed out by Napoli are the increasing fragmentation and autonomy of the audience. He asserts that these two tendencies are present in all new communication media and, therefore, also in the Internet: "the Internet may represent the apex of audience autonomy" (2003: 147). He believes that this increasing fragmentation and autonomy lead in turn to increasing problems in the audience measurement process and, as a result, to a worsening of the quality of the audience product.

Within the Spanish-speaking world, perhaps the most interesting work on the Internet audience is that of Javier Callejo (2001). In his book *Investigar las Audiencias*, he focuses on the analysis of audience research and devotes most of the book to the issue of Internet audience research. Callejo (2001: 30) thinks Internet audience research presents certain problems, and he asserts that:

> What was thought to be the audience starts to dilute. The new communication media bring new ways of communicating [...]. Other ways of communicating generate new audiences and, obviously, the need to study the audience differently, to rethink what is usually done.

Callejo points out in his analysis issues such as the interactivity allowed by the Internet and the fragmentation that it presents. These issues make it possible to consider the Internet more as a communication medium (in which what is sought after is the link or the contact with others) than as an information medium (in which what predominates is the passive exposure to content). In this sense,

> the very concept of audience begins to creak. First, the interactivity breaks with the idea of passivity that predominates when the term 'audience' is used. Second, the fragmentation of the audience breaks with the massive character that has been associated with it. (Callejo, 2001: 273)

However, Callejo asserts, this may change due to the commercial interests surrounding the Internet.

Callejo considers the Internet to be essentially an advertising medium, although his conception of advertising is very broad, as it includes everything ranging from self-representation in a chatroom, or self-advertising, to the advertising of commercial companies, or commercial advertising in the customary sense. He also believes it to be the commercial medium *par excellence*, given that the advertising and the satisfaction of the demand created by that advertising can be just one click apart in the same medium, thus instantaneously converting audience into consumer.

In this sense, he believes that in the increasingly commercialized online environment, "the pressures to transform the Internet user into a commodity are strong. And first it is necessary to transform it into an audience" (2001: 185). In order to demonstrate efforts to transform the user into a commodity, Callejo examines the Spanish studies that offer a picture of the Internet audience, detecting in these studies a tendency toward inertia in how the new medium and its audience are approached. He argues that the Internet presents enough peculiarities to warrant the development of new methods for studying it and its audience. Some of the peculiarities he mentions include: the global nature of the medium, the problems associated with drawing representative samples, the potentially intrusive character of the measurement process, and resistance to being measured on the part of the users themselves.

In summary, Callejo sees the Internet audience as occupying an ambiguous place when compared to the audiences of traditional mass media, and he believes that this ambiguity requires new approaches to its study. He argues, "by demanding new ways of researching its audience, it may also generate new approaches to looking at the audiences of the other media" (2001: 265). He concludes his book with an assertion that the issue of audience research poses other issues of greater scope:

> It is no longer just an issue of debating what and how large is the audience, but also of debating what is a communication medium or, at the least, whether it makes sense to continue speaking of mass communication media. (Callejo, 2001: 284)

In spite of the above efforts to examine and analyze the Internet audience from within the academy, the truth is that scientific production on the subject is rather limited. This is without a doubt partially due to the youth of the Internet phenomenon and to the complexity and ambiguity that the object of study, the Internet audience, presents. However, there is another reason to account for the lack of studies addressing the Internet audience: the very idea of the 'audience,' as well as its study within the field of communication, continues to be very much conditioned by television. Even in recent works produced within the field of audience studies, one perceives a tendency to look more at the past than at the present or the future (Neuendorf, 2001). The tendency is to study the audience from the point of view of television and, furthermore, to apply the classic television model, without fragmentation, without new technological devices, and without new business models. Of course, it is clear that in spite of the momentum with which the Internet has entered the field of communication in recent years, television still remains the medium of reference. As Callejo says (2001: 61), "the communication medium that is dominant in each historical moment has a notable influence in the general conception of the audience." But that should not impede us from opening the study of the audience to new realities that appear to possess an enormous transformative potential and examine in this manner the appropriateness of the concept of the 'audience' when it is applied to these new communication realities.

This book aims to contribute to the literature on the Internet audience. The works mentioned above offer some fundamental ideas that, no doubt, will reappear later in this book, namely:

- the ambiguous nature of the Internet audience,
- the centrality of the World Wide Web when speaking of the Internet audience,
- the importance of commercial interests to any understanding of the Internet audience,
- the audience fragmentation produced by a complex medium such as the Internet,
- the issue of interactivity and the diminishing asymmetry between sender and receiver,
- the limitations and possibilities of Internet audience research.

However, in order to organize and articulate the various issues that appear in a dispersed manner in the works summarized here, it is necessary to select a perspective, a point of view, to structure and give meaning to the study on which we are embarking.

The Institutional Approach to the Study of the Audience

When we speak of audiences, we frequently do so as if we were referring in an unambiguous way to a concrete, stable, and observable entity. However, research on communication media has paid great attention to the concept of the audience and has proposed numerous approaches for its study (Jensen & Rosengren, 1990; McQuail, 2000).

Audiences themselves, and the frameworks used to study them, have come in many configurations (McQuail, 1997; Webster, 1998).

If we go back to the origins of research in mass communication, to the Payne Foundation's studies on cinema and Lazarsfeld's work in the Princeton Radio Research Project, we find the audience converted into a legitimate object of scientific study. According to Mosco and Kaye (2000), the conception of the audience that emerges from the first scientific studies of the media is that of a passive mass subject to the influence of communication media and of propaganda. If we take Mosco and Kaye's interpretation of these early studies to be correct, then we can describe the scientific-academic study of the audience in subsequent decades in terms of a progressive distancing from this earlier conception. This evolution can be attributed to: technological and institutional changes in the media, modifications to the approach and techniques of study, and the progressive discovery of the role of social groups and of the much-debated activity of the audience (Clarke, 2000; Huertas, 2002; Mattelart & Mattelart, 1995; Morley, 1993; Power et al., 2002). We have now arrived at a moment when the majority of academic production on audiences has focused on analyzing the activity, power, and interpretations of the audience. To this end, research has privileged qualitative methods and micro-level approaches. Cultural studies, reception studies, ethnography, focus groups, and in-depth interviews have generated new theoretical and methodological approaches and have become essential elements for understanding the academic literature on the audience.

In this sense, the project proposed here departs from the most habitual approaches currently used, as it does not propose a micro-approach and does not aspire to analyze issues related to the reception or interpretation of messages. If the uses and gratifications approach (Katz et al., 1974) reversed the effects tradition and aimed to analyze what the audience does with the media, I would like to reverse the uses and gratifications approach and aim to analyze what the media do with the audience. But, instead of taking my cues from the effects tradition, I take an institutional perspective. The institutional point of view focuses neither on how audiences receive messages nor even on how communicators make messages. Rather, it focuses on how communicators make audiences. (Ettema & Whitney, 1994: 4)

Therefore, the study proposed here focuses, in concrete terms, on how communicators create or construct audiences through measurement. From an institutional perspective, the audience is inseparable from the measurement methods that constitute it. In other words, I plan to analyze audience measurement as an instrument for the creation of the audience, which, in turn, is an essential element for the understanding of the functioning of the media as social institutions (Ang, 1991).

In an institutional conception of communication, "actual receivers are constituted—or, perhaps, reconstituted—not merely as audiences but as institutionally effective audiences that have social meaning and/or economic value within the system" (Ettema & Whitney, 1994: 5). In other words, the study of audience measurement becomes a study of the media as institutions and of the role that measurement plays in the economic and social functioning of those institutions. Within this approach, "audiences are seen to be the product of something like a manufacturing process, but they also are seen to be the site of contestation among media firms, measurement services, advertisers, interest groups, government and other agents of institutional power" (Ettema & Whitney, 1994: 16). This is the general perspective that inspires this work.

The institutional approach is focused on impersonal relations on a macro-level and is developed through separate lines of analysis. For Ettema and Whitney (1994), these lines of analysis can be reduced to three fundamental divisions: (1) the economy of the media, which includes the classical current as well as that of critical political economy; (2) interorganizational studies of the media industry; and (3) the analysis of the media as political institutions. However, as far as the analysis of the audience and of the mechanisms of its measurement is concerned, the political economy of the media is, according to Eileen Meehan (1984), the current which has contributed the most to the development of an institutional analysis. More concretely, she asserts that the essential corpus of the institutional approach applied to the study of the audience and its measurement is constituted by work in political economy which attempts to respond to the question "what is the commodity produced by the mass communication industries?"

According to Meehan (1984), in the literature on the political economy of the media we can find three different answers to this question:

1. The media industry produces messages.
2. The media industry produces audiences.
3. The commodity produced, bought, and sold is constituted solely by audience data, or ratings.

The first response, according to which the messages constitute the commodity, assigns to the media the role of mediator between the economic base and the politico-ideological superstructure, and allows for the analysis of the economic and political roles of the media by means of concepts such as 'ideology,' 'representation,' and 'hegemony.' This approach, which is carried out fundamentally through textual analyses and through organizational analyses—in which internal restrictions on production, external commercial restrictions, and professionalism are studied—aspires to explain why cultural products reproduce the dominant ideology.

As far as the approach of this study is concerned, these works ignore, for the most part, the issue of the role of audience data in the process of the production of the message-commodity and carry out only a methodological analysis of audience measurement tools. As Meehan (1984: 217) claims,

> with the focus on the commodity message, researchers have treated ratings in much the same way as broadcasters; that is, as imperfect but basically scientific measurements of audience size and type which could be influenced by manipulations of program schedules. The critique, then, has centered on issues of methodological adequacy and proper interpretation of ratings ...

Audience measurement is thus presented, through this first perspective, as an industry abstracted from historical conditioning factors and from the imperatives of the capitalist economic system, and its study is reduced to a methodological analysis focused on the precision of the data obtained and on their scientific validity.

The limitations of this first response to the question on the commodity produced by the media industry opened the door to a second answer, which places the audience at the center of the analysis, and according to which the most important product of media is the audience. The introduction of this second perspective can be found in the work of Dallas Smythe (1977), for whom talk of 'ideology' is too ethereal and who prefers to inquire into the economic function of the media industry. According to Smythe, the messages produced by the media are merely bait with which to attract the audience which, once organized into salable categories, is bought by advertisers. Smythe (1977: 3) therefore proposes that we go beyond messages:

> I submit that the materialistic answer to the question—What is the commodity form of mass-produced, advertiser-supported communications under monopoly capitalism?—is audiences and readerships (hereafter referred to for simplicity as audiences).

According to Smythe, for the majority of the population in a system of capitalistic monopoly, all the time that is spent awake is spent working. Of the time spent outside of the workplace proper, the largest block of time is made up of the audience time that is sold to advertisers. This time is not sold by the workers but rather by the mass communication media. The mass communication media produce this commodity through advertising, explicit and hidden, mixed with 'programs' which, according to Smythe, constitute the focus of attention of the bourgeois theoreticians of communication. The audience members themselves pay more for the production of the commodity than the very communication media that sell the commodity. Besides their time and attention, the audience members pay for the reception equipment, electricity, and a surcharge on the advertised products.

For Smythe, what advertisers buy are audiences[3] with certain characteristics, which pay attention to given media in a given moment and which, in the end, learn to buy certain brands of consumer goods and create a demand for advertised products. The production of the audience becomes, from this point of view, a fundamental mechanism of media functioning. And since the audience becomes a commodity, those who purchase it, advertisers, need to be certain that they are getting what they pay for. This is the reason for the existence of a subsector within the media industry, that of audience and market research companies and departments, with the role of researching the product: the audience. The presence and development of the audience measurement business thus become evidence that the audience is being manufactured and sold, since, as Bill Livant (1979: 105) argues, "the main impetus to the rise of measurement is the rise of commodity production. Where something begins to be measured it is an almost sure sign it is being traded." Meehan (1984: 220) summarizes this view in the following manner:

> Advertisers want audiences; networks capture audiences; raters measure audiences; advertisers buy audiences from networks. Yet, the audience not only fails to receive compensation for its participation in these transactions, but actually pays for much of the production process by investing capital in television sets, by absorbing advertising costs hidden in the prices of advertised brands, and by paying for the electricity to run the machinery necessary to make one available for sale.

Without doubt, Smythe's work represents a new step in the understanding of the media industry and of the role of audience measurement in granting those audiences with a fundamental value from the institutional point of view. In fact, his view has made itself felt in the academic setting, and it is also shared within the world of professional media. For example, Ang (1991) begins her book *Desperately Seeking the Audience* recalling an interview with a researcher from NBC who bluntly explained that the ultimate goal of her work was to provide advertisers with audiences. From the academic setting, to use just one of many available examples, Curran and Seaton (1997: 181) assert: "Commercial television produces audiences not programmes. Advertisers, in purchasing a few seconds of television time, are actually buying viewers by the thousand. [...] Hence advertisers regard programmes merely as the means by which the audiences are delivered to them."

If the audience is a product generated by the media, how is it that the process of audience manufacture remains removed from the restrictions and pressures that affect the production of other commodities in capitalism? Is it possible to understand the process of audience production without understanding how this process is articulated, what agents intervene, what interests are at stake, what sorts of pressures are exercised, and what are the limitations of audience construction? To answer these questions, Meehan (1984) proposes a third answer to the question about the commodity produced by the media industry: ratings. From this point of view, it is not the audience that is bought and sold in the media market but information about the audience. To be able to examine this process of buying and selling data,

> the internal economics of the ratings industry as well as relationships with client industries and client firms must come under the most careful scrutiny. Similarly, we must probe behind the image of rating firms as technicians simply applying scientific procedures in order to discover the relationships between such procedures and actual production practices. (Meehan, 1984: 221)

In sum, to Meehan ratings must be regarded as products or commodities shaped by business exigencies and corporate strategies.

In other words, this third response regarding the commodity produced by communications media asks us to go beyond methodological analyses and the examination of the economic logic that conditions the organization and functioning of the media. It demands that we enter the audience production industry and examine its logic, dynamics, actors, and configurations. This would make it possible to study how, even though the different agents participating in the audience measurement market have shared interests in the production of measurements (each one receives some kind of benefit), they nonetheless need independent measurement organizations to guarantee the neutrality of the process. Given that the measurement market requires a certain amount of stability for its functioning, it is possible to analyze the monopolistic tendencies of the audience measurement market or the predominance of syndicated studies. Similarly, by studying the dynamics of the measurement industry it is possible to understand why the barriers to entry to the audience measurement market are so high and why the strategy normally used by new competitors in the market consists of developing measurement procedures that can be claimed to be more scientific than the existing ones, in order to, on this basis, build alliances, obtain patents, and generate clients (Buzzard, 2002; Meehan, 1984).

From a political economy perspective, and with respect to the question regarding the commodity produced by the media industry, an institutional approach to the study of the media audience takes shape. This approach places the audience and the process of its measurement in a privileged place when analyzing the mass communication media. None of the three answers to the commodity question offers a complete view of audience measurement and the role it plays in the institutional functioning of the media. Each response privileges a single perspective and, therefore, focuses on a concrete aspect of measurement. Nevertheless, these three responses complement one another and serve, when taken together, to articulate the work proposed here.

In more concrete terms, each of the three sections that follow is related to one of the three responses offered to the question about the commodity produced by the communication media. However, I have altered the order to better articulate the rest of this book:

1. The *second* answer, *the media produce audiences*, focuses on the central role played by audience production in the economic processes that drive the functioning of the mass media and, additionally, asserts that the presence of audience measurement becomes evidence of the manufacturing process. By studying the origins of Internet audience measurement and the context in which it comes into being, I hope to understand how and under what circumstances the process of manufacturing the Internet audience has been commenced, whether that process is similar to analogous processes in traditional media, and to what extent these similarities indicate that the Internet is similar, at least in its economic functioning, to those media.

2. The *first* response, *the media produce programs*, speaks of audience research as an imperfect but basically scientific practice and criticizes that practice from a methodological point of view. If scientific practices are shaped by the reality they aim at studying and by the interests that underlie them, then studying the measurement methods applied to the Internet will help us understand the interplay between the reality of the new medium and of its audience and the interests that underlie the application of those methods.

3. The *third* response, *the media produce ratings*, aspires to examine the institutional factors that shape the field of audience research, its actors, their interests, and the dynamics generated by those interests. Applying such an analysis to the devel-

opment of Internet audience measurement should thus lead us to a better understanding of the process of institutionalization of the new medium. I will examine the extent to which, independently of the technology of the media or the reality of the audience, the interplay of interests and agents creates a logic that governs the industry, and I consider to what extent that logic is the same as that which governs the audience measurement industry in traditional media.

These three responses together, in spite of the fact that they were developed for media existing before the advent of the Internet, offer us a complete platform from which to address the study of audience measurement on the net. They allow us to analyze audience measurement in terms of its role in the constitution of that audience and the institutionalization of the new medium, in terms of its methodological development, and in terms of the dynamics of the measurement industry. To each of these three points I will dedicate a section of this book, with the objective of offering as complete a panorama as possible of my object of study. But it is first necessary to analyze each of these three perspectives in some detail. That is the goal of the following chapter.

Chapter 2

The Three Axes

Audience Reality and Audience Measurement

Smythe's (1977) approach, according to which it is possible to understand the communications media as mechanisms for the production of audiences that are bought and sold, provides a stimulating point of view for the study of communications media as a whole and of audience measurement in particular. Nonetheless, this approach cannot be applied in a generic sense to all communication processes, and not even to all the possible configurations of mass communication. Its application is restricted to certain given historical realities in which communication processes present a series of specific characteristics as a result of technological, economic, and social conditioning factors.

From a conceptual as well as a historical point of view, audience analyses tend to be based on the model of face-to-face interpersonal communication (Radway, 1988; Schudson, 1978). In a communicative situation that is similar to, for example, the ideal speech situation postulated by Habermas (1984), the assignment of the roles of sender and receiver has an arbitrary nature that depends not on the functioning of the communication process itself, but rather on how we decide to punctuate that process. That is, it depends on when or where we decide that the communication process starts and, as a result, on whom we designate as the initiator of the process. In a situation in which all of the participants have the same capacity to participate in the communication process, the message and the feedback would be essentially the same.

However, the ideal speech situation is a counterfactual reality; it is not so much an empirical reality as it is an ideal model with which to compare the real situations that we might wish to analyze. The assignment of sender and receiver roles in real situations, therefore, turns out not to be completely arbitrary, since in normal situations the symmetry required by the ideal situation is not present. In fact, the development of the mass communication media has meant a progressive distancing from this situation in which the sender and receiver roles are easily interchangeable. It is this progressive distancing that, in part, allows us to speak of audiences.

We can take the origin of the audience as involving physical presence in a given place, where a division of social roles is produced between performers (i.e., senders) and spectators (i.e., receivers). In fact, the first uses of the term 'audience' referred to situations involving a formal and presential encounter between a figure of power—a sovereign, a judge, a figure with political power—and a person lacking that power—a subject, a defendant, or a citizen (Mosco & Kaye, 2000). In other words, the asymmetry between sender and receiver appears already inscribed into the historical and conceptual origin of the audience itself.

Of course, the idea of the audience has changed dramatically with the advent of each medium (Livingstone, 2003). McQuail (1997) finds the origins of the media audience in theater, musical performances, games, and spectacles of antiquity. This early audience displays a series of characteristics that differentiate it from the audience of the mass communications media:

> Most important, the audience of classical times was localized in place and time. An audience occupied an 'auditorium', a space [...]. This meant that the audience was necessarily small by modern standards (though it could number thousands). It was potentially active within itself and interactive with performers. Performances were always 'live', in the fullest possible sense. (McQuail, 1997: 7)

That is, the audience was bound by time/space constraints, but those very constraints facilitated the generation of feedback.

The appearance of mass communication media as we know them today resulted in important changes in terms of how audiences for older media were conceived. Schramm and Roberts (1971: 57) describe how,

> when mass media came into being [...] the principal differences between the new media and the more traditional media were in scale and in operation. [...] The enormity of these differences, the startling power of the mass media to leap space, telescope time, and make information portable and

preservable, gives them a kind of social impact that the more traditional media never had.

In this manner, new modes of communication come into being, and the mass communication media generate communicative processes that accentuate the inequalities between senders and receivers. That inequality manifests itself in two major facets. First,

> the mass media require an organization to operate them. [...] Consequently, the mass media have taken on many of the characteristics and social constraints of other large social institutions and organizations. (Schramm & Roberts, 1971: 57)

That is, senders become a different, more complex entity. Second,

> there is a fundamental difference in feedback from receiver to sender of messages. In personal communication, feedback is usually quick and extensive; in mass communication, usually slow and weak. (Schramm & Roberts, 1971: 58)

As such, the modern communication media seem to be marked by a growing asymmetry between senders and receivers. Senders become social organizations and institutions with a complex technical, human, and economic scheme, and the feedback processes become more difficult (Thompson, 1995).

Historically speaking, it is possible to consider the mass audience as having come into being with the utilization of the printing press, which allowed for communication over distance, through space and time, and the creation of a dispersed readership that consumes the same texts in private. At the beginning of the eighteenth century, we already encounter periodical publications with large regular readerships. However, it is in the nineteenth century, with the processes of urbanization, the development of means of transportation, an increase in standards of living, growing literacy, and improvements in printing technologies, when the printing press becomes a true mass medium, a sizeable industry that is directed at a large public and that, financed by advertising, successfully reaches the market at accessible prices (McQuail, 1997).

With the advent of film, a new kind of audience appears, an audience with some of the characteristics of the audience that existed prior to the appearance of the modern media of communication (physical presence within a specific space, and, therefore, the possibility of interaction among members of the audience) with elements that define the audience of mass media (large size, an identical message in each showing, and impossibility of interaction with the sender). It is with the emergence of radio and, especially, television, however, when the concept of the mass audience achieves its ultimate expression. These are media able to reach millions of people simultaneously, heterogeneous and anonymous people, situated in disperse locations. With the development of radio and television, the idea of the mass audience assumes a central role both in the institutional workings of the media and in the efforts to study and analyze those media.

Therefore, the idea of the asymmetry of the communication process seems to be inscribed into the very concept of the audience, and the idea of the mass audience appears to refer to a concrete historical configuration of communication processes linked to certain technological devices. However, the issue of the need for knowledge about the audience requires careful examination. While, from a conceptual point of view, knowing the audience seems to be essential to any communication process, the truth is that the particular way in which that knowledge is obtained also depends on specific historical circumstances. Even though every communication process involves some manner of knowing the audience—which we can refer to in generic terms as 'feedback'—audience measurement, with its various techniques and apparatus as we know them today, is born in a specific historical context. James Beniger, in his work *The Control Revolution: Technological and Economic Origins of the Information Society* (1986), is one of the authors who have offered a more detailed and carefully articulated framework for understanding the historical origins of audience measurement.

If we want to place the issue in perspective, it is possible to situate the development of audience measurement within what Beniger (1986) calls the Control Revolution. According to Beniger, around the mid-nineteenth century, in advanced capitalist societies, a Control Crisis developed as a consequence of the changes brought about by the Industrial Revolution. This Control Crisis took place when innovations in information processing and communication technologies did not keep up with innovations in the production of energy and in the use of that energy in manufacturing and transportation that characterized the Industrial Revolution. This crisis eventually generated, at the end of the nineteenth century and the beginning of the twentieth century, a Control[1] Revolution which would eventually bring about the Information Society. The Control Revolution is characterized by

> a complex of rapid changes in the technological and economic arrangements by which information is collected, stored, processed, and communicated, and through which formal or programmed decisions might effect societal control. (Beniger, 1986: vi)

The progressive bureaucratization of modern societies is the most evident manifestation of this revolution, which is accompanied by a whole series of technological devices to collect, store, process, and transmit information. These devices take shape in three different areas: the control revolution in mass production, the control revolution in distribution, and the control revolution in mass consumption.

According to Beniger, technical improvements in printing methods, the later introduction of radio and television, and the progressive development and rationalization of advertising activities are manifestations of the Control Revolution in the sphere of mass consumption. Beniger shows, for example, how the cereal and canned food industries, upon applying improvements in their production processes, found themselves unable to efficiently sell the huge amount of goods generated in their factories. For this reason, at the turn of the twentieth century they began to utilize mass advertising, to create brands, and to package their products for individual mass consumption. In this manner, by taking advantage of the mass media, they were able to control the consumption of their products and to solve problems of overproduction, becoming in the process some of the largest advertisers in the market, a ranking that did not correspond to the real size of these industries. Smythe (1977: 3) mentions this same idea regarding the ability of mass media to control the demand of products when he says that mass communication media are "engaged indispensably in the last stage of infrastructural production where demand is produced and satisfied by purchases of consumer goods."

This process of controlling mass consumption is not complete until the loop of the control process is closed, until the feedback that comes from consumers is gathered. Therefore, the role played by mass media and advertising is not fulfilled until mechanisms are developed for managing the information that comes from consumers. It is after 1900 when these feedback technologies attain what could be called maturity. They are the techniques that gave birth to market and audience research. Obviously, the feedback in question is of a peculiar type, since it serves the control function for mass media and for the different agents implicated in the advertising market. Audience research is thus born as an instrument of control of the advertising activity that allows the mass media, in turn, to control mass consumption in a market economy that tries to solve a control crisis through mechanisms of gathering and analysis of information.

We can now understand how to apply Smythe's (1977) answer to the issue of the commodity produced by the media. When Smythe says that the commodity produced by communication media is the audience, he is referring to communication processes in which there is an obvious asymmetry between senders and receivers, where there is a mass audience, and where there exist clear commercial interests that aim to control, through advertising in those media, the process of mass consumption. That is, Smythe's response refers to the concrete historical articulation that communication media have acquired in Western capitalist societies, particularly in North America.

However, almost from the moment in which the mass media system is consolidated, the mass audience itself begins to erode through a progressive specialization and proliferation of media vehicles (Maisel, 1973). At the same time, the increasing ability of the audience to control the reception process through the use of technological devices, such as remote controls and VCRs, makes the audience more and more elusive, generating more anxiety within the media system, a system that needs to "desperately seek the audience" (Ang, 1991). And in a media system in which the supply grows exponentially due to the proliferation of vehicles and communication technologies, and in which the competition for attracting the audience is increasingly stronger, the need to study and measure the audience is, if anything, more relevant. To some authors (Adler, 1997; Davenport & Beck, 2001; Lanham, 1993), the growth in the supply of content has led to the emergence of a new economy, the Attention Economy. In this economy, attention is the scarce resource that governs the functioning of the economic system. Attention is not an elastic good—we can only pay attention to one thing at a time and only for a certain amount of time—and the supply of information does not stop growing. Competition for attention becomes the central issue of the economy and, therefore, the need to measure and quantify it becomes increasingly pressing.

In this situation, even though economic interests maintain and increase the need to measure the audience, what is certain is that the media system moves in a direction in which the two other elements that are fundamental to the process of audience manufacturing, the asymmetry in the communication process and the large size of the audience, are put into question. This progressive erosion of the mass audience is even more visible with the advent of digital media and, in particular, of the Internet. The characteristics of these media, their seemingly unlimited ability to generate and store content, and the diminishing asymmetry they introduce in sender–receiver relations, make it necessary to take seriously the idea of the disappearance of the mass audience (Neuman, 1991). The audience of these new media is situated in an ambiguous and complex place. It would seem that the Internet does not fulfill the necessary requirements for the existence of the audience-commodity manufacturing process. However, the Internet audience is measured and, as Livant (1979) has said, if something is measured it is because it is being traded. It is necessary to thoroughly analyze the origins of Internet audience measurement in order to understand the degree to which it is possible to apply Smythe's approach to the new medium and in this way fathom its internal logic and its process of institutionalization. This will be the goal of Section II of this book.

Measurement Methods

The first answer to the question about the commodity produced by the media, the one that asserts that the media produce programs or content, gives rise to studies that are interested in audience measurement only from a methodological point of view. Along these lines, in Section III of this book, I will focus on the methods used in audience measurement.

When communication takes place face to face, or among a small number of participants, the instruments available to the sender to know the audience's size, composition, and reactions are multiple and direct. To the extent that the communication process differs from that interpersonal ideal and the receivers are numerous and not physically present, the procedure becomes more complicated. In fact, as the communication process becomes more complex, as the sender goes from being an individual to being an organization, and the audience that acts as receiver changes from a small group with physical presence to a disperse and numerous audience, the need grows to create a whole institutional fabric to develop methods and procedures for the study of the audience.

As Foucault asserts in his analysis of the intertwining of knowledge and power through discursive practices that transform certain parts of reality into knowable and controllable objects, power mechanisms go hand in hand with "the production of effective instruments for the formation and accumulation of knowledge—methods of observation, techniques of registration, procedures for investigation and research, apparatus of control" (quoted in Smart, 2002: 80). This general approach can also be applied to the study and research of the audience.[2] Audience measurement is a manifestation of the development of those instruments for the creation and accumulation of knowledge linked to power relations. They are instruments that do not aim at offering the audience feedback opportunities with the goal of creating a richer and more fulfilling communication process. Instead, they spring out of instrumental actions that aim at goals situated beyond the communication process itself. In this sense, the instruments used are linked to certain interests and those interests influence the final form of these instruments. As Andy Ruddock (2001: 6) states in a very explicit way:

> To be blunt, the nature of the questions one asks will be guided by the persons or institutions paying for or supervising the research. These initial motivations are likely to shape not only the questions you ask but also crucially the methods you use to gather your answers. In combination, the methods and their motivations will also exercise a determining influence over the way in which you view your data and the conclusions you will reach.

That is, the agents interested in developing instruments for the collection of knowledge on the audience will be the ones who will finance and make possible the existence of those instruments and, at the same time, will determine the questions that are asked, how the data are interpreted, and the concrete form that observation methods, registration techniques, and research procedures will take.

In principle, the whole range of social research methods and techniques are available for the study of the audience, since both qualitative and quantitative methods can be used to accumulate knowledge on media audiences. However, commercial audience research has traditionally favored the use of quantitative methods and, in particular, the measurement[3] of the size and composition of the audience. The reason needs to be sought within the economic interests that lay behind the research. If what the research process seeks is to obtain an image of the audience that can be utilized within the advertising market, this image must show a certain degree of stability and a lack of sharp edges. It has to produce what Ien Ang (1991) calls a "streamlined audience." We can say that commercial audience research seeks to collect all the possible information on the object of study, but that, to the extent that the research serves a control function within the media economic system, it becomes necessary to apply rationalization and preprocessing procedures to the collected information. As Beniger (1986: 15) says, "rationalization might be defined as the destruction or ignoring of information in order to facilitate its processing."

In order for audience research to fulfill its role in the economic fabric of the media, not only the information that is collected is important. Just as important is the information that is eliminated or ignored to facilitate the processing that leads to the construction of the audience. Therefore, the methods used in commercial audience research must always remain within the threshold within which they offer enough information about the audience to make it valuable but not so much as to make it unmanageable. That is why, even though it is possible to defend qualitative methods as offering a more complete and detailed view of the audience, quantitative measurement methods actually end up being more relevant to the specific function that commercial audience research serves.

In addition, the need to know the audience and the methods used to obtain that knowledge also vary depending on the business model to which the medium is linked. If we consider that in every communication process some kind of exchange takes place (Callejo, 2001), in business models based on pay-per-content the exchange is obvious and direct. Within this type of model, the pressure on the sender to know the receiver is reduced at two different levels. First, the sender receives money and, because of this, the survival of the organization can be guaranteed. Second, since it is an exchange that leaves a trace, the monetary transaction, it is possible to have an idea, even if not a very precise one, of the size of the audience without the need to develop specific measurement methods. In business models based on advertising revenues, in which content is free, the pressure to know the audience, to develop tools for measuring and researching the audience, becomes stronger since nothing is known of the size of the audience—because there is usually no trace of a transaction—while the economic survival of media organizations under this model depends completely on the size and characteristics of that audience.

The business models followed by different media are in turn influenced by the kind of technology on which they are based. For instance, when radio was introduced it was difficult to see the business possibilities of a medium in which there was no charge for content, since, in contrast with print, it was a medium that lacked materiality and was based on broadcasting, making it effectively impossible to establish a specific link between sender and receiver (Smulyan, 1994). The massive response from listeners to certain promotional initiatives organized by radio stations opened advertisers' eyes to the commercial possibilities of a medium that would, from then on, be based on the advertising revenue model (Beniger, 1986). It was, therefore, the technological nature of the medium that shaped its business model, and it is that technological nature that has also determined the evolution of audience measurement methods from their origins through the present.

The print media were the first media in which interest in measuring the audience led to the development of standardized measurement methods. Print media display a number of characteristics that determine to a great extent how they should be measured. They are based on an obvious material support, paper. Also, they are often packaged in finished products, issues, that have a certain periodicity. That is, in opposition to radio and television (Williams, 1992), print is not a flow medium. Thanks to these characteristics, it was easy for any editor to have information on the number of copies printed and thus obtain a rudimentary quantification of their publication. As Guadalupe Aguado (1996: 19) mentions in her analysis of the historical development of print circulation monitoring in Spain,

> the importance of showing the quantitative reach of the print media was increasingly felt as advertising became the main financial support of the print sector. As advertisers increased their advertising expenditure, they also started to demand guarantees of the profitability of those expenditures. Due to these demands, a struggle erupted among editors trying to demonstrate the advantages of their publications as advertising vehicles. The chosen element to show this was the press run, that is, the number of copies coming out of the printing presses.

Therefore, the quantification of the press run of periodicals became the first and rudimentary form of measurement that allowed advertisers to obtain some guarantee regarding their advertising investment. To the extent that the number of printed copies was used to establish the price of advertising it was subject to interested manipulation on the part of publishers. Besides, these figures said nothing about the actual circulation of the publications nor about the number of readers and their profiles. Even though new mechanisms were soon set in place to give advertisers circulation data, in the end the need to know the readers, their number and profile, implied a shift in the point of information gathering, from the place of production or sale to the place of consumption.

This displacement of information gathering from the point of production to the place of consumption became essential with the birth of radio and television. Even though techniques for the research, study, and control of the audience—and not just of the circulation of publications—were soon applied to the print media (Beniger, 1986; Chaffee, 2000), it is with radio and television that these techniques achieved full expression (Beville, 1988). These developments around radio and television are explained to a great extent by the lack of materiality of those media. While the print media have a material base that is easy to quantify and control, radio and television communication generates obvious uncertainties, since it is impossible to establish and quantify a clear and explicit link between messages and audiences. That same lack of materiality in broadcasting favored a business model exclusively based on advertising, which, as I mentioned above, creates a pressing need to measure an audience with which there is no explicit link but on which rests the economic viability of the media.

Since radio did not allow for the quantification of consumption through records at the point of emission, it was necessary to start collecting information on the radio audience at the point of consumption. In order to collect such audience information, standardized questionnaires were used and administered through mail, in person, and by phone. As the radio audience reached a certain size and a certain degree of dispersion due to the formation of networks, the surveys started to confront problems of representativity and validity. It is then that statistics, with its advances in the nineteenth century (Porter, 1986), became an essential tool for the study of the audience. Especially important were the developments introduced around 1930 on the theory of representative samples for the administration of surveys (Beniger, 1986). Thanks to these advances, it was possible to offer advertisers valuable information on a large and dispersed audience without having to use samples that were unmanageable from a logistic or financial point of view.

Beyond the lack of a link between sender and receiver, radio and television have another peculiarity that makes them different from the print media: they operate in a flow (Pérez Ruiz, 2002; Williams, 1992). This creates a relationship with advertising that is different from print media's relationship with advertising. In radio and television, time becomes an essential element when it comes to planning the insertion of advertising. It is not only necessary to know the vehicle (i.e., publication, station, etc.) into which the advertisement will be inserted. It is also necessary to know the time at which it will be inserted, since the flow of the audience can be very different at different times of the day. That is why audience measurement in radio and television had to go beyond the techniques applied to the print media and to start designing the techniques that gathered information on media consumption at different times of the day.

Two main techniques were developed: diaries and meters. In diaries respondents are asked to recall their exposure to radio or television at different time intervals throughout the day. This requires a significant effort on the part of respondents, which can lead to low cooperation rates and a decrease in the value and quality of the information, if it is not recorded in a thorough and honest manner. Besides, to remember precisely the different radio and television stations one has been exposed to throughout the day is not an easy task. This is one reason why diaries, though used for the first time in 1934, did not consolidate as a technique for audience measurement until many years later (Beville, 1988).

The lack of consolidation of diaries was to a great extent due to the existence of another data gathering technique that took advantage of the technology of receiving sets to obtain information on radio consumption. The audimeter, originally invented by Claude Robinson in 1929, reinvented by Elder and Woodruff in 1934, and redesigned by A. C. Nielsen, was first used as a commercial tool for the production of ratings around 1942. With the audimeter, the problems of precision associated with diaries were solved, and the demand on respondents' cooperation became much lower. To a great extent, the introduction of audimeters contributed to the development of panels—studies in which fixed samples were used over a certain period of time. Unlike surveys, panels allow for the observation of the evolution of sample members' behavior. However, panels were not implemented just because of the additional information they could provide, but because of the logistical problems that one-time-use samples with audimeters would have caused. If it is relatively easy to administer a questionnaire to different samples in the successive waves of a survey, it is not at all efficient to install audimeters in a sample of homes only to immediately remove them and then reinstall them in a new sample of homes.

Despite the similarities in the possibilities for audience measurement in radio and television, the fate of audimeters in each medium has nonetheless been very different. Radio soon underwent a process of expansion and fragmentation, both in the number and nature of the stations available and, what was perhaps more important to the fate of audimeters, in the number and nature of receiving sets. The popularization of car radios (Beniger, 1986) and the development of pocket radios (Blanch, 1999) ultimately eliminated the use of radio audimeters, since the audiometer could not keep up with the process of miniaturization and mobility of radio receivers, and it was impossible to create a census of radio sets from which to draw a statistically representative sample to install the audimeters (Miller, 1994). If we add to this a growing and more complex variety of radio stations, it is easy to understand why radio had to make do with measurement techniques, such as diaries, that could not achieve the degree of detail and precision offered by audimeters.

Meanwhile, television audimeters would progressively become more sophisticated in their functioning and information gathering possibilities (Jauset, 2000). The big qualitative leap took place with the development of people meters, audimeters that went beyond the gathering of information on the activity of the television set, and allowed for the gathering of information on the people that were in front of that set.[4] This change can also be seen as a move from the home to the individual as the unit of consumption. While the activity of the television set offers some valuable information on the family's television consumption, the needs of advertisers and marketers cannot be satisfied with this level of detail. They require a much more precise profile of the audience, and the people meter allowed for the production of that profile.

Television audience measurement has, like the measurement of radio, also been subjected to pressures generated by the evolution of the medium and the technological developments that surround it. The introduction of new technological devices such as remote controls and VCRs (Ang, 1991), together with the proliferation of networks, channels and stations have called for improvements in measurement procedures in order to account for the new reality of the medium. The increases in sample size and in the precision of the information gathered by audimeters, both in terms of exposure time and in terms of the ability to register the activity of peripheral devices, have been some of the changes introduced in television audience measurement.

In sum, throughout the twentieth century, the evolution of mass media, both in technological and business terms, has generated a parallel evolution of audience measurement methods and techniques. Each medium presents peculiarities that make certain measuring methods more apt than others for measuring their audience. When it is possible to quantify the medium at its origin, as is the case with print media, the measurement will be less dependent on statistical methods for the drawing of samples, which, even when statistically sound, always imply a certain amount of error. At the same time, the further the point of measurement from the point of consumption, the less will be known about the final size and the exact profile of the audience. In addition, those media that cannot be quantified at the point of emission or sale require representative samples to obtain information on a large and disperse audience. The specific methods or techniques for information gathering will depend on the possibilities afforded by the medium, and on the resources, both logistic and economic, that measuring organizations have at their disposal. Finally, the variables that need to be measured depend both on the nature of the medium and on the needs of the advertising industry that underlie the measuring effort.

Audience measurement in traditional media presents, therefore, a methodological corpus created through decades of work (Aguado, 1996; Beville, 1988; Blanch, 1999; Guerrero, 2002; Huertas, 1998; Jauset, 2000; Méndez & Lamas, 2003; Webster et al., 2000). The Internet—and, in particular, the World Wide Web—presents a series of peculiarities that place it apart from traditional mass media. It is a medium whose link with the audience leaves a trace, in contrast with radio and television, though this trace is very complex and difficult to analyze. It does not operate as a flow, as do radio and television, nor is it configured around discrete products such as the print media, with their issues and copies. All these make for a special relationship between the Internet and advertising, with its criteria and modes of insertion. The advent of a new medium such as the Internet, therefore, calls for an examination of the methods used to measure its audience, and of how adequate those methods are when they are applied to this new and changing reality. This will be the goal of Section III of this book.

The Audience Measurement Industry

Audience measurement uses similar methods to those used in the social sciences in order to offer information to the agents invested in the advertising market. However, as Ettema and Whitney state (1994: 10), audience measurement cannot simply be seen as a more or less scientific mechanism to obtain knowledge, since it responds to certain specific goals and it is shaped by certain specific interests:

> In some measure, institutionally constituted images of the audience all depend on some measure. That is, they all depend on social scientific measurement technologies [...] Those employing measurement technologies usually claim that their methods provide accurate and detailed images of actual receivers [...] However, such claims gloss over the fact that measurement technologies and the audiences that they construct always serve particular purposes and reflect particular interests.

That is, the construction of the audience, the process of its manufacture, depends on an array of methods that are designed to obtain a high degree of validity, though they cannot help but respond to the specific interests and goals that shape the particular form of these measurement technologies. If, in order to understand the field of audience measurement, it is necessary to analyze the conditions that make possible the manufacture of the audience and the methods used to do so, it is also necessary to examine those interests that underlie the measurement process, the agents that embody those interests, and the dynamics those agents generate in order to give form to audience measurement. Such an examination is what Meehan (1984) proposes when she says that there is a third answer to the commodity question: ratings or audience data. That is, since we understand that the process of audience manufacturing is not a natural process and it is realized through a series of measurement procedures that depend in turn on the interests of certain social agents—measuring companies, media, advertisers, and other intermediaries in the advertising business—we can say that, in fact, the whole measurement structure ends up producing a product which is not the audience itself, but data on the audience. It is thus necessary to analyze the dynamics that lead to the production of audience data, of ratings.

In response to this need, Meehan (1984) proposes to broaden our view so as to include not just the measurement methods but also the organizations that produce the audience data, their economic structure, their products, and the relations they have with other agents interested in the measurement process. In this sense, Meehan (1984) points to both the continuity and discontinuity between the interests of the media industry and the interests of the advertising industry when it comes to audience measurement. Both industries are interested in the production of audience measures that can be bought and sold. Despite this, the price that some agents pay and other agents receive in the commercial exchange involving audience measurement will depend on how that measurement is carried out and on what results are obtained. That is why neither of the two industries can trust the other to carry out the measurement. From that lack of trust springs the need for independent measuring organizations.

This need for independent measurement to reconcile the interests of the different agents and to become a neutral ground on which to establish business exchanges does more than explain the need for a third agent in the process of production and sale of audience data. It also explains the preference for a specific way to structure the measurement. Even though it is possible to perform the measurement process in any thinkable way—from case studies promoted by one company or organization to the single and homogeneous measurement of the whole market sponsored by all the agents involved—in fact there is a preference for studies that cover most of the media offerings and that are sufficiently homogeneous. Méndez and Lamas (2003: 67) summarize the issue as follows:

> The birth and development of audience research stems from the need to find objective measuring elements [...] that can be used as a coin of exchange in the buying and selling of advertising space [...] This main goal of the research determines some of its more relevant organizational characteristics. Usually there is only one measuring procedure per medium per country, and that measuring procedure covers most vehicles within that particular medium, and this helps to make this measure 'official' and to give credibility to the coin of exchange, at the same time that available resources are optimized since they are used for a single study.

That is, just as we found in our discussion of audience research methods that quantitative approaches are preferred over qualitative ones—even though the latter have the potential to offer richer information on the audience—it is also possible to see, when we analyze the way measurement is structured and organized, how there is a preference for homogeneous and large-scale measurement procedures—even though custom studies might offer a richer picture of the object being measured. Because, as Peter Miller (1994: 61) explains,

> the custom study's information richness advantage is balanced by two disadvantages: Its unique information cannot be compared directly with that produced by other studies and its sponsorship by one client threatens its claim to objectivity.

In other words, custom studies have credibility problems because they respond to the specific interests of the organization that finances them—interests that cannot be hidden behind the reputation or the scientific quality of the research company that carries out the study. At the same time, they do not allow the data obtained to become a coin of exchange because they cannot be compared to the data obtained in other studies. That is why advertisers demand studies that simultaneously measure as many vehicles as possible and that offer a similar degree of detail on each vehicle, even if that means not offering very detailed information.

The organization of audience measurement around studies that cover most of the vehicles available to advertisers and whose data serve as a coin of exchange in advertising transactions creates a tendency toward monopolies in the audience measurement market, and "although a number of different firms provide statistical representations of media audiences, only one firm tends to dominate the distribution of comprehensive audience data for each media technology" (Napoli, 2003: 18).

Therefore, the logic that rules the dynamics among the different agents involved in the audience measurement process privileges those situations in which a single source becomes the reference for the market. In order to achieve that position of reference it is necessary to convince both the media and advertisers that the performed measurement is the best possible, and to do so it is necessary to appeal to the 'scientific' and 'practical' validity of the measurement. There has to exist an appeal to the correctness of the measurement process in terms of its ability to reveal the actual audience, and there must be some evidence that the information obtained in the measurement process is functional in terms of the day-to-day needs of the industry, is easy to understand and manage, and does not interfere with established routines (Miller, 1994).

Despite the monopolistic trend within the measurement market, if one looks at the industry's history it is possible to see how these monopolies always seem to be in a precarious situation (Beville, 1988; Buzzard, 1990, 2002). As soon as a monopoly is established, it is challenged by new competitors that sometimes succeed in replacing them. And the strategies that these competitors follow seem to respond to a specific pattern: methodological variations are created in order to differentiate similar products, and these differences are then promoted as ways of obtaining more objective, exact, and scientific measurements. In particular, Meehan (1984) mentions a series of steps that can often be found in the competitive environment of audience measurement: first, the development of a new measurement procedure or a variation on an existing procedure; then, the shaping of the innovation in order to manipulate differences in demand; finally, the promotion of the innovation as a step forward in the progress of science at the same time that alliances are built with the companies whose interests would be better served by the innovation. According to Meehan (1984), there is another possibility, introduced by AC Nielsen, to develop an innovation on which a patent can be obtained and to use that patent to keep the market under control and prevent new competitors from entering the market or, at least, limit their possibilities.

Therefore, the interplay of interests around audience measurement promotes the creation of independent measuring entities that serve as arbiters in the audience market and produce the coin of exchange of audience data. In order to be able to establish the measurement data as a currency it is necessary to privilege a certain type of study in which the offerings of most media vehicles are covered in a homogeneous way. And since the measurement industry is ruled by this currency logic, there is a tendency to form monopolies based on the 'scientific' and 'practical' validity of the measurement procedure of reference. This same appeal to the validity of the measurement serves, in turn, as a tool for the entry of new competitors into the measurement market.[5]

All these ideas refer to the audience measurement industry of traditional mass media, and it is therefore necessary to examine these same dynamics in the context of the Internet and the World Wide Web. In audience measurement of traditional media, there is a long tradition that has created a relatively stable situation and has allowed for the examination of these dynamics with the perspective of decades (Buzzard, 2002). However, in the case I am studying here, and considering the short span of time since the emergence of the medium, the examination of these issues becomes more complex. The constant evolution of the object of study and the lack of consolidation means that we are confronted with a field in frenetic activity.

Besides examining whether the logic surrounding the single currency, that is clear in the measurement of other media, is also applicable to audience measurement of the Internet and the World Wide Web, it will additionally be necessary to examine whether the strategies followed by the agents involved in the measurement process are similar to the ones described above. In addition, if the appeal to the validity of the measures seems to be an essential element in those strategies, it will be necessary to analyze the extent to which there are attempts to adapt the measurement process to the specific characteristics of the new medium in order to make them more scientific and valid. For instance, we need to know whether the global nature of the Internet or the huge supply of vehicles that it allows for become arguments in this game of interests among measuring organizations, media, and advertisers. All these issues will constitute the focus of Section IV of this book.

Conclusions to Section I

This book proposes an analysis of Internet audience measurement and, in particular, of the origins of that measurement, of the methods used, and of the industry dynamics that shape it. But I have not chosen this object of study because I would like to improve or criticize the methods used or because I would like to display the panoply of research techniques available to the practitioner of audience measurement in the new media environment. Instead, I aspire to use the analysis of audience measurement as a way to examine issues of deeper theoretical and practical implications. Knowledge about the audience, or the interest in the other, is an essential part of every communication process. Even though organizational studies seem to reveal that media professionals do not necessarily have a clear image of the audiences they address, images of the audience play a fundamental role in the organizational strategies and institutional interactions of the media. As Ettema and Whitney assert (1994: 8),

> while newspaper reporters and television scriptwriters may not have audience images dancing in their head as they write their stories, newspaper managers may have circulation and market research data and television programmers certainly have ratings data on their desk as they decide whether such stories should continue to be written at all. Thus 'audience images' reappear, if we look for them, not in individual daily work routines but in organizational strategies and interactions within the overall arrangements of the institution.

In the case of mass media audiences, these images take a peculiar form since the lack of physical co-presence and of clear links between senders and receivers make the reality of 'the other' especially elusive. That is why the reality of the audience is only manifested through research that usually takes the form of measurement of the size and profile of the audience. And it is through this measurement that the audience acquires an institutional presence.

In other words, it is thanks to audience measurement that the audience takes a central role in the institutional functioning of the media. As Ang's (1991) work shows, this institutional relevance of the images of the audience produced through research is not exclusive to those mass media that follow a commercial logic. Audience measurement has also become a substitute for worn-out discourses on the public service role of non-commercial television, becoming in this way an ideological support for public broadcasting systems. Hence, in order to study the audience from an institutional point of view, it is necessary to study its construction through measurement. And when we study the institutional role of the audience of a medium we are at the same time conducting an analysis of the medium itself, since "media reproduce by producing audience. The audience produces the media that reproduce it" (Callejo, 2001: 60). By studying the audience, we are studying the medium.

The Internet and the World Wide Web are recent, complex, and constantly evolving phenomena. To analyze the measurement of their audience, the origins of that measurement, its methods, and its organization, will in fact allow us to study the characteristics of these new media, of their process of institutionalization, of their place in communicative practices and processes, of their differences and similarities with respect to other communication media. And since "precisely one of the problems that the Internet has when it comes to its being considered a more or less conventional medium is the lack of standardized and widely accepted procedures for the empirical observation of its audience" (Callejo, 2003: 19), the analysis of Internet audience measurement, of the procedures for the empirical observation of its audience, leads us to an examination of the degree to which the Internet and the World Wide Web can be regarded as conventional communication media.

In order to structure our route, I have specified three statements that can serve as hypotheses which, taken together, will allow for a complete analysis of the object of study. These statements are as follows:

1. The birth of Internet audience measurement coincides with the historical moment in the development of the medium in which

it starts to show some of the characteristics that define the mass media that precede it.

2. The methods applied in Internet audience measurement, and in particular those applied to World Wide Web audience measurement, display clear similarities to those applied in audience measurement in traditional mass media but show obvious limitations when trying to respond to the peculiarities of the new medium.

3. As is the case with audience measurement in traditional mass media, the economic interests that surround Internet and web audience measurement make it necessary to search for audience data that can become a coin of exchange in the economic transactions within the medium.

Regarding methodological issues, because I analyze such wide and complex phenomena as the Internet and its audience from an institutional point of view, I have considered that the most appropriate way of covering my object of study and analyzing it from the chosen perspective is to resort to secondary information sources. Even when using secondary sources, the size of the phenomena is such that it is impossible to exhaust all those sources and to examine all of the development of such a global medium and of its audience measurement. That is why, for each of the statements and hypotheses that shape each of the following chapters, I have privileged certain sources of information and certain areas of study.

For the first statement, I will, in particular, examine three essential characteristics of the Internet that will allow for its comparison with traditional mass media:

1. The existence of asymmetry between sender and receiver in the communication process.

2. The popularization process in which the user population attains a significant number.

3. The existence of commercial interests, specifically of advertising interests, that seek to exploit the business potential of the medium.

I will start with an examination of the evolution of the Internet from its origins in order to decide whether, and in which moment, we can compare the Internet with traditional mass media. Since the analysis I propose here refers to the articulation of the Internet and the World Wide Web as communication media and most of the developments that lead in that direction have taken place in the United States, most of the sources used in the second section focus on that country. In order to show whether the Internet presents the aforementioned characteristics, I have paid special attention to the existing literature on the history of the Internet, online advertising, Internet technology, and Internet culture. I have also used, to the extent that they were accessible and reliable, data available online.

For the analysis of the second statement, I will examine whether the different methods and techniques used in World Wide Web audience measurement take into account the peculiarities of the medium and are able to offer valid and rigorous measures of its audience. In order to articulate this analysis, I will use the following structure for each of the methods to be examined:

a. General description of the method
b. Measuring organizations
c. Sampling issues
d. Data gathering and analysis
e. Metrics and results

Since the third section of this book will focus on measurement methods, and these do not show relevant differences in their various local applications, the analysis will not refer to any particular geographic area, but to the formal characteristics of those methods.

Regarding information sources, I have used a combination of existing literature with the analysis of documents and measures produced by measuring organizations. Most of the literature I have used comes from publications based on ESOMAR–ARF conferences. ESOMAR, formerly known as the European Society for Opinion and Marketing Research and currently named The World Association of Opinion and Marketing Research Professionals, and ARF, Advertising Research Foundation, organize annual global conferences on audience measurement. These conferences bring together the organizations and professionals who are at the cutting edge of audience measurement methods. Since 1998, ESOMAR and ARF have been paying attention in their conferences to the development of Internet audience measurement. The proceedings of these conferences are probably the richest and most up-to-date sources on Internet audience measurement methods.

In order to analyze the third statement, in Section IV I will examine the dynamics of the Internet audience measurement industry since its inception and how the interplay of interests has shaped the measurement process with the ultimate goal of obtaining a standard to provide stability to economic exchanges. In particular, I will analyze the different interests that come together in online audience measurement, and I will examine, on the one hand, the role of measuring organizations and, on the other hand, the role of their clients in giving shape to the measurement process.

Although I adopt a global perspective, in the analysis of the dynamics of the Internet audience measurement market I have focused my attention on the United States, since it is the point of reference in the evolution of the World Wide Web, and it is where most of the technological and business developments surrounding the web have taken place, where Internet audience measurement has been most relevant, and where there are more abundant, accessible, and well-organized information sources for the analysis of the dynamics I would like to study.

Besides the sources used in the previous two chapters, for the analysis of the third statement in Section IV, I have used documents produced by the different organizations created by the relevant agents with the goal of developing those measures. I have also used information from periodicals available on the Lexis-Nexis database. In particular, I have focused on three periodicals—a newspaper, a magazine that covers the developments surrounding the Internet from different points of view, and a trade magazine from the field of advertising—that I feel offer sufficient, and to a certain degree, complementary information on the object of study:

- The *New York Times*: Newspaper of reference in the United States, with a daily circulation of over a million copies.

- *The Industry Standard*: Magazine published by *Standard Media International* between 1998 and 2001. It became, in spite of its short life and its variable periodicity, a publication of reference for the Internet industry, and it offered a detailed coverage of business, technology, and social developments in the online world.
- *Advertising Age*: Published by the *AdAge Group*, it is the magazine of reference in the advertising world in the United States. It began publication in 1930, and it is published weekly.

In order to retrieve the documents necessary for this study, I performed searches, using Lexis-Nexis, in these three publications. The terms searched for were 'Internet Audience,' 'Web Audience,' 'Internet Ratings,' 'Web Ratings,' and 'Audience Measurement.' The searches were restricted to the twelve-year period from September 1, 1993 to August 31, 2005. They retrieved a total of 493 documents: 204 from the *New York Times*, 50 from *The Industry Standard*, and 239 from *Advertising Age*. Besides these generic searches, several specific searches were performed—for names or concepts that had appeared in the analysis—in order to complement the information gathered. In this manner, a total of over 600 documents were analyzed.

The Constitution of the Audience

The goal of this section is to examine the first of the three statements proposed above, that is, that Internet audience measurement appears at the time when the Internet starts showing some of the fundamental and defining characteristics of traditional mass media. By analyzing these characteristics and the birth of Internet audience measurement, I will in fact be analyzing the constitution of the Internet audience.

As we saw above, audience measurement is, according to Smythe's (1977) proposal, an essential element in the process of manufacturing and selling the audience. But, as it was also mentioned, this understanding of the role of audience measurement has its own field of application in a concrete and specific historical development of communication processes. Therefore, audience measurement is closely linked to different business interests that, in a particular historical moment, take advantage of the possibilities opened by the mass communication media to manage demand and mass consumption. In turn, these mass media are defined by the asymmetry they establish between senders and receivers, and by addressing large numbers of individuals. Even though all three of the elements mentioned (asymmetry, large numbers of individuals, and business interests) intertwine in the historical process that leads to the advent of audience measurement, I will examine each of them separately in order to obtain a more detailed and complete picture of the birth of Internet audience measurement.

If we want to understand the origins of Internet audience measurement, it is necessary to examine the evolution of the medium from its origins to the moment in which its audience starts to be measured. Only then the changes that take place in the process will become apparent. Even though the origins of the Internet can be traced back to the late 1960s, online audience measurement starts in the mid-1990s. Understanding the differences between the Internet of the 1990s and the Internet of previous decades calls for an examination of the historical evolution of the medium, of its origins, of the interests that were behind its creation, of the roles of the various agents that participated in its development, and, especially, of the transformation that the medium underwent at the beginning of the 1990s and of the role played by the World Wide Web in that transformation.[1] In the process, it will also be necessary to pay attention to the technological innovations introduced in the Internet from its inception. Only then will we be able to understand not just the birth of Internet audience measurement, but also the methods used in the measurement of the audience, which will be examined in detail in Section III, and the degree to which those methods are appropriate for a medium that presents specific technological characteristics which are different from those of traditional mass communication media.

After examining the history of the medium, I will analyze each of the three essential traits which, according to my approach, lead to the birth of Internet audience measurement. Finally, I will briefly examine the role played by online audience measurement in the mid-1990s. With it, I will be performing an analysis of the advent of a new reality, the Internet audience, and of its main characteristics.

CHAPTER 3

A Brief History of the Internet

The Origins: ARPANET

On October 4, 1957, the Soviet Union launched Sputnik, the first artificial satellite in history. This launch caused much concern in the United States, since it meant that the USSR might gain control over outer space. The then US president, Dwight Eisenhower, decided to mobilize all available scientific resources in order to match and outperform Soviet military technology capabilities. Eisenhower was aware of the existing rivalry among the different branches of the US military and of the danger that that rivalry could pose to his efforts to compete with the Soviet Union. That is why he decided to create within the Department of Defence an agency that was to be independent from the different branches of the military and that would be in charge of coordinating the scientific efforts to match the Soviets (Hafner & Lyon, 1998). This is how the Advanced Research Projects Agency (ARPA) was born at the beginning of 1958.[1] With a budget of around 500 million dollars, ARPA was to be responsible for developing all space research in the country, as well as advanced research in strategic missiles. However, at the end of 1958, the US government created the National Aeronautics and Space Administration (NASA), which took charge of all space research and also took with it most of ARPA's budget. ARPA now had to rethink its goals and objectives and, after a process of consultations with its own employees, decided to devote itself to high-risk research projects and to seek collaboration within the academy (Naughton, 2000).

At the beginning, the research carried out by ARPA was focused on antimissile defence and on technology for the detection of nuclear tests. However, the US military asked ARPA to start doing research in the field of behavioral sciences. In 1961, the Air Force decided to donate to ARPA a spare computer from a project devoted to time-sharing computing.

In 1962, ARPA hired J. C. R. Licklider as director of its Control and Command Research section. Licklider was a scientist from the Massachusetts Institute of Technology (MIT), interested in the issue of time-sharing computing and obsessed with the interaction between human beings and computers and with the communication possibilities of that interaction (see Licklider, 1960; Licklider & Taylor, 1968), and these interests influenced the future work of the agency. During his tenure in ARPA, from 1962 to 1964, he also shaped the informal and non-bureaucratic style of the agency, supported the creation of joint research projects with different universities, and created the Information Processing Techniques Office (IPTO), the branch of ARPA that was in charge of computing technology and which would start ARPANET.

In 1965, Bob Taylor became the head of IPTO and found in his Pentagon office three different terminals to access each of the three time-sharing computers managed by ARPA: one in Boston, one in Santa Monica, and a third one in Berkeley. Taylor started thinking about a system that would make the use of the different computers compatible and facilitate a more efficient use of the agency's resources. In 1966, Taylor received one million dollars from the head of ARPA to create a compatible network that allowed for access to the different time-sharing computers from a single terminal, promoted the exchange of resources and results among scientists, and permitted communication among computers using different languages and operating systems (Hafner & Lyon, 1998). The ultimate goal was to optimize the computing resources of the different projects financed by ARPA. Taylor hired another MIT scientist, Larry Roberts, to launch the network. In the first published description of the project, Roberts and his assistant explained the reasoning behind the creation of the network:

> Currently each computer center in the country is forced to recreate all software and data files it wishes to utilize. In many cases this involves complete reprogramming of software or reformatting of data files. This duplication is extremely costly... With a successful network, the core problem of sharing resources would be severely reduced. (Quoted in Abbate, 1999: 96)

However, the role of the network as a tool for sharing computing resources only made sense for a short period of time. Within a few years, the advent of microcomputers revolutionized the world of computers and made large time-sharing machines obsolete.

At the beginning, the network project was based on the connection of the large time-sharing computers (hosts) via telephone lines. But in 1967 Wesley Clark, a researcher at Washington University, proposed a different network architecture. This architecture left those large computers out of the network and connected them to the network through a series of smaller computers called interface message processors (IMPs). This system created a network of computers that could speak the same language and that could be exclusively devoted to managing the traffic of the network, and it avoided excessive demands on the hosts or on the people in charge of them.

Aside from the general architecture, however, ARPA did not have a clear idea of how the network would function. This was until, in 1967, ARPA members attending a symposium in Tennessee heard a British scientist talk about packet switching, an idea that would turn out to be essential for the creation of the network. Interestingly, the idea of packet switching was born in parallel, independently, and almost simultaneously on both sides of the Atlantic.

In the US, the idea was born from the work of Paul Baran. He was a scientist at RAND Corporation, a think tank created in California in 1946 with the goal of helping the United States develop its nuclear capabilities. The Corporation was funded, for the most part, by the Air Force. In 1959, Baran started working on a project aimed at improving the survival possibilities of the American military command-and-control systems in case of a nuclear attack. This project has often been mentioned as the starting point for the creation of the Internet, and it has been assumed that the net responded to the command-and-control needs of the American military. However, that perception does not seem to be backed by most detailed accounts of the origins of the net. Even though Baran's ideas are essential if we want to understand the gestation of the Internet, the truth is that the creation of ARPANET, the embryo of the Internet, was a response to the need for sharing the scarce available computer resources among research groups that were separated from each other (Hafner & Lyon, 1998; Naughton, 2000).

The central idea of Baran's project was to create a communications network able to keep working under the most extreme circumstances in order to coordinate the military response to a hypothetical nuclear attack. Baran thought that the communications networks that existed at the time would not be able to survive a powerful attack, and he decided to design a new type of network. Baran started with a few fundamental ideas: to avoid centralization, since it made networks highly vulnerable; to build a network of distributed nodes, each of them connected with its neighbors; and to obtain a certain degree of redundancy in the connections. He soon arrived at the conclusion that the network would be robust enough if every node were connected to three others. He also realized that the network would have to be digital since, on the one hand, the nodes of the network would have to be computers able to obtain information on the state of the network and, on the other hand, with the analog communication technology prevalent at the time, the signals would quickly degrade in a network with so many connections (Abbate, 1999). Finally, Baran introduced a new idea in the network's design: breaking the messages into component blocks. The use of this idea would allow for the use of cheap and simple nodes in the network, increase the security of the network by making the interception and interpretation of messages more difficult, and increase the flexibility and efficiency of transmissions. Each node would pass the blocks of information to the next node through the most efficient root; thanks to a system for constant monitoring of the state of the network. Once the destination was reached, the blocks would be rearranged to compose the original message. Baran had the final design ready in 1962. It consisted of a network of nodes that received and transmitted the information blocks through microwave transmitters set on small towers. The distance between the nodes was to be around 20 miles, and they would run on fuel, since it was assumed that the power grid would be destroyed by a nuclear attack (Naughton, 2000). Baran made his design public in 1964, and, even though the experts working for the telecommunications monopoly AT&T (American Telephone and Telegraph) considered that the proposed network would never work, in 1965 the RAND Corporation asked the Air Force to build an experimental version of the network. When the Pentagon decided to proceed with the implementation, the task was assigned to the Defence and Communications Agency (DCA). However, the DCA did not seem to understand or appreciate the project, and Baran decided to stop the development of his design before it could be ruined by the DCA. The network proposed by Baran was never built.

In the UK, Donald Davies, from the British National Physical Laboratory (NPL), became interested at the beginning of the 1960s in the possibility of communication between computers via telephone lines. As time-sharing computing was developing, the terminals used to connect to the computers were situated at a distance from them. Sometimes it was necessary to use the telephone system to connect the terminals to the computers. Davies realized that was not an efficient system. One of the issues that caught his attention was the problem derived from transmitting large packages of information that could clog the lines and keep smaller packages waiting. In order to solve this problem, Davies conceived in 1965 a system similar to the one designed by Baran: messages would be broken into smaller packages that would contain not only a piece of the original message, but also information on the origin and destination of the information, a control number to make sure that there were no losses of information in the transmission process, and a sequence number that allowed for the ordering of the packages to recompose the original message. When he presented his ideas publicly in 1966, a representative of the British Ministry of Defence told him about the similarities of his design and Baran's design (Naughton, 2000).

Once ARPA found out about the ideas of Baran and Davies, it became clear how the intended network would function. In 1968, ARPA started the process of accepting bids from companies wanting to build the network. It ended up awarding the project to Bolt, Beranek, and Newman (BBN), a small technology firm based in Boston and full of MIT graduates. The IMP network had to be invisible to users and, therefore, it had to be quick—a message had to be able to go from one host to another in less than half a second—and reliable—since it was not expected to achieve the degree of redundancy in connections proposed by Baran. The task faced by BBN was not an easy one.[2] However, the first IMP was installed at the University of California Los Angeles (UCLA) on August 30, 1969, and the second one was ready on October 1 of the same year at Stanford Research Institute (SRI). Before the end of the year two more nodes were installed, one at the University of California at Santa Barbara and the other one at the University of Utah. Between 1969 and 1971, fifteen ARPANET—the name given to the network—nodes were created, most of them within research centers linked to the Defence Department's projects. In 1971, new IMP models were introduced that allowed for the connections to the network of up to sixty-three different devices, which multiplied the growing possibilities of the network and made it possible to connect to the network different machines, not just host computers. With the new IMPs, it was also possible to connect to the network those research centers that did not have an ARPA time-sharing computer (Abbate, 1999).

Even though BBN was in charge of creating the network and making it functional, the research centers where the large computers that had to be connected by the network were located were responsible for establishing the system of connections between these hosts and the smaller IMPs. In order to do this, the Network Working Group (NWG) was created. Most of the members of the group were students from the universities with nodes connected to the network, and their role was to coordinate the process of developing the connections between hosts and IMPs. Since there seemed to be no clear idea about how to establish those connections, a shy student within the NWG wrote in April 1969 a preliminary proposal with the title Request for Comments (RFC). He wanted his document to be the starting point of an open debate among NWG members. His approach was so well received that the RFC became the usual form of communication for the proposal, revision, and acceptance of the technology standards of the network. This way of communication meant that nothing was secret, that solutions were sought through collaboration, and that everything produced belonged to the public domain.

Two of the goals of the NWG were the design of a method to allow network users to log into a remote computer and another method to allow the exchange of files among the different computers in the network. In this manner, the TELNET protocol was born in 1969, allowing users to control a computer remotely. Similarly, the File Transfer Protocol (FTP) was born in 1972, allowing the exchange of files between computers. Another result of the NWG's work was the Network Control Program, proposed in 1971 and later renamed the Network Control Protocol (NCP), which permitted connections among host computers and which would be fundamental for the functioning of the network.[3]

Even though ARPANET had originally been created with the goal of allowing the research groups associated with ARPA to remotely use the computers located in other centers, the truth is that three-fourths of the network's traffic was being generated by electronic mail (e-mail). ARPANET was being transformed into a communication tool. This transformation process bestowed the network with a new meaning at the same time that it was losing its foundational function as a way of sharing computing resources due to the popularization of microcomputers. E-mail, the way we understand it today, was born in 1970. That is, the e-mail in which messages are exchanged among different computers, because at least since 1960 there existed e-mail systems within time-sharing computers with which users of the same machine could leave messages for each other (Naughton, 2000). Ray Tomlison, a BBN employee, had created a program for the exchange of messages between users of the same computer and another program for the exchange of files among different computers. In July 1970, he decided to combine both tools and made the first exchange of mail messages between two computers within his office (Naughton, 2000). In order to allow the exchange of messages among network computers that used different languages, Tomlison's e-mail program was included in the FTP. Ever since, and with constant improvements in the software, e-mail has become one of the essential tools of the network.

At the end of 1972, ARPANET was made up of thirty-seven nodes, whose access was restricted to research centers that worked for the Pentagon, and it was functioning with enough reliability to allow ARPA to carry out a public demonstration of the possibilities of the network. By that time there were other active networks in France and the United Kingdom based on the idea of packet switching. In the United States, there were also a radio communications network in Hawaii (ALOHANET) and another one that used satellites (SATNET).

The next step in the development of the net was to find a way of connecting ARPANET with other networks. This project was called *Internetting*; the goal was to create a network of networks, and in order to do this it was necessary to define an architecture that would allow all the different networks to operate together. Vinton Cerf from Stanford University, and Robert Kahn from ARPA, with the help of an international group of scientists started the development of that architecture. It was based on a simple principle: instead of reconfiguring all the networks to make them compatible, the only thing that was needed was the use of computers that could act as gateways among the different networks. The sole function of these gateways was to transfer the information packages from one network to the other. In this way the network would be expandable *ad infinitum*, since all that was needed to connect any network was to make sure that some kind of gateway was established. In 1973, Kahn and Cerf created a series of standardized communication protocols to make this architecture function. Thus, the Transmission Control Protocol (TCP) was born. This protocol, besides applying the gateway architecture, established a way for information packages to be wrapped inside an electronic envelope. With this arrangement, the gateways would only have to read the envelopes and send them to their destination and would not be required to examine the content of the packets or to check that these arrived safely at that destination. When a host received some information, it would send a confirmation message to the computer from which that information came. The Internet architecture had been born.

The TCP was reorganized in 1978 and gave way to the TCP/IP (Internet Protocol), on which the Internet still runs today. Splitting the original protocol into two combined protocols involved assigning each with its own specialized functions. The TCP was in charge of breaking the messages into packages with their corresponding electronic envelopes, of organizing them at their destination, of detecting errors in the transmission, and of resending any information lost in the process. In turn, the IP was responsible for locating a particular computer among all those connected and specified a system of names, addresses, and routes within the net.

Since the beginning of the 1970s, ARPA, which changed its name to Defence Advanced Research Projects Agency (DARPA), started thinking about the need to transfer the control of ARPANET. The goal of the original project had been more than achieved, and ARPA as an organization was not designed to manage complex technological infrastructures but rather to generate innovative research projects. The obvious candidate to take charge of the network was AT&T, but the telecommunications giant rejected the offer. That is why in 1975 ARPANET was transferred to another military agency, the DCA. The DCA would be in charge of making all decisions regarding the network, while BBN would still work as a contractor in charge of the technical side of the network. The most significant change following the transfer of the network from ARPA to the DCA was, apart from an increased bureaucracy, the growing use of ARPANET by the American military (Abbate, 1999). The network that had been until then the exclusive territory of academics, engineers, and students became an important tool for the military activities of the United States. Otherwise, the network kept on functioning and growing at a healthy rhythm.

Thus, in a little more than ten years, and with the funds and help of the US Department of Defence through ARPA, a digital computer network was established—a network that allowed for a more rational and efficient use of the computer resources devoted to military research and that made possible the connection to other networks with different structures and functioning systems. The network, with its distributed and flexible architecture, and working with a packet switching system, was able to function with the reliability, speed, and robustness planned in its original design. Even though the influence of the military was not direct in its design and implementation, the truth is that the design favored military values (resistance, flexibility, and high performance) above commercial values (simplicity, low cost, or attractiveness for the user). This design allowed ARPANET to acquire a growing value as a military tool from the late 1970s onward. However, the academy—researchers, professors, and students—had a huge influence on the development of the network and introduced into it its own values, decentralization of authority, information exchange, and camaraderie (Abbate, 1999). It was a network with very restricted access, in which the users were almost exclusively the researchers, engineers, and students in charge of making it function. And, since its main original goal was to improve the use of computer resources and to allow computers to communicate with each other, the big surprise that it produced in the first years of functioning was the advent of e-mail. It soon became the most popular tool of the network, and this led to the network being perceived more as a tool for communication among people than as a tool for sharing computing resources.

The 1980s: Growth and Demilitarization

The 1980s were characterized by the growth of the network; thanks to its connection with other networks and the progressive disappearance of military control over ARPANET, until it was transferred to civil hands. A first step in the decline of military control over the network was its division into two different networks. As military use of ARPANET grew, the Defence Department began to question the procedures for controlling access to the network. Since it became apparent that it was impossible to implement a rigorous control over users and network access, and due to security reasons, at the beginning of the 1980s the DCA decided to split ARPANET into two separate networks. One of them, MILNET, would be used exclusively by the military, while the other one would be devoted to research under the name of ARPA-Internet (Castells, 2001). As it was necessary to maintain some kind of communication between the two networks, the DCA decided to implement the TCP/IP and to eliminate the obsolete NCP (Naughton, 2000). The transition took place on January 1, 1983, and, from them on, connections to ARPANET-Internet from the civil world became much easier, both because of technical reasons (the implementation of the TCP/IP made it easy to connect other networks) and because of administrative issues (with the disappearance of the military component from ARPA-Internet, security restrictions could no longer act as a burden for the growth of the network).

And the growth of the Internet during these years was not restricted to those networks created under the umbrella of ARPA or of other government agencies. This growth was influenced by a series of practices of interconnection born outside official institutions. The restrictions on the use of ARPANET had generated a series of movements among those who did not have access to the new computer networks. In 1979, a group of students from Duke University and the University of North Carolina developed a communication system among computers that ran on the UNIX operating system. Two AT&T employees had created this operating system in the 1970s. UNIX became extremely popular among computer aficionados. It was also widely used within AT&T and this led the company to develop a tool that would allow engineers to modify remotely the software of the company's computers running on UNIX. This way, in 1979 AT&T introduced a version of UNIX, the UNIX-to-UNIX Copy (UUCP), that allowed a computer to call another computer and upload software onto it. This was the tool that facilitated the creation of the new communication system among computers (Naughton, 2000). The system used homemade modems to call from one computer to a second computer, to examine the changes introduced in the files of this second computer, and to copy these changes to the first computer. The creators of this system presented their idea in January 1980 and named it Usenet News. In this manner, newsgroups, a new tool for the exchange of information and ideas, were born. A user could connect from her own computer to another computer that hosted one or more newsgroups, read the contributions of other members of the group, download articles or commentaries to her computer, and then respond to them, etc. The development of Usenet was slow at the beginning, but once it was connected to ARPANET-Internet the growth gained momentum and soon reached thousands of newsgroups on the most diverse topics.

Another example of these alternative movements for computer connectivity was the Bulletin Board System (BBS). In the late-seventies, two members of the Chicago Area Computer Hobbyists' Exchange (CACHE) created the software that runs bulletin boards. The software allowed two personal computers, not UNIX, to communicate directly via telephone lines using modems. Once the software was installed in the computer, anyone could create a bulletin board, connect the modem to the telephone line, give out the telephone number of the new bulletin board at some pre-existing bulletin board, and wait for other users to come and add their commentaries or their information. In 1983, another programmer developed new BBS software called Federal Interagency Databases Online (FIDO). His goal was to create a network of bulletins. By 1986, it had more than one thousand nodes and ten thousand users (Naughton, 2000).

Another popular alternative network was BITNET. This network took advantage of a tool within IBM's operating system that allowed the exchange of programs among programmers. This tool was modified to allow for the exchange of messages. In 1981, with the support of IBM, students from the City University of New York and Yale University created an experimental connection between the two universities using this tool. The connection permitted the exchange of e-mail messages and even real-time conversations, instant messaging, using regular phone lines (Abbate, 1999).

All these alternative networks ended up being connected to ARPANET and became part of the Internet; thanks to the gradual adoption of the TCP/IP and to the attitude of ARPANET-Internet managers, who allowed the exchange of e-mail and newsgroups between these networks and ARPANET-Internet. But in the early 1980s, there was also a proliferation of private and public networks, both American and European, each of them with their corresponding gateways to connect to ARPA-Internet. And this proliferation ended up blurring the border between the network financed with public funds by the US government and the macro-network made up of all the networks connected to it. A decisive contribution to this proliferation was made by the development of Ethernet, a protocol—born out of an ARPA-funded project—for the transmission of data among computers in a local network. Ethernet facilitated the creation of intranets and local area networks (LANs) in universities and companies.

If there is one institution that is key to any explanation of the expansion of the Internet, the increasingly open access to it, and its definitive transfer to civil control, it is the National Science Foundation (NSF). The NSF was created as a US government agency in 1950 with the goal of promoting scientific development through the funding of research projects and the support of sciences education. In the 1970s, the NSF had already considered the need to create a computer network for scientific use. In 1980, the NSF approved a proposal to allow computer science departments to have access to a telecommunications network. CSNET, as the network was named, had a three-level structure: ARPANET; Telenet, a commercial service for the exchange of information, created by BBN and based on packet switching; and PhoneNet, a system of connections using the telephone lines. Those centers with ARPA projects would use ARPANET, those that could afford a full-time connection would use Telenet, and those with fewer resources would use PhoneNet. The network became functional in 1982 and was funded by the NSF until, in 1985, it could be supported by the contributions of the different universities and private research centers connected to CSNET.

The success of CSNET led the NSF to consider the creation of a new network that could serve not just computer science researchers, but also the scientific community in general. This is how NSFNET was created in 1984, with a high-speed backbone sponsored by the NSF and several regional networks connected to it. With NSFNET the connections with international networks grew rapidly from the late 1980s onward. By the end of the decade, the Internet was a conglomerate of very different networks, and 250 of them were not American. ARPANET was not anymore the center of the Internet. In fact, NSFNET was working better than ARPANET, at a higher speed and with more users. At some point, the DCA considered the creation of a new network to substitute ARPANET. But it ended up choosing another option, that is, to dismantle a technologically obsolete ARPANET, connect ARPANET nodes to NSFNET regional networks, and put the NSF in charge of the network's backbone. Following this plan, ARPANET ceased to exist on February 28, 1990. The Pentagon removed the network for good from the military environment and asked the NSF to manage it. But the NSF's control over the network would not last for long.

Thus, in the 1980s, the military's oversight of the Internet ended up disappearing and the network fell into civilian hands. This development eased access to the net. However, the management of the Internet remained in the hands of the government, and commercial activities on ARPA-Internet were explicitly prohibited. The size of ARPA-Internet increased; thanks to the total implementation of the TCP/IP, the connection of new international networks, the proliferation of intranets or LANs, the promotion of access from all American universities, and the birth of alternative computer networks. However, and in spite of the growth of the infrastructure of the network, the communication tools available through that network did not develop at the same rhythm. They were difficult to use, and unattractive because of their purely textual character, which contrasted with the development at that same time of graphic user interfaces for personal computers. Another big hurdle that the Internet presented was the difficulty of finding specific pieces of information. From the beginning, the managers of ARPANET had enormous difficulties in creating a catalog of the resources available on the net. With the growth in the number of connected networks, the number of users, and the amount of information available online, the problem of information search and retrieval acquired a new dimension. Thus, Internet use at the end of the 1980s was still limited to those minority circles with extensive computer knowledge and with the need or the passion to overcome the limitations of use presented by the net.

Privatization and World Wide Web

Even though the Internet was released from military control, it was still managed by a government agency and it was focused on scientific research and teaching, since commercial activities were prohibited by the NSF's Acceptable Use Policy. But with telecommunications embarked on a process of privatization and the technology needed for the creation of computer networks open to the public domain, the NSF started the privatization of the network. This process culminated on April 30, 1995, when the Internet was transferred to private hands after the closure of NFSNET. This transfer of the net to private hands launched a process of commercialization that would thoroughly transform the net.[4]

But if we had to point to a particular event that shaped and determined the development of the Internet, that event would be the birth of the World Wide Web. This new application attracted millions of users and transformed the perception of the net, from a research tool or a tool for the transmission of personal messages via e-mail to a medium for entertainment, shopping, or self-presentation. The World Wide Web appeared at the beginning of the 1990s in the scientific and academic environment of the Conseil Européen pour la Recherche Nucléaire (CERN), the European Laboratory for Particle Physics in

Geneva, Switzerland. Berners-Lee, a British physicist and computer consultant working at CERN, took advantage of the unstructured academic environment of the laboratory to develop his own ideas about the combination of hypertext and computer communication. The goal of Berners-Lee was the creation of a communication system that would allow for the linking of documents in a simple and non-sequential manner and that would facilitate the location of the information stored in the system. Through the 1980s he matured his project, culminating his work with the creation of the World Wide Web.[5]

The system developed by Berners-Lee was based on a client–server relationship. That is, a computer would act as a client that makes, through a specific program (a browser), a request to another computer (the server). By the end of 1990, Berners-Lee had been able to develop a prototype of a web browser and a web server. In order to make the relationship function he had to elaborate a series of new tools, beyond the browser, to allow for the creation, location, and transfer of information among computers that often were not compatible. The final result of his effort was made up of three fundamental pieces:

1. The HyperText Transfer Protocol (HTTP): A new communications protocol that managed the connection between clients and servers.
2. The HyperText Markup Language (HTML): A language based on tags for the creation of hypertext documents.
3. The Universal Document Identifier (UDI):[6] A system that provided the necessary information about where the required data were stored and that facilitated the location of documents.

The manner in which these three pieces were developed allowed for them to be used on the TCP/IP on which the Internet ran. Besides this, the UDI permitted the use of the web to access the resources already available over the Internet: newsgroups, file transfer, systems for the cataloging of information, such as Gopher and Wide Area Information Servers (WAIS),[7] etc. During 1991 and 1992 new versions of the web browser were developed in different places and institutions. By January 1993 there were fifty web servers on the Internet. It was not a spectacular growth.

But everything changed when at the beginning of 1993 a group from the National Center for Supercomputing Applications (NCSA) at the University of Illinois, led by the student Marc Andreessen, developed a browser that required very little learning, was able to use images and insert them within texts, and was easy to download and install. The creators of the browser, most of them students, named it Mosaic and produced versions of it for UNIX, PC, and Macintosh. In a few months it was estimated that several hundreds of thousands of copies of different versions of the browser were downloaded from the net. It was not the first web browser, but it was the first that could function on almost any computer, that was user-friendly (it had buttons, drop down menus, bars to move through documents) and that, in addition, was able to display images inserted in the text—thanks to a modification of the HTML language introduced by Mosaic programmers.[8] Soon the number of users, the number of servers, and the amount of information available on the web multiplied. In about one year, it is estimated that there were 1 million installed copies of Mosaic, and the number of web servers grew from 64 to 1248 (Abbate, 1999).

Andreessen, the leader of the team of programmers behind the creation of Mosaic, left the NCSA and moved to Silicon Valley. There he ended up getting in touch with a famous entrepreneur within the computer world, the founder of Silicon Graphics, Jim Clark. Together, in April 1994 they started the Mosaic Communications company, later renamed Netscape. After hiring the team of programmers who created Mosaic, they developed, in a few months, the browser that would shape the definitive expansion of the web, Netscape Navigator. The browser designed by Netscape was ten times faster than Mosaic and more sophisticated—it allowed, for instance, for the secure transmission of data, an essential element for online commerce.

The Navigator browser was another astounding success. It was distributed to users for free over the net, since the business model was based on flooding the individual user market with free browsers and obtaining revenues for business licences and server software (Clark, 2000). Within four months, Navigator took 75% of the browser market. But it was Netscape's Initial Public Offering in August 1995 that marked the beginning of a new era in the spectacular growth of the diffusion and use of browsers and the web.

Thus, at the beginning of the 1990s there took place a fundamental transformation of the Internet. On the one hand, the control and management of the net left for good the government's umbrella and was transferred into private hands. This transfer opened the door to the commercialization of the Internet. On the other hand, the advent of the World Wide Web and the development of the tools associated with it made it possible for any user without any special computer knowledge to easily access all the information and communication resources available over the Internet. But, as the web became the center of the Internet and web browsers became the most common way of accessing it, transformations in the communication processes established over the Internet also took place due to the specific characteristics of the web and its browsers. The web introduced new ways of communicating over the Internet, facilitated the use of the net, leading to its popularization and, to a great extent, also facilitated and promoted its commercialization.

Thus, we can already see sketched here the characteristics that turn the Internet into something similar to traditional mass communication media: asymmetry, popularization, and commercialization.

CHAPTER 4

Asymmetry, Popularization, Commercialization, and Measurement

Constituting the Internet Audience

In what follows I will analyze each of the three characteristics that lead to the constitution of the audience. To a certain extent, it can be said that the creation of organizations that act as senders is closely related to the process of commercialization, that the advent of large-size publics, or audiences, is closely related to the process of popularization, and that the difficulty in generating feedback is related to the advent of communication processes that show high levels of asymmetry. However, the three elements examined here are also closely interrelated among themselves in the historical development of the Internet. Nonetheless, for the sake of analytical clarity, I will examine each of them separately. Once this has been done, the origins and functions of Internet audience measurement will be discussed.

Asymmetry in Internet Communication

When I talk about asymmetry in communication I am referring to processes that are clearly different from the interpersonal communication ideal and in which there is an obvious differentiation between senders and receivers. This obvious differentiation, as we saw before, is an essential element that needs to be present before we can start speaking of audiences. It is a basic characteristic of all mass communication media, in which there are organizations that act as senders and publics of a certain size that act as receivers and who have limited options when it comes to generating feedback. The existence of this asymmetry in the communication processes taking place over the Internet is a development that becomes particularly prominent at the beginning of the 1990s due to the advent of the World Wide Web. Hence, it seems necessary to pay close attention to the moment in which this change takes place.

ARPANET was conceived as a tool for the efficient management of computing resources and not so much as a communication tool. In addition, in the origins of the net, ARPANET's user population was made up of those academics, researchers, and engineers in charge of its creation. As Abbate (1999: 5) says:

> in the early days of the ARPANET, the distinction between producers and users did not even exist, since ARPA's computer experts were building the system for their own use.

ARPANET was basically a tool for communication among computers and it was used by its own creators. This is why the first tools to be used over ARPANET's infrastructure were tools aimed at the management of the computers connected to it, tools that allowed having remote control over a computer (TELNET) or the transferring of files between computers (File Transfer Protocol, FTP).

As mentioned before, almost from the birth of the net, tools aimed at facilitating communication among the net's users, and not only among the computers constituting it, started to appear. The Internet can be defined as a series of computer networks that communicate among themselves through a series of protocols or languages and that support a series of tools and make it possible to establish different types of communication processes. With the Internet it is possible to send electronic mail messages, to chat, to read or contribute to bulletin boards and newsgroups, and to browse the web, among many other things. Each of these activities takes place in the Internet or through the Internet, but each of them presents certain peculiarities that make them different from each other, both from the point of view of the technological elements that sustain them and from the point of view of the possible uses they facilitate.

I will now briefly describe the different communication tools that became available over the Internet in the 1970s and 1980s, and examine the degree to which the communication processes they allow present a certain degree of asymmetry.[1]

Electronic mail (e-mail). Available over the Internet since the early 1970s, e-mail allows for the sending of texts or files through a specific address system. E-mail messages are sent from a mail address with the format name@domain.extension. In the message it is necessary to specify the destination address or addresses. The message is sent from a computer through the Transmission Control Protocol / Internet Protocol (TCP/IP) to a mail server that redirects it to the destination mail service. The person or persons to whom the message is sent can connect through the net to their mail server and download the message onto their computer. It therefore generates communication processes that, even though they can involve a great number of people, are fundamentally private, since information goes from point to point over the net and nobody can access it unless they are the designated recipients. Besides this, the possibility of generating feedback, of becoming a sender in the communication process established through e-mail, is very ample. It only requires a click on the 'reply' button and then typing in a message addressed to the original sender of the message, and/or to other recipients. E-mail is therefore an interpersonal (or even group) communication medium, in which even though it might be easy to identify senders and receivers, the roles are easily interchangeable.

Chat and instant messaging (IM): These tools allow for the establishment of live conversations, usually textual in nature, though it is increasingly possible to use voice and/or images. Regarding chat, one of its most popular systems is Internet Relay Chat (IRC), which has thousands of channels on the most diverse topics which any user can join and thus contribute to the ongoing conversations. It is also possible to create 'private' spaces in order to converse only with those participants that the user decides to invite. With an IM it is possible to create a list of contacts and have the system alert us when any of the contacts log on to the Internet and have their IM activated so we can initiate a live conversation with them if we choose to do so. Thus, both chat and IM allow for the establishment of synchronous conversations with certain degrees of privacy and with a variable number of participants, depending on the wishes of the user. In any event, they are communication processes that are very close to the ideal interpersonal communication process, in which there is no obvious asymmetry in the communication and where it is difficult to differentiate between senders and receivers.

Newsgroups:[2] They are online 'spaces' specialized in particular topics in which users send messages and establish asynchronous conversations, not live, about issues related to the particular topic of the newsgroup. Conversations are organized in 'threads' that allow users to easily follow the discussions. These discussions can be moderated and filtered or they can be completely open and unregulated. Server administrators decide which groups they want to host in their computers and they receive participants' messages. When users who subscribe to a particular group connect to the server hosting the group, they can automatically download to their computer the messages received by the group since their last connection to the server was terminated. The most widely known network of newsgroups is Usenet. Thus, newsgroups generate participatory communication processes in which it is possible to read what other participants contribute and to easily add information or comments. Therefore, and even though it is possible to use them in a completely passive way as a tool for consuming information, newsgroups have since their inception created communication processes in which it is not easy to talk of senders and receivers, or in which those roles are easily interchangeable.

As we can see, the communication tools available over the Internet before the advent of the World Wide Web show some basic traits that make it difficult to talk about asymmetry in the communication process. Regardless of the number of people involved, of the role they play, and of the synchronous or asynchronous nature of the communication, they generate essentially participatory communication processes that are co-created by the participants and that allow for fluent feedback. To what degree is the World Wide Web different from these other tools?

In the web the user's computer performs, through the TCP/IP, a HyperText Transfer Protocol (HTTP) request to a web server so that it can search for a particular page or perform a search in a database. Once the page is found or the search completed, the server sends it back automatically to the user's computer so that she can view it through a web browser. The page can contain text, images, multimedia files, executable programs, etc.

When Berners-Lee conceived the World Wide Web he was in fact putting together two fundamental tools: the Internet and hypertext. The hypertext idea had been proposed, in a more or less explicit way, by different researchers (Vannevar Bush, Douglas Engelbart, Ted Nelson) throughout the twentieth century.[3] However, Berners-Lee gave to his conception of hypertext in the web a special twist (Naughton, 2000: 239):

> Namely the idea that *documents should be editable by their readers*. Berners-Lee's idea of a browser therefore was not just an interface that would provide passive viewing, but something that would allow users to create their own inline links even as they were reading a document. This is the one part of his vision which did not survive beyond the CERN version.[4]

Berners-Lee proposed the web as a system in which any content could fit, in which any user could, easily and without needing much technical knowledge, provide content and obtain content. This is why the first browser developed by Berners-Lee combined browsing and editing capabilities. As Gillies and Cailliau (2000: 193) explain,

> Another big difference between Tim's [Berners-Lee] first browsers and modern ones is that with the NeXT [Berners-Lee's] browser it was just as easy to write pages as to read them.

It was conceived so that web users could be both consumers and producers of content. The web was supposed to be based on collaborative work. In his story of the creation of the web, Berners-Lee (1999: 30) says: "I was looking at a living world of hypertext, in which all the pages would be constantly changing." As Naughton (2000) mentions, that was precisely the facet of the web that did not survive beyond its original conception at the Conseil Européen pour la Recherche Nucléaire (CERN).

Even though the first browser developed by Berners-Lee worked both as browser and as editor and allowed for the editing and altering of the information as it was being read, it only worked on NeXT computers, a kind of computer that was very sophisticated for that time but had very limited diffusion. Due to a lack of resources and time, Berners-Lee could not develop a browser–editor compatible with the different computer systems and languages that existed at the beginning of the 1990s (Berners-Lee, 1999). A student working at CERN developed a line-mode[5] browser that could be installed in all the computers in the laboratory, from UNIX to PCs. Even though this browser allowed Berners-Lee (1999: 35–36) to show the scientific community the value of the web, it also meant a sacrifice:

> This was a big step, but it was achieved at some sacrifice in that we decided not to take the time to develop the line-mode browser as an editor. Simply being able to read documents was good enough to bootstrap the process. [...] But it left people thinking of the Web as a medium in which a few published and most browsed. My vision was a system in which sharing what you knew or thought should be as easy as learning what someone else knew.

Throughout 1992 new graphic, point-and-click, browsers were created outside the CERN. One of them was developed by a group of students at the Technological University of Helsinki, and it ran on the X Windows operating system, quite popular at the time. However, and in spite of an explicit request from Berners-Lee, they did not add editing capabilities to the browser. Another browser, Viola, was created by a student at the University of California-Berkeley and ran on UNIX machines. Even though it was a pretty advanced browser, Viola's installation was rather complicated.[6] Again, Berners-Lee (1999: 61–62) lamented the path that browsers' development was taking:[7]

> Although browsers were starting to spread, no one working on them tried to include writing and editing functions. There seemed to be a perception that creating a browser had a strong potential for payback, since it would make information from around the world available to anyone who used it. Putting as much effort into the collaborative side of the Web didn't seem to promise that millionfold multiplier. As soon as developers got their client working as a browser and released it to the world, very few bothered to continue to develop it as an editor.
>
> Without a hypertext editor, people would not have the tools to really use the Web as an intimate collaborative medium. Browsers would let them find and share information, but they could not work together intuitively. Part of the reason, I guessed, was that collaboration required much more of a social change in how people worked. And part of it was that editors were more difficult to write.
>
> For these reasons, the Web, which I designed to be a medium for all sorts of information, from the very local to the very global, grew decidedly in the

direction of the very global, and as a publication medium but less of a collaboration medium.

When it was becoming clear that Mosaic, the browser developed at the National Center for Supercomputing Applications (NCSA) of the University of Illinois, would become the browser of choice, Berners-Lee once again asked the developers of Mosaic to add editing capabilities to the browser they had created. However, to Berners-Lee's incredulity, they answered that it was not possible to develop an editor for Mosaic, and they began the diffusion of the browser as it was (Berners-Lee, 1999). It seems that what impeded the creation of a browser–editor was not so much an insurmountable technical hurdle as a very different view of what the web should be in the future. Marc Andreessen, the student who led the Mosaic team, was not seeking a tool for the collaborative participation of Internet users; he was seeking to extend the use of the Internet and of the tools available through it to the largest possible number of people. In order to do that, his first goal was to create a browser whose installation and use were very simple and to make browsing attractive for users. This is why the browser developed by Andreessen's team, with its graphic interface, its buttons to move back and forth, its bars to move up and down, and the possibility of including images within the text, was designed to become a popular tool for the consumption of information. With the evolution of browsers and the advent of new models (Navigator, Explorer, etc.), each of them more advanced than the previous one, this tendency was only accentuated and the idea of making the World Wide Web a tool for participative communication and collaboration would almost completely disappear.[8]

Contributing to this tendency were issues such as the increasing complexity of the web's resources and the system for the identification of documents (Universal Document Identifier [UDI] or Uniform Resource Locator [URL]). Since the web was conceived as a flexible technology, the possibility of including in it all kinds of information in different formats was soon a reality. From an Internet basically designed as a textual tool, a quick transition took place to a web in which it was possible to include images and create documents with a strong visual component. It was even possible to add sound and video files, or to execute programs thanks to the Java language.[9] Web content started to move away from the simple production of texts within the reach of any user and the use of the natural language as the main communication tool. It became a much more elaborate and visual product that led communication to a domain closer to that of traditional mass media than to the one of participative interpersonal communication.

In addition, one of the main problems of the Internet prior to the advent of the web was not the lack of content, but the difficulties in finding content. If information cannot be found or located it is, in practical terms, as if it did not exist. The web soon led to the multiplication of the amount of information available over the Internet and, especially and thanks to the system for document identification, allowed for that information to be sought and found more easily. The web became, in sum, a wonderful tool for the publication of information (Clark, 2000). Thus, the web user could easily become an information consumer, a receiver.

As we can see, with the advent of the World Wide Web starts a significant transformation of the communication processes over the Internet. Even though the web was conceived as a communication tool that maintained the open and participatory spirit of the other communication tools available over the Internet, it was soon transformed into a technology that presented clear similarities to traditional mass media. In particular, the web became a tool that generated communication processes characterized by the asymmetry between senders and receivers. However, this transformation of the characteristics of communication via the Internet was not only due to the specific development undergone by web technology. To a great extent it was also due to the process of popularization of the Internet, which went from being an environment restricted to researchers, academics, and computer aficionados to a technology with massive use and open to the public at large.

Popularization

Apart from the existence of communication processes that present an obvious asymmetry between senders and receivers, there is a second trait that characterizes those situations in which audience manufacturing takes place. This is the presence of large-scale exposure to a given communication medium. To the extent that audience manufacturing derives historically from the need to control mass consumption, it is necessary that the number of people who use a particular medium be large enough for that control mechanism to be established and to work properly. Obviously, the specification of what number is large enough is to a great extent arbitrary or contingent to particular historic circumstances. However, what I aim to show here is that by the beginning of the 1990s a process of popularization of the Internet and the web took place and that this process opened the door to the manufacturing of the audience.

In spite of the technological success achieved with the creation of ARPANET, the truth is that the resources it offered went underused for years. The use of the network and its servers was rather complicated, help systems were inadequate, interacting with other users was not an easy task, there was no system to give users knowledge of the content and tools available at the different nodes of the network, access was restricted to a few research centers, and computer experts were required to establish and manage the connections. This situation would gradually change, however, and be transformed step by step to the point of making of the Internet a medium with large number of users.

The fundamental pillars that allowed for the popularization of the net started to be established in the 1980s with its expansion and with the interconnection of many diverse networks. If in 1982 there were 15 different networks connected to ARPA-Internet, in 1986 there were more than 400 (Abbate, 1999). However, the real take off, in all respects, took place at the beginning of the 1990s, especially with the advent of web browsers.

Regarding the infrastructure of the net, we can examine the number of hosts connected to the Internet and see how they had surpassed a million at the beginning of the 1990s. In particular, by 1993 there are already 1.3 million hosts connected (see Figure 1).

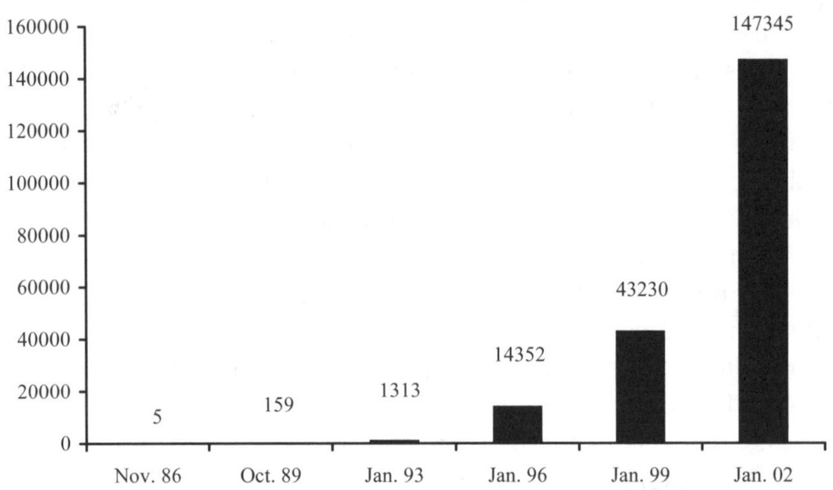

Figure 1: Number of Internet Hosts (in thousands). Source: Zakon (2005).

However, the existence of millions of hosts connected to the Internet is not enough to reach millions of users. It is also necessary to have a significant number of personal computers so that users can establish connections to the Internet. As we can see in Figure 2, starting from the early 1980s there was a sustained growth in the number of available computers, which reached by 1990 the 51 million mark in the United States and the 100 million mark in the world.

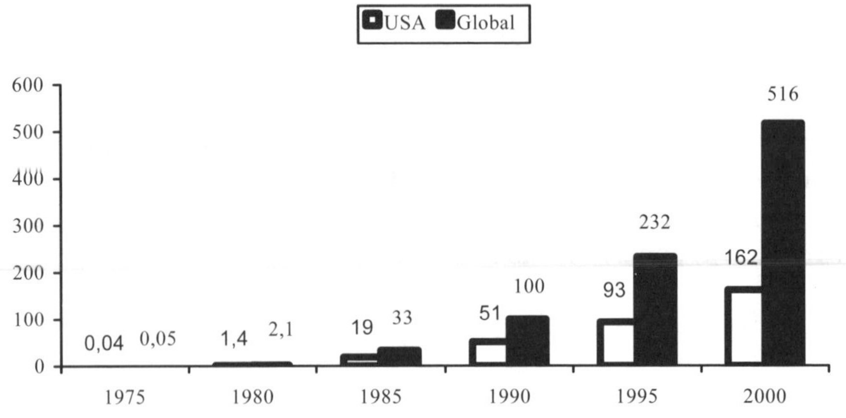

Figure 2: Number of computers (in millions). Source: eTForecasts (2002).

But even the existence of a network with millions of servers and the high rate of diffusion of personal computers do not necessarily mean that the net is popular. It is still necessary to be able to establish connections between personal computers and the network's servers. Before the complete privatization of the Internet and the advent of the World Wide Web there were already some active online services, such as AOL, Compuserve, and Prodigy. These services offered access to private networks with different kinds of content. It is estimated that these online services had, by the end of 1994, around 4 million customers worldwide. With the privatization of the Internet these online services were able to offer access not only to their own networks, but also to all the other networks connected to the Internet. In this manner, by the end of 1995 and after having introduced graphic browsing and having allowed access to the Internet, these services had about 12 million customers around the world (Morgan-Stanley, 1996). Apart from online services, Internet Service Providers (ISPs) started to pop up in the early 1990s. These ISPs offered Internet connections for a fee, and it is estimated that there were 1800 of them around the world by 1995 (Clemente, 1998). In this way, the connection between client computers and servers became available to millions of potential Internet users.

Thus, by the early 1990s the Internet had a huge size in terms of the number of hosts connected, and there was also the possibility, through commercial services, of connecting to it the millions of personal computers available in the world. Nonetheless, it was also necessary for the net to be attractive enough to lead potential users to take the step that would turn them into actual users. However, of the existing computers tools, the ones available for using the net were among the least sophisticated. As Mark Andreessen, the leading figure behind the creation of Mosaic and Netscape Navigator said:

> The Mac was a huge success, and point-and-click interfaces had become part of everyday life. But to use the Net you still had to understand Unix. You had to type FTP [File Transfer Protocol] commands by hand and you had to be able to do address-mapping in your head between IP addresses and host names and you had to know where all the FTP files were; you had to understand IRC [Internet Relay Chat] protocols, you had to know how to use this particular news reader and that particular Unix shell prompt, and you pretty much had to know Unix itself to get anything done. And the current users had little interest in making it easier. In fact, there was a definite

element of not wanting to make it easier, of actually wanting to keep the riffraff out. (Quoted in Naughton, 2000: 243)

All this would change with the advent of the World Wide Web and its browsers, especially those developed after 1993. With these the Internet became easy to use. They did not require much knowledge about computers, online content became available to users in a graphic, intuitive, and attractive environment, it became very simple to locate any online resource, and the new tools opened the door to millions of individuals and companies willing to place the most diverse content online. In sum, the Internet became a mass phenomenon. In this context, Mosaic, the browser created by the NCSA, became the software with the fastest diffusion in history (Naughton, 2000); the first Netscape browser was downloaded from the net by around 6 million users in six months (Clark, 2000); and the Explorer browser developed by Microsoft was downloaded by 3 million users in eight weeks (Clemente, 1998). In addition, the number of registered web domains grew from 26,000 in 1993 to 1.3 million in 1997 (Clark, 2000). In fact, in less than two years the web went from being almost non-existent to taking about a fourth of all the traffic on NSFNET, as given in Table 1.

Table 1. Traffic in NSFNET backbone (%)

Date	FTP	Telnet	Netnews	IRC	Gopher	E-mail	Web
06/1993	42.9	5.6	9.3	1.1	1.6	6.4	0.5
12/1993	40.9	5.3	9.7	1.3	3.0	6.0	2.2
06/1994	35.2	4.8	10.9	1.3	3.7	6.4	6.1
12/1994	31.7	3.9	10.9	1.4	3.6	5.6	16.0
03/1995	24.2	2.9	8.3	1.3	2.5	4.9	23.9

Source: Naughton (2000).

Thus, coinciding with the advent of the World Wide Web and the privatization of the network, the Internet became an everyday phenomenon for millions of individuals, and it was open to users from all over the world. If in 1987 it is estimated that there were around 1 million Internet users (Abbate, 1999) and in 1994 around 3 million (Clark, 2000), the figures of growth for the user population from that year on are truly remarkable (see Figure 3).[10]

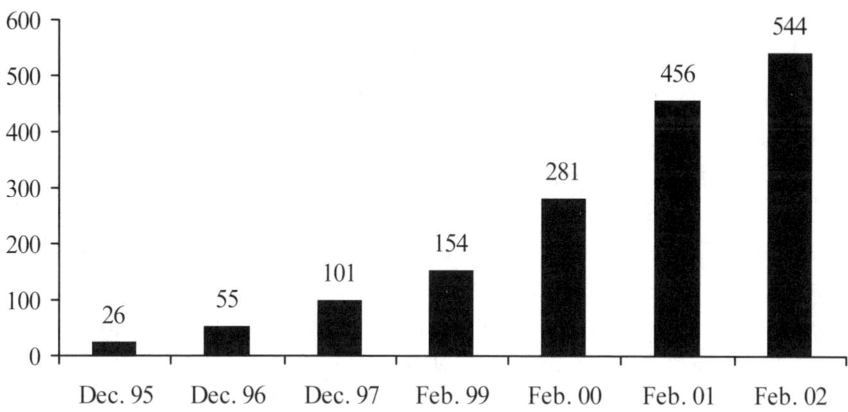

Figure 3: Number of Internet Users in the World (in millions). Source: Fundación Auna (2002) based on NUA 2002.

Therefore, we can say that it is at the beginning of the 1990s when the Internet, in all parameters but especially in the number of users, became a mass phenomenon. The creation of a network of networks of enormous size, the large number of personal computers available, and the incipient penetration of home connectivity thanks to online services and ISPs created an environment mature enough for the quick popularization of the Internet. This popularization was possible, to a great extent, because of the privatization of the network, which lifted all kinds of access restrictions, and the advent of the World Wide Web, which with its browsers transformed the use of the Internet and put it in the hands of large numbers of individuals. But this whole process was to a large degree facilitated and stimulated by the business interests that entered the Internet with force at the beginning of the 1990s.

Commercialization

The process of audience manufacturing is born in connection with business interests related to advertising and mass consumption. As long as control over the network remained in government hands, be it civil or military, the use of the net for business purposes was contained. However, the progressive privatization and commercialization of the Internet soon turned it into a field of expansion for those advertising interests that usually accompany audience measurement.

The processes of popularization and commercialization of the Internet took place in parallel. With the gradual privatization of the infrastructure of the Internet at the beginning of the 1990s, the net was opened to a wide spectrum of the population, and its commercial and entertainment uses became normal and accepted. In this process, commercialization affected all facets of the Internet. First, the management of the telecommunication backbone of the network was transferred to telecommunication companies. Second, commercialization was solidified by the advent and proliferation of ISPs that allowed for connection to the network from all types of locations, including homes, in exchange for a fee. Third, the computer industry entered into a competitive race in the market of hardware and software for network access. And, last but not least, a gradual commercialization of the network's content took place, and the Internet became a tool and a space for the most diverse businesses, from direct sale to the production of content accompanied by advertising.

Even though already in 1974, Bolt, Beranek, and Newman (BBN), the firm in charge of the technological development of ARPANET, had created Telenet, the first commercial computer network independent of government agencies,[11] the commercialization of the network's infrastructure was carried out by the National Science Foundation (NSF) starting in 1987. In that year, NSF funded a not-for-profit company, named Merit Network, in which participated the University and the State of Michigan. Merit Network was to take charge of the management of NSFNET. When the NSF decided to include in the network T1 lines, with higher bandwidth, MCI and IBM joined Merit Network to create a not-for-profit service named Advanced Network Services (ANS) that ended up managing the net—IBM provided packet switching technology, while MCI provided the lines. When in 1991 it became necessary to introduce a new improvement in the network's capacity, the government gave permission for ANS to include a new extra space within the network that would allow ANS to create its own network for commercial services. Thus, in 1991 large companies, such as IBM and MCI, were in charge of managing, through ANS, the network's infrastructure and were allowed to create their own commercial network within the existing non-commercial one. On top of this, from the late 1980s onward, commercial networks that used their own private backbones to provide services to their customers had started to appear. In July 1991, different private telecommunication networks created the Commercial Internet Exchange (CIX) to coordinate the traffic of these networks. At that moment the NSF proposed the total privatization of the Internet structure, the creation of a series of access nodes managed by big telecommunication companies that would favor the advent of commercial ISPs, and the creation of a new network (National Research and Education Network, NREN) to serve the needs of universities and research centers. In 1993, the National Information Infrastructure Act assumed the ideas proposed by NSF, and in April 1995, NSFNET ceased to exist. In this manner, the gradual commercialization of the Internet backbones began in the early 1990s and was completed in 1995 with the total privatization of the net's infrastructure (Abbate, 1999; Thomson, 2000).

The next level in the commercialization of the Internet was led by the commercial ISPs. The advent of these providers was facilitated by a series of technological issues, such as the fact that the hardware and software systems used by the academic and military pioneers of the net could be used almost automatically for the commercial exploitation of the network without requiring any new technological developments. It was also facilitated by the attitude of the Internet's managers—the NSF and other government agencies—who allowed for the creation of an access market within a loosely regulated, very flexible, and decentralized framework. Ever since the 1980s there have existed online services, that is, companies (such as Prodigy, Compuserve, or America Online) that have offered access to the content stored in their own networks, even though they did not offer access to the Internet. But it was the advent of web browsers that definitively opened the door to the creation of large numbers of ISPs. In this way, the ISP market in the United States was, in the mid-1990s, made up of a large number of small local providers (especially in rural areas), some national providers related with well-known companies (such as IBM or AT&T), and some emergent providers that went through the transition from the management of private networks to the Internet access market (these were the online services mentioned above).[12] At the end of 1998, 95 percent of the US population was in a position to access the Internet through an ISP and 92 percent of the population could choose in their area of residence from among seven or more different ISPs (Greenstein, 2000).

The opening of the net to any citizen interested in using it led the computer industry into a race in pursuit of a new market, that of the products that facilitated the access to the network. Ever since 1977 ARPA had financed the inclusion of TCP into the UNIX operating system (Abbate, 1999), and since 1985 the TCP/IP had also been included as part of UNIX thanks to the DCA's efforts (Naughton, 2000). The Pentagon had favored the appearance of private companies devoted to the manufacturing and selling of routers—the computer in charge of managing the network's traffic (Abbate, 1999). In this manner, and thanks to the Pentagon's effort to include the TCP/IP in American computers, most of these computers were ready to function online (Castells, 2001). Therefore, the computer industry was by the early 1990s in the right situation to take advantage of the business opportunities opened up by the Internet. However, even though the sale of personal computers and other hardware devices for managing Internet access was favored by the net's privatization and commercialization, it was the commercial interests surrounding software that caused a larger impact at the beginning of the 1990s. The creation of Netscape, the huge success of its web browsers, and its spectacular Initial Public Offering (IPO) in August 1995 caused an authentic revolution within the world of software (Clark, 2000). Coinciding with Netscape's success, the largest world manufacturer of software, Microsoft, made the Internet its first priority and took a radical turn in its strategic objectives. According to Netscape's founders, this change took place because of Netscape's success; according to Microsoft managers, the radical change of priorities had nothing to do with Netscape and was the result of an internal reflection process. In any case, the Internet and, in particular, the World Wide Web, became from that moment on key for understanding the development of the global software market. The Internet and the World Wide Web also led to a fierce fight for supremacy within this market, a fight that ended up taking Microsoft to court (Cusumano & Yoffie, 1998).

Regarding the use of the Internet's infrastructure for commercial purposes, the Acceptable Use Policy of the NSF prohibited the use of the net for purposes other than research or projects financed by the government. However, with the creation by ANS of a commercial services network, thanks to the extra bandwidth of the net, the door was opened to the commercialization of the content and services available through the Internet. As soon as the telecommunications infrastructure of the net went into private hands and access began to be provided by commercial ISPs, the net became a target of entrepreneurs, advertisers, business people, and content providers ready to take advantage of the business opportunities opened by it.

Given the complexity and flexibility of the medium, it is obvious that there are many different ways in which the Internet and the World Wide Web can be used as a business tool. In fact, both the Internet and the World Wide Web are central elements if we want to understand the new economy, the network economy that characterizes the most recent evolution of capitalism (Castells, 2001). My focus, however, will be on the penetration of advertising on the Internet since the work here centers around the issue of the audience, its manufacturing and its measurement, and those processes are usually linked to advertising activities.

The use of the Internet for advertising purposes began long before the advent of the web. The first documented case dates from 1978, when an employee of a computer company used e-mail to announce to ARPANET users the presentation of one of their new products (Kelly, 2001).[13] This commercial use of e-mail generated angry protests among Internet users and received a strong response from the network's managers in which it was reminded that the use of the Internet for commercial purposes was strictly prohibited.

Even though the first attempt at using the Internet for advertising purposes dates back to the 1970s, the best-known controversial use of the Internet as an advertising tool dates from April 1994. Two Arizona lawyers, Canter and Siegel, used an automatic system to send an advertisement to thousands of Usenet newsgroups. The utilization of Usenet for advertising purposes generated angry responses on the part of users, who decided to take action against the lawyers (Armstrong, 2001).

As we can see, the first advertising activities over the Internet used the communication tools that were available online. However, those activities were limited or blocked because the network was controlled by government agencies, the predominant online culture was the academic, hacker, and libertarian, and the communication processes generated were based on the egalitarian participation of Internet users. To the extent that, in the early 1990s, all those factors underwent a radical transformation, advertising found a receptive field for its expansion. Perhaps the prominence achieved by the Canter and Siegel affair in the history of the Internet derives from its symbolic character as the last attempt to stop the process of commercialization of the Internet. In October 1994, just a few months after the Canter and Siegel affair, the first advertising banner on the web appeared on the Hotwired magazine website (Zakon, 2005). Users could no longer stop the spread of Internet advertising. Figure 4 shows the beginning of the take off of online advertising expenditure.

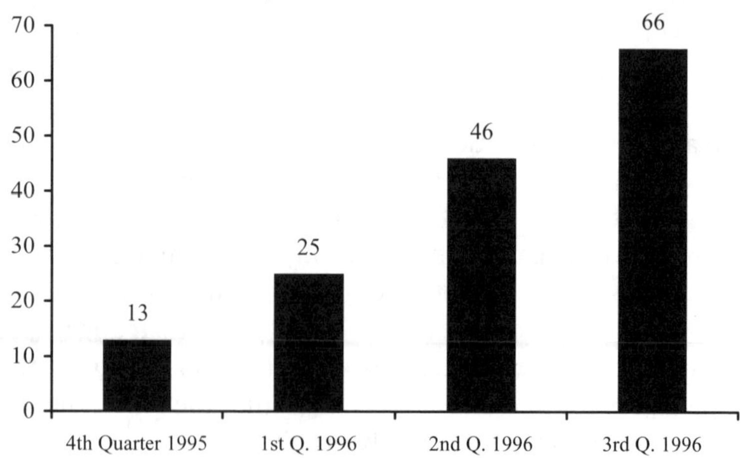

Figure 4: Online Advertising Expenditures (millions of dollars). Source: Meeker (1997) based on Jupiter Communications.

Due to its special characteristics, the Internet had ever since its inception the potential to become an ideal vehicle for advertising messages. It combined, within a single medium, the ability to serve both of the two main tendencies in the development of advertising: on the one hand, it offered global advertising able to reach any place on the planet with the message of international brands; on the other hand, it also provided for segmented advertising addressed to population groups with defined characteristics adequate for the commercialization of specific products. Over the course of the last few decades, advertising has been swinging between these two tendencies, which seem opposed but are in fact complementary. First, the Internet can serve the tendencies toward the globalization of advertising, whose doctrine was launched in 1983 by Theodor Levitt (Mattelart, 2000), in the sense of contributing to the exploitation of international markets through the launch of global standardized brands. Second, the Internet can serve the fragmenting tendencies in advertising which aim at obtaining the maximum economic profit by adjusting the offer to the individual profile of customers (Turow, 1997). The possibility of using the Internet to support either of these advertising tendencies explains, at least in part, why advertising interests took the Internet by storm once it was released from government control, reached a critical mass of users, and thanks to the World Wide Web became a visual, attractive, user-friendly, and basically unidirectional medium.

But that assault required a convincing speech to get started. In May 1994 Edwin Artzt, the then president of Procter & Gamble, the largest advertiser in the world, delivered a speech in front of the American Association of Advertising Agencies (AAAA). In his speech, entitled *The Future of Advertising*, Artzt depicted a scenario in which traditional media would be substituted by interactive personalized media that, and this was the worrisome part, would carry no advertising. Even though Artzt was for the most part thinking of interactive television, which in 1994 seemed destined to become the new medium of reference, his thoughts could be perfectly applied to the Internet and the World Wide Web. Artzt accused advertising agencies of ignoring this emergent reality and asked them to adapt to the new interactive environment if they did not want to end up disappearing. He finished his speech encouraging advertising agencies to start the assault on new media: "Let's grab all this new technology in our teeth once again and turn it into a bonanza for advertising" (quoted in Turow, 1997: 162).

Since this advice, or warning, came from the largest world advertiser, advertising agencies had no other option but to pay attention. Together with the Association of National Advertisers (ANA) they immediately created Coalition for Advertising Supported Information and Entertainment (CASIE), an organization whose main goal was to convince those companies in the interactive television and Internet businesses that consumers would not be willing to pay for these new media and that advertising would therefore become vital for their survival. CASIE soon defined three main lines of action: to promote a regulatory framework that favored the use of advertising in the new media, to study the diffusion of new media among consumers, and to find methods for measuring consumers' activity in relation to those media. Advertising agencies were aware that measuring the Internet audience would help their clients and themselves, that the credibility of the measurement would only be maintained if it was carried out by independent entities, and that the birth of an independent audience measurement system would become a turning point in the development of the new media. As Turow (1997: 170) states,

> CASIE members and advertisers that supported them made it clear that serious money could come to the interactive media only if a rating system was put in place that satisfied the researchers and planners at major agencies.

We therefore find in the mid-1990s an Internet that has already been penetrated, at all levels, by commercial criteria and interests. The infrastructure, the access, and the hardware and software tools needed to establish that access became a source of business for the most diverse kinds of companies. The network itself became an essential tool for the establishment of new businesses. And the advertising market became aware of the importance of the new interactive media and was ready to use it for its own benefit.

The Birth of Internet Audience Measurement

By the mid-1990s, the Internet hardly resembled the project initiated by ARPA in the 1960s, and it already possessed the characteristics that define the constitution of the audience of traditional media:

- With the advent of the World Wide Web arrived a very powerful communication tool that established communication relationships characterized by the asymmetry between senders and receivers.
- The process of popularization of the Internet, favored by the advent of the World Wide Web, and by the privatization of the network, made it possible for Internet users to be counted by the million.
- The privatization of the Internet allowed business interests to disembark in the new medium at all levels and with full force.

Thus, in 1995 we have a network in which the World Wide Web becomes a central element and in which there are more than 25 million users in the world. Its growth is not unnoticed by an advertising industry that sees the new situation as a threat and that decided to grab the new medium "in its teeth."

In this context, the birth of Internet audience measurement takes place in 1995. And since the World Wide Web was the tool that made possible the establishment of asymmetrical communicative relationships, and the one that stimulated the processes of commercialization and popularization of the Internet, it was around the World Wide Web that the initiatives to measure the Internet audience centered.

In March 1995 Arbitron, the company of reference in the field of radio audience measurement in the United States, reached an agreement with two other companies to start the Interactive Information Index, an audience measurement service for interactive television developed under the supervision of CASIE (Turow, 1997). That same month Caddis International announced the creation of Webtrack, an initiative to offer audits of websites' traffic and information about the use of these websites and the demography and attitudes of their users (Hong & Leckenby, 1996). In April appeared the Internet Profiles Corporation (I/PRO), and NetCount, of Digital Planet (Meeker, 1997).

I/PRO collected the IP addresses of website users and gathered demographic information on them through questionnaires that were shown to users prior to their access to the sites' content. NetCount, in turn, was oriented toward advertisers, and it gathered information on the traffic of the different pages that made up websites and also on the click-through rates that different advertisements achieved. In July 1995 the NPD Group launched PC-Meter, the first electronic panel on the Internet. It had a sample of 500 homes that downloaded to their computers a software tool for monitoring their online activity. That same month, Nielsen and two other companies joined forces to launch a new online audience measurement service, ANYwhere Online. In August 1995 Virtual Office introduced WebWatch, another measurement service that gathered information on the number of visits to a website, the time spent in each page, and the clicks on the different advertisements. That same month C/net introduced new software for controlling the traffic of websites. In September 1995 Nielsen announced a strategic alliance with I/PRO, which, with the support of CASIE, the Advertising Research Foundation (ARF) and the Magazine Publishers of America (MPA), had the goal of allowing them to become auditors of website traffic (Hong & Leckenby, 1996). In October of that same year, the Audit Bureau of Circulations (ABC), the leading organization in the monitoring of publications' circulation in the United States, started to run tests for the realization of website audits (Meeker, 1997).

As we can see, in the space of a few months a whole new sector took shape: an Internet audience measurement industry and, in particular, a World Wide Web audience measurement industry. It is an industry in which there are a series of new young companies willing to conquer an emerging market elbow to elbow with the titans of audience measurement in traditional media—Arbitron, Nielsen, ABC, etc. As we can also see, the new sector is born with close links to advertising market interests and aspires to become an essential tool for the managing of advertising in the new medium.

However, besides serving as a tool for the advertising market to rationalize the exploitation of a new market, Internet audience measurement also displayed other facets and functions that should be pointed out here. The highly competitive character of the web's origins turned audience measurement into a tool for other interests that, even though related to the issue of advertising, are not easily reduced to it. Audience ratings became from their inception a self-promotional tool used to convince users to visit a particular website, with the argument that lots of people were already using that website (Coffey, 2001). In a new environment in which brands, prestige, and quality stamps were still undefined, audience figures became a valuable self-advertising tool. This is not a phenomenon specific to the web. For example, Blanch (1999: 119) mentions how the first systematic studies of the radio audience in Spain "served not so much to analyze the new medium, they served or were used to create ads in which the leadership in this area was remarked." But the special characteristics of the new medium turned this use into something very common.

Apart from the psychological value that a user may derive from knowing that a particular communication vehicle is used by many other people, the Internet is also influenced by what is called the 'network effect,' which is particularly relevant in those sites in which user participation goes beyond mere exposure to content or the simple purchase of a product for sale. When the value a user assigns to a website depends on the number of users that already use this website it is said that that website presents 'network externalities' or 'network effects.' In this manner,

> as the number of visitors grows, more and more users find that website attractive because of their ability to interact with other users and the ability to share and contribute to member generated content (e.g., book reviews generated by readers at Amazon.com). The greater member base creates opportunities for advertisers and vendors to market a range of products and services to those members. Accumulation of data about member profiles and transactions profiles makes it possible to attract even more vendors and advertisers to tailor the products and services to members, thus making it even more attractive for members to join the virtual community created by the firm. (Rajgopal et al., 2000)

The network effect generates a kind of virtuous circle of positive feedback, in which a large audience attracts more audience and, on top of that, attracts more advertisers—which means more resources for the website and more information on products for the user—and sellers of services, which augments the attractiveness of the website, increasing the audience, etc.

Thus, the ability to obtain and, especially, publicize favorable audience figures became a wonderful tool for many organizations in their strategy to establish an advantageous position in an incipient, competitive, and unstable market. But there is another side to the use of Internet audience measurement that should be mentioned here.

When the relationship between business interests and audience measurement is discussed, the focus of attention has usually been placed on the advertising market. However, the advent and development of the World Wide Web presents a series of distinctive peculiarities that lead us to widen the focus of attention in order to include in it another element that was very influential in the interest in web audience measurement. I am referring here to the stock market and the venture capital market. Even though advertising soon became a relevant source of income for those companies that operated online, those companies sought from their inception the aid of venture capitalists and, following this, capitalization through the stock market (Perkins & Perkins, 1999). In this way, and due to a series of contextual factors, from the mid-1990s a new phenomenon developed, which has been called the 'Internet bubble.'[14]

In the venture capital market and the stock market the usual procedure is for investors to choose among the different investment options by examining the financial situation of the companies in which they could place their money (Jiménez-Blanco, 2003). However, in the market of Internet companies, due to the youth and peculiar structure of the market, the non-financial information regarding those companies acquired an enormous relevance. Many researchers have tried to determine which non-financial factors influenced the valuation of Internet companies in the mid-1990s. Among all of these factors, one stands out remarkably, that of audience data.[15] Demers and Lev (2001: 334–335) summarize the situation as follows:

> In the absence of an established history of profit generating ability, the 'top line' (i.e., revenues) has become an important focal point in the financial analysis of companies in this sector. Most Internet analysts (including venture capitalists and others who are interested in the performance evaluation of web companies) have also come to rely upon non-financial measures of web traffic activity as indicators of the current performance and future cash generating ability of these intangible asset based firms. [...] Web traffic measures have become standard Internet company performance benchmarks that are now commonly reported in the business press,

voluntarily disclosed by companies at the time of their earnings announcements and frequently mentioned as valuation parameters in analysts' reports.[16]

Regardless of whether or not it could be shown that audience data and profit generation potential were related, in the world of the Internet bubble audience ratings became bait used to convince investors that they were in front of the business opportunity they were dreaming of. Internet audience measurement played, at least for a few years, an extra role beyond the one of providing information for the managing of the advertising market.

In sum, it is possible to assert that Internet audience measurement was born in 1995 and that it focused on the World Wide Web. The origin of this measurement is closely linked to the interests of advertisers and advertising agencies. In this sense, its birth barely differs from the birth of audience measurement in other media. However, it is necessary to point out that, once the measurement started, Internet audience measurement also became an instrument for the self-promotion of the different websites and for the determination of the stock market value and investment potential of Internet companies.

Conclusions to Section II

As I mentioned at the beginning of this section, my goal was to analyze whether Internet audience measurement begins when the net starts to show some of the fundamental characteristics that define traditional mass communication media. We have seen how, in fact, the measurement starts when the Internet shows the three characteristics analyzed. We have seen the process of constitution of a new reality, that of the Internet audience. As Callejo (2001: 17) points out,

> the audience is a product that, at the least, requires four elements to be present: a) a society of consumers; b) mass communication media or, at least, media that address previously unknown receivers; c) advertisers interested in knowing the impact of their advertising expenditures; and d) empirical research.

Thus, it is possible to say that the Internet audience is born in 1995, when all four elements mentioned by Callejo are already present.

The birth of the Internet audience was closely linked to the development of the World Wide Web. In a sense, the few years that go from the creation of the web by Berners-Lee in 1990 to the Initial Public Offering of Netscape in 1995 constituted an accelerated historical transformation of the Internet in which converged all the defining elements of the net. First, a computer communication system characterized by its flexibility and its openness to participation was created by a scientist working in a research institution financed with public funds. Then, we see the involvement of students, such as Marc Andreessen, creator of Mosaic, who took advantage of the work of Berners-Lee and developed more attractive and easy to use tools that could appeal to a large number of people. Finally, we see the arrival of purely business interests, embodied by Jim Clark, who soon realized the business potential of the web and created Netscape with the goal of "making a thousand million dollars" (Clark, 2000), which opened the way to the 'Internet bubble.' Academics, students who are computer aficionados, and entrepreneurs joined forces in a chain, which, to a large extent, represents a faster version of the evolution of the Internet from its origins to the mid-1990s. These five years are the ones that, basically, made the Internet what it is today.

There is no doubt that the web technology, in and of itself, would not have been able to transform the Internet the way it did had it not been for the existence of other parallel and contemporary phenomena that facilitated that transformation. These phenomena include the disappearance of government oversight of the Internet and the existence of the computer and telecommunication infrastructure required for the popularization of the net. But the importance that the web has achieved since its inception leads to talk, as it often happens, of the Internet and the World Wide Web as the same thing.

This lack of distinction also takes place when the issue of the audience is addressed. As we saw above, in the review of the literature on the Internet audience, it is normal to encounter references to the Internet audience that, in fact, exclusively refer to the web audience. But when the concept of the audience is applied to Internet communication tools other than the web there is something strange in that use of the word. That is because even though in certain communication tools or processes established through the Internet—newsgroups, bulletin boards, e-mail lists, newsletters, spam—we can perceive in an incipient way the conditions of possibility for the manufacturing of the audience, the truth is that only in the World Wide Web do those conditions appear in a clear and defined way. That is why the immense majority of the developments that have to do with Internet audience measurement and that start taking shape in 1995 are in fact attempts to measure the World Wide Web's audience.

Along those lines, what remains of this book will focus on the analysis of the measurement methods applied to the World Wide Web and on the development dynamics of the World Wide Web audience measurement industry. As we have seen in this chapter, it is possible to say that in the mid-1990s the web already possessed the essential traits that define a mass communication medium. However, both because of its technological foundation and because of the nature of its development, the World Wide Web also possesses characteristics that clearly differentiate it from other mass communication media. In the following chapters, I will analyze which measurement methods are usually applied for the measurement of the web audience, and to what extent those methods adapt to the specific characteristics of the medium.

Measurement Methods

In the previous section we saw how the World Wide Web had acquired by the end of the 1990s the general traits that allow us to start talking of it as a mass communication medium. It is, therefore, at that point when we can start applying to the web Smythe's (1977) ideas, according to which the commodity produced by the mass communication media is the audience.[1] As was mentioned at the beginning of this book, however, the process of audience manufacturing in the mass media relies on an elaborate institutional fabric and on the application of a series of more or less scientific measurement methods that facilitate the transformation of the audience, which is an abstract and undetermined entity, into a concrete product that can be traded in the advertising market. Thus, the study of the web audience, and of its measurement, must also include an analysis of the measurement methods used, of their validity, and their rigor.

As was discussed before, the evolution of the measuring methods used to manufacture the audience of a medium depends, for the most part, on two different issues: the characteristics of the medium whose audience is to be measured and the interests that underlie the measurement process. Regarding the specific characteristics of the medium, the World Wide Web possesses a series of technological and usage traits that make it different from traditional mass communication media. Regarding the interests that underlie the measurement process and that condition its forms and evolution, it is safe to say that web audience measurement responds, for the most part, to the same interests that underlie the audience measurement process of traditional mass media. The fact that web audience measurement has been used as a self-promotional tool by different websites, or as an indicator of the value of the shares of online companies, does not mean that its development responds, essentially, to interests other than the production of an audience that can be traded in the advertising market. However, the technological and usage peculiarities of the web lead to a relationship with advertising interests that presents some special characteristics. In this way, the influence of advertising interests over web audience measurement may generate certain dynamics that are different from the ones appearing in the audience measurement of traditional mass media. This is why, before getting into a detailed analysis of the different methods used to measure the web audience it seems necessary to, on the one hand, analyze which technological and usage peculiarities of the web might influence the concrete shape that those methods might take and, on the other hand, to which extent web advertising presents peculiarities that might influence the configuration of the different audience measurement methods.

Once these specific characteristics of the web medium have been addressed, we will be able to enter an analysis of the different methods for measuring its audience and examine to which extent they adapt to its distinctive traits. Through this analysis, I will be carrying out an analysis of the validity and rigor of the web audience measurement methods, and will also be examining the validity of the second statement, which asserts that the methods used to measure the web audience display clear similarities to those applied in the audience measurement of traditional mass media, but show obvious limitations in responding to the peculiarities of the new medium.

CHAPTER 5

Peculiarities and Classification

The World Wide Web and Its Differentiating Traits

The World Wide Web, considered as a mass communication medium, presents a series of technical and usage peculiarities that clearly distinguish it from traditional mass media. From a general point of view, we can say that the web is the first mass communication medium based on a digital network made up of computers. In his examination of the technical specificities of the new digital communication technologies, Neuman (1991) mentions a series of characteristics that define this type of technology: decreasing cost, decreasing distance sensitivity, increasing speed, increasing volume, increasing channel diversity, increasing two-way flow, increasing flexibility, increasing extensibility, and increasing interconnectivity. However, I am not going to carry out here an analysis of the generic differences between these new digital communication technologies and traditional analogical technologies. Rather, I am going to focus on those traits of the World Wide Web that might have a repercussion on the ways in which the audience is measured. Even though an analysis of the general characteristics of the web as a digital technology is not required at this point, it is necessary to examine web technology in order to observe those peculiarities that may determine the way in which the audience is measured and which problems or possibilities that measurement may present:

Globalization: Traditional mass media, as was mentioned before, have the power to leap across space and telescope time. However, they have usually had a limited reach, be it local, regional, or national. And even though over the decades they have generated internationalization and globalization processes (Herman & McChesney, 1997), the truth is that none of them possesses a global character as marked and defined as that of the web (Carey, 1998). Web content is available, at least in principle, from any location in the world and it, therefore, generates intrinsically global audiences. As a consequence, the traditional organization of audience measurement based on national markets does not adjust easily to the new medium. The transition from national to global audiences generates a series of new problems that need to be solved. For instance, the ability to measure the audience by using random samples from a manageable universe, as was the case until now, ceases to exist. The need arises for representative global samples, which implies a methodological, logistic, and economic challenge of significant proportions. The issue of the global harmonization of measuring procedures, from the definition of the universe to the metrics, appears as a fundamental question in order to account for the global nature of the web audience.

Access locations: The fact that World Wide Web communication takes place through computers means that web access locations are as diverse as the places where there are computers connected to the network. And since computers are flexible machines, with multiple uses, those places can vary quite broadly. As was mentioned before, when talking of radio audience measurement, the multiplication of access locations can have very significant repercussions when the goal is to measure the audience by using receiving devices. In the audience measurement of traditional media, only television audience measurement panels measure the audience through receiving devices. This is possible because television is a medium closely linked to the home. That is why even though television audience measurement panels leave out of their coverage the television consumption that takes place outside the home, this lack of coverage is not significant enough to cause a grave deficiency in the measurement. This does not happen with the web, since the use of computers connected to the network in the workplace, in libraries, and in other public places turns out to be very significant. In particular, the fact that in many workplaces and educational centers computers have become essential tools for the work being carried out and, on top of this, that the connections to the network available in these places have traditionally reached higher speeds than the ones available in the home, makes it impossible to ignore the use of the web from such locations if the goal is to obtain an appropriate measurement of the web audience.

Neither a flow nor a closed product: In opposition to the content of radio and television, web content does not take the form of a flow. It is not clearly marked by time limitations. Rather, it is available for a certain period of time, which may be years, for users to request and consume it. In this sense, the web presents traits that clearly distinguish it from radio and television and that, therefore, demand an alternative model for measuring its audience. On the other hand, while print media are essentially closed products, with a certain periodicity and concrete physical and spatial limits, the web is a much more flexible and complex medium. The limits between vehicles and issues (i.e., specific products or editions) of those vehicles are not at all obvious in the web, and both periodicity and space limitations are more virtual than real online. All this calls for an adaptation of the measurement to the specific characteristics of the web.

Trace: Communication processes established over the web are based on the request and reception of files between client and server computers. Such requests and receptions of files leave a trace that is possible to track and measure. For instance, when a server receives a file request it generates a new text file, called a log-file, in which several information items are recorded—what was requested, when it was requested, from which Internet Protocol (IP) address it was requested, etc. The fact that communication through computers always leaves a trace, as opposed to what happens with communication over traditional media, leads many people to think that web audience measurement should be easy and accurate, since the contact between medium and audience is recorded. As we will see below, the issue is much more complicated than it might seem, and questions such as what exactly is measured, how it is measured, and what escapes the measurement process turn out to be rather complex and noteworthy.

Vehicle proliferation: The web is an open system that makes it easy to create vehicles within it. One of the main characteristics of the web is the facility with which it is possible to open a new communication outlet. Even though usage dynamics may lead most users to simply be information consumers, as was mentioned when the issue of the asymmetry in web communication processes was discussed, the truth is that it is very easy to be present on the web as a content provider. This is the case partly because it is not financially burdensome (it is not necessary to create a whole organizational structure to be present on the web) and partly because the very technical specifications of the medium make it very difficult to impede anyone from becoming an online content provider. This is why when the measurement process has to deal with the size and profile of the audience of the different web vehicles it is almost impossible, as opposed to what happens with previous mass media, to cover most of them.

Multiplicity of access platforms:[1] Even though computers are the most common platform for accessing the web, and this already presents a challenge for the measurement based on receiving devices, the truth is that there exist other access platforms that in the future might constitute a significant share of web access activity. Technologies such as web television, PDAs, and cell phones with Internet access will make it more complex to measure the web audience through the monitoring of access platforms (Foan, 2001).

Regarding the relationship between the web and advertising, we can say it is a complex issue. The flexibility of the medium, the many different ways in which content can be presented, the capacity of the medium to be something more than a simple platform for the dissemination of information, and the large number of activities that can be performed through the medium lead the form and functions of web advertising to take on a level of complexity way beyond what can be expected in traditional communication media.

The specific ways that advertising might be displayed on the web are very diverse (Lavilla, 2002; Zárraga, 1997): the creation of websites by the companies that advertise online, the introduction of advertising content into the content of other websites through the use of banners (which, in turn, can take many different forms and sizes), the promotion of links in the results of search engines in exchange for a fee, the creation of specific 'microsites' for particular advertising campaigns, the introduction of interstitial advertisements, etc. Even though advertising in traditional media also takes multiple formats, the web presents a much more open field, in fast evolution, in which possibilities seem endless and consolidation difficult.[2] In this manner, while audience measurement in traditional mass media possesses a more or less precise guide regarding what needs to be measured, regardless of whether that is possible or not, audience measurement in the web has to deal with very diverse advertising objects susceptible to being measured and with certain characteristics that do not appear in the advertising of traditional media, such as the ability to interact or the location of sponsored links within search engines' results.

Besides the multiple forms it may take, another relevant characteristic of web advertising is that it is easily separated from the content that accompanies it. That is, when an advertisement is inserted in a print publication, or when a spot is inserted in a broadcast, the link between content and advertisement is the same for each and every member of the audience. But when a user makes a page request over the web, the advertisement that accompanies the content can vary from user to user, from request to request (Álvarez & González-Quijano, 1998). The linking of advertising and content can be made independently and individually for every member of the audience. This possibility, allowed because of the flexible structure of the web, is achieved through (1) the use of advertisement servers, computers in charge of managing advertisements and their placement in specific pages requested by users, and (2) by the creation of advertisement server networks, server networks in charge of managing the advertising insertion for different websites, and, therefore, taking from content providers the ability to manage advertising space the way it is done in traditional media (Agulló, 2000). While in print media it is often assumed that the audience of a particular advertisement is the same as the audience of the particular vehicle or page where it is inserted, and while in broadcasting it is often assumed that the audience of a spot is the equivalent to the audience of the program in which it is inserted, in the web it is not possible to sustain that assumption, since content and advertisement are not linked to each other in a fixed manner. As Cormier and Haering (2003: 188) assert:

> In all other media, the definition of a media vehicle's audience is systematically used as the definition for the audience that is exposed to advertising. The Internet is the only medium to distinguish between Media OTS [Opportunities to See] and Advertising OTS.

In this way, and with the aim of managing advertising campaigns, it seems important to develop specific measures for advertisements that do not necessarily have to imply the measurement of the audience of the vehicles where they are inserted.

We can say that the management of advertising in the different communication media requires the measurement of the audience at a number of levels. First, it requires knowledge of the total audience of the medium: how many people use a particular communication medium, such as television, and their profile. Second, it requires the measurement of the audience of specific vehicles or media outlets: what is the audience of X network or Y newspaper. Third, and even though this may turn out to be difficult with print media, it requires information about the audience of specific content: what is the audience of program X. And fourth, to these traditional measurement needs the web adds the necessity of measuring the audience of particular advertising products that appear separately of any specific informational content: what is the audience of the banner X?

But, besides this, the web's relationship with advertising presents another peculiarity that is absent in traditional media's relationship with advertising. For advertisers, the web can become something more than a mere platform on which to insert advertisements in their multiple forms. In traditional mass media, this is almost the only relationship established between advertising and the media. Advertising in traditional media is based on the assumption that exposure to certain advertisements not only can lead to an increase in brand awareness and to an improvement of brand perception, but that it can also ultimately lead to increased sales. The interactive possibilities of the web, the fact that interaction leaves a trace in the computers that take part in it, the possibility of expanding the information offered by an advertisement by linking it to another page or website, and the ability of the web to become a platform for directly selling products and services, all open the door for the web to become more than just a place where advertisements can be inserted. Since this is the case, advertisers might be interested not only in measuring the exposure to a particular advertisement, but also in measuring the whole process, from exposure to the final sale of a product or service (Madinaveitia & Agulló, 1998). Advertisers' interest in this entire process is manifested in the different ways in which advertising is priced. In the early days of online advertising the pricing model was that of a flat fee rate paid in advance as a sponsorship of a website. Soon a new model was in use, that of CPMs (cost per thousand), a model commonly used in the advertising activity of traditional media. From early on, however, pricing models based on interactivity measures were also in use. In particular, the most common form was the one based on clicks—cost per click or CPC.[3] It is also possible to take into account the amount of time spent on the website to which the user is directed after clicking on an advertisement, or the number of clicks performed on that website, etc. Models based on sales or outcomes, in which the price depends on the number of actual business transactions generated by an advertisement or the number of forms filled out, have also been used—these are referred to as cost per action models or CPA. There are also mixed models, in which a certain amount is paid based on exposure (CPMs) plus another amount depending on the number of times that users follow the links inserted in the advertisement (CPC) plus an extra amount per sale generated through the advertisement (CPA) (Hoffman & Novak, 2000). Obviously, these models are only applicable in those cases in which it is possible to link the advertisement to another site or microsite of the advertisers, and in which it is possible to finalize online the purchase of the product or service. In addition, the pricing models that take into account issues beyond mere exposure to advertising generate mistrust among content providers, since the ability of an advertisement to attract the audience's interest, to lead to a click, and to generate a sale, is something that cannot be controlled by content providers and depends, for the most part, on the quality of the advertisement and of the product or service being advertised. As Callius et al. (2005: 138) put it,

> direct response cannot be a major part of the revenues because it just is not fair for the medium. The media has no control over the pricing of the

advertised product, the advertising agency's creative work or even the fact that the advertisers might be trying to sell a crappy product.

Partly due to this problem and to the limited scope in which mixed models can be applied, the most common pricing model for web advertising has been the one based on exposure (i.e., CPMs). However, the existence of other models poses the need to develop measurements that go beyond the simple exposure of the audience to a particular advertisement.

Thus, even though it is possible to assume that the web possesses the general characteristics of the mass communication media in which the manufacturing of the audience takes place, the truth is that it also presents certain specific characteristics, both from a technical point of view and from the point of view of its relationship with advertising, that seem to demand new solutions and methods for the measurement of its audience. My aim here is to carry out an analysis of the extent to which the existing methods for measuring the web audience account for these peculiarities and adapt to them.

In fact, when we talk about research methods and the web, we can do so from a number of very different points of view. First, it is possible to consider the web as an object of study, the same way that traditional media were also considered objects of study. In this sense, it is possible to apply to the web the research tools, techniques, and methods used for the study of other communication media.[4] Second, the web has become a new tool for research-data gathering, since it can be used to carry out online surveys, online focus groups, etc. The major advantage of the use of the web as a data-gathering tool is that it is often cheaper and more efficient than traditional tools—telephone, mail, face-to-face interviews—particularly when the research deals with issues related with the web itself. Third, some novel research techniques have been applied to study the web, such as usability studies—analyses, based on observation, of the use that people make of different webpages' designs.[5]

To a certain extent, web audience measurement combines all these aspects. First, the web itself, and its use, becomes the object of study and measurement. Second, the web can function as a tool for the gathering of the data used in the measurement. Third, web audience measurement opens the door to the development of methodological innovations that allow for the adaptation of the research process to a new communication reality. In order to measure the web audience, it is possible to use the audience research methods and techniques traditionally used for other media. But it is also possible to take advantage of the possibilities offered by the new medium to research its audience with new methods and techniques. If we carefully examine the audience measurement methods applied to the web, it will be possible to see to which extent methodological innovations that take into account the peculiarities of the web have been introduced, and to what extent the measurement methods follow the model of those applied to previous communication media.

In this section, I will perform an analysis of the measurement methods applied to the web audience, and I will examine to what extent they present limitations or misfits in their adaptation to the new medium. It is obvious that each measurement method presents limitations when it is applied to previous media, but, even though I will mention these limitations, my analysis will focus on those limitations that are specific to the measurement of the web audience.

The Measurement Methods and Their Classification

The classification system most commonly used when discussing web audience measurement methods is the one that distinguishes between site- and user-centric methods (FitzGerald, 2002; Foan, 2001; O'Connell, 2002). Even though this classification has become standard within the field of web audience measurement, the truth is that the basis for that classification is rather sketchy, to say the least. It is asserted that site-centric methods are those in which websites become the focus of attention, while user-centric methods are those in which the focus of attention is the web users. However, using the 'focus of attention' as the criteria under which methods are classified does not seem to be very appropriate, since the 'focus of attention' is not so much an intrinsic characteristic of the methods as a characteristic of the use to which the results of the measurement are put. For example, electronic measurement panels offer information both on websites and web users. Whether the focus of attention is placed on sites or on users depends on the way in which we use the results obtained from the panel, not on the nature of the measurement method used.

As a way of explaining the basis for the aforementioned classification, it is often asserted that site-centric methods are those based on the analysis of log-files, while user-centric are those that use some variation of the electronic panel technique. This kind of distinction, rather than offering a way of classifying the methods, creates a label for each method. In this way, we can find authors (Lamas, 2002) and organizations (FAST/ARF, 2000) who add to site- and user-centric methods a third group, that of advertisement-centric methods, since it is possible to measure—based on the information provided by advertising servers—the audience of specific online advertisements. There are even authors (Goosey, 2003; Salgado, 1997) who talk of browser-centric methods; that is, those based on the measurement of the activity of users' web browsers. In this manner, and depending on the point of the communication process from which the information is collected, new types of methods are added to the classification. And since the web is a complex medium in which a trace is left by the communicative contacts performed through it, it allows for the collection of information on such contacts at many different places and, therefore, the list of types of methods can be extended almost *ad infinitum*. There are also measurement methods, such as electronic measurement panels, in which the collection of information can be performed at a variety of points and in which the nature of the information collected can be very diverse. In sum, we seem to be facing a mere listing of the different methods, whose variations generate new labels, rather than a real classificatory scheme.

This is why I would like to propose here an alternative system of classification that takes as its starting point a distinction made by FAST/ARF (2000) between passive and active research and applies it, though not literally, to the classification of web audience measurement methods. Passive research is characterized by the lack of interaction between researchers and the subjects whose behavior is being researched, while in active research that interaction exists and, therefore, the participation of the researched subjects is required. If we take this idea as our starting point, we can say that there are three types of methods for measuring the web audience: passive, active, and mixed. In the case of passive methods, information on the activity of users is collected without requiring their collaboration; thanks to the trace left by the interaction of the different machines involved in the communication process. In the case of active methods, the measurement depends on the collaboration of the subjects being researched and on the information provided by them. In the case of mixed methods, the collaboration of the subjects is needed, at least in the initial stages of the research, and the information provided by them is combined with the information collected from the machines used in the communication process.

In turn, and within these main groups, we can find different methods or specific techniques. Within the group of passive methods, and depending on where and how the information is collected, we can talk of website log-files analysis (which is usually referred to as site-centric method), advertisement server log-files analysis (usually referred to as advertisement-centric method), and analysis of the log-files obtained through the use of tags that activate the information collection process when they are read by a web browser (usually referred to as browser-centric method).

In the case of active methods, the information used in the measurement comes from web users themselves and it is usually obtained through surveys. Since the web itself can become a tool for the collection of data provided by its users, it is necessary to add to traditional surveys, using personal or telephone interviewing, the possibility of doing online surveys.

In the case of mixed methods, there is a combination of the information provided by users and by the activity registered by the computers taking part in the communication through the web. The usual procedure for the combination of these two types of information is the implementation of electronic measurement panels, with their different variations.

We can, therefore, propose a classification of the different methods for measuring the web audience that will allow us to analyze their main characteristics, their strengths, and their weaknesses. This is summarized in Table 2.

Table 2.   Classification of web audience measurement methods

Type	Source of information	Method
Passive	Trace left by the information transaction among computers	Website log-files analysis Advertisement-server log-files analysis Analysis of log-files generated by the use of tags
Active	Information provided by web users	Online surveys Offline surveys
Mixed	Combination of the trace left by computers' information transactions and the information provided by web users	Electronic measurement panels Global macro-panels

CHAPTER 6

Passive Methods

In this chapter I will proceed to examine those audience measurement methods that I have called passive and which are based on the information provided by the interaction between computers. I have included here the three main varieties of these methods: website log-files analysis, advertisement server log-files analysis, and the analysis of the log-files generated by using tags that can be read by web browsers. This list does not aspire to be exhaustive, since new measurement options appear periodically. There are already other possible applications of passive methods, such as the initiatives aimed at measuring webcasts through the trace generated in the transaction between computers, or the initiatives directed at the analysis of the log-files generated by specific Internet Service Providers (ISPs).[1]

In this section I will analyze in greater detail the first of the three methods, the analysis of website log-files, and in the analysis of the other two methods I will focus on those issues that differentiate them from the first one, with the objective of not making unnecessary repetitions.

As we will see, and in spite of the potential of passive methods to become powerful tools for web audience measurement, the truth is that for the most part they do not go beyond being a tool for measuring circulation, often not very precisely, and show obvious limitations when trying to quantify and qualify the audience.

Analysis of Websites Log-Files

The first passive method I will describe here is the one based on the analysis of the log-files of servers where a website is hosted.[2] Log-files are text files that include information on requests and exchanges of information between the client computers of web users and the servers that host the available information. I include below an example of a log-file, though, as we will see, there are different log-file formats that contain different types of information (Fleishman, 1996).

Table 3. Example of a log-file

01:50:17 216.126.148.89 - ICICWEB1 GET /pdq.html - 200 16391
295Mozilla/4.0+(compatible;+MSIE+4.01;+Windows+98)
http://cancernet.nci.nih.gov/pdqsrch.shtml

01:50:17 216.126.148.89 - ICICWEB1 GET /images/pdq.gif - 200 793
290Mozilla/4.0+(compatible;+MSIE+4.01;+Windows+98)
http://128.231.164.190/pdq.html

01:50:18 216.126.148.89 - ICICWEB1 GET /images/banner1.gif - 200 4067
294Mozilla/4.0+(compatible;+MSIE+4.01;+Windows+98)
http://128.231.164.190/pdq.html

01:50:18 216.126.148.89 - ICICWEB1 GET /images/news.gif - 200 1054
291Mozilla/4.0+(compatible;+MSIE+4.01;+Windows+98)
http://128.231.164.190/pdq.html

Source: Haylock (2003).

Log-files were originally created to allow system administrators to monitor the system and solve any problem with its functioning. Nowadays, they are also used as a way of measuring web use. As we will see, the use of such files to measure the audience of the web presents certain strengths but also difficulties and significant limitations.

Even though we often speak in a generic way of log-files, it is possible to distinguish among four different types of log-files that may be used to collect information on the traffic generated by a website (Bertot et al., 1997; McDunn, 2001):

1. *Access logs*: These collect the most relevant information on server activity, including the IP address of the computer making the request to the server, the date and time of the request, and the content of the request (i.e., text files, images, etc.).
2. *Agent logs*: These collect information on the browser making the request, the version of the browser, and the operating system of the computer making the request.
3. *Error logs*: These include information about any problem in the process of requesting and serving files between server and

client computers, from "file not found" to "document contains no data" or "transmission interrupted."

4. *Referrer logs*: These collect information on the pages that have links to the different documents stored in the server. In the case that a user makes a request through the result of a search on a search engine, both the search engine name and the words used in the search are saved in the referrer logs.

All this information available through the log-files can be saved in different formats, such as, for example, *Common Logfile Format* or *Extended Logfile Format* (Burton & Walther, 2001), depending on the server type and on the changes system administrators may introduce in the process of collecting the information. As a whole, log-files may include the following information:

- Date and time at which the information exchange between server and client takes place.
- IP address of the computer making the request.
- User name, though only in those cases in which it is necessary to type in a user name, usually with a password, in order to gain access to the requested content.
- Website's domain name.
- Name of the specific computer where the content is stored, in the event that the website is stored in more than one computer.
- IP address of the web server.
- Type of request made, usually GET (obtain information).
- Uniform Resource Locator (URL) of the information requested to the server.
- Status code. There are four series of status codes: the 200s, which refer to the success of the exchange of information; the 300s, which mean redirection; the 400s, which mean error on the side of the client; and the 500s, which refer to errors in the server. For example, the status code 200 means "successful transmission," while 404 means "file not found."
- Search performed in order to get to the website. In the event that the request is performed from a search engine, it is possible to collect the keywords that were used in the search.

- Size, in bytes of information, of the request to the server.
- Size, in bytes of information, of the response of the server.
- Response time, that is, the time it takes the server to respond to the request made by the client.
- Server port through which the request was made.
- Protocol used in the transaction.
- Browser, including type, version and, often, the operating system on which it runs.
- *Referrer*, that is, the page in which the link that generated the request was located—if the request to the server was made by clicking on a link.
- *Cookie*, or unique file sent by the server to the user's browser, which is read by the server every time the same browser is used to make a request to that server.

Measuring Organizations

Since the information used to perform the measurement, in the form of log-files, is stored in the servers where the website of interest is stored, the analysis can be easily carried out by the managers of the website themselves. In order to conduct the analysis, it is possible to develop customized tools that, properly programmed, can offer valuable information on the traffic of the site. There are also several software tools in the market specifically developed for this kind of analysis. However, the audience or traffic measurement of a website when carried out by the website's own managers does not generate the necessary credibility, since the different interests at stake can lead to manipulations of the data. Besides, the complexity of the analytic process requires specific and standardized criteria that are not always followed by website managers. That is why, since the inception of audience measurement on the web, there have appeared various organizations and companies that perform audits of the analyses of log-files, whether by performing the analysis themselves (following standardized and public procedures) or by examining (against norms widely accepted) the procedures followed by the websites in doing the analysis. These auditors can be of different types but, in most countries, the organizations in charge of monitoring the circulation of print publications have taken the initiative.

Sampling Issues

Log-files analysis can be thought of as a census, since it does not rely on samples and collects all the activity generated by the server where the website is hosted. Therefore, there are no problems of statistical representativeness, of sample design and size, of non-response rates, of response bias, etc. In this way, it allows for the focusing of the analysis on the most specific and minute elements of a website (e.g., a particular text within a particular page) regardless of the number of users that request them from the server. It also collects information generated by requests coming from any location—not only the home, but also workplaces—and from any country (FitzGerald, 2002).

There are obvious limitations that must be mentioned, however, when talking of the census-like character of website log-files analysis. Even though all the exchanges between client computers and servers are recorded in the log-files, the truth is that there are occasions in which the request by a user of a page stored in the server might generate no activity in the latter. This is due to the use of cache memory. Requests of pages stored in cache—browser or proxy caching—do not show up in the log-files. In the case of browser caching, the computer of the user stores certain pages, which have already been requested from and served by the server, in the hard drive. If the user makes a new request for one of those pages from the same browser and the page has not been modified since the last time it was requested, this page will be viewed in the browser without the intervention of the server and, therefore, without recording any activity in the log-files. In the case of proxy caching, the pages are stored in proxy servers—that is, servers that are located between the user's computer and the website's server from which the page is requested. When the user makes a page request, this page is served from the proxy server without the intervention of the website's server, which will not register any activity in its log-files. A server on which a website is stored can prevent the use of cache memory,[3] but it will then loose the advantage that cache memory offers—improved access speed—and the website might lose users due to its slow functioning.

There is also an additional limitation: the analysis of website log-files has to focus on specific websites, without yielding a panoramic view of the medium. Log-file analysis cannot offer a general vision of the medium because only those websites that voluntarily collaborate with the measurement process are included in the results. Since the data needed for the analysis are stored in the servers of the website, the managers of the website have to give permission and provide the records needed for the analysis. To this we need to add that the quantity of information generated by the log-files is often larger than the information stored in the websites themselves. Its analysis is a complex and fastidious process, as we will see now, and this makes it impossible to audit all the websites available online, not even all the relevant sites in a particular category.

Data Gathering and Analysis

The information gathering process in log-files is completely automatic, without any intervention on the part of researchers or researched subjects. In some cases, a certain initial preparation might be necessary in case the analyst wants to change the format in which the log-files are stored in order to adapt them to the specific needs of the measuring process.

However, the analysis of the information contained in the log-files is rather complex, and it is full of nuances that may lead to unintentional errors or intentional manipulations. In order to make this information useful, a whole process of cleaning and refining is necessary. I am going to describe that process here following the specifications proposed by I/PRO, a pioneer organization in the development of website traffic audits. The following description can be considered a complete and ideal process, which is not necessarily followed in all its terms when website log-files analyses are carried out:[4]

1. At the beginning of the process, the unrefined hits are received; that is, information on each of the files that makes the webpages that have been requested. These files may be HTML pages, images, multimedia files, style sheets, etc. Even though when the measurement of the traffic of websites was initiated, unrefined hits were used as a measurement unit, their use was abandoned as a metric since the only information they offer is the number of files that configure the pages requested to a

website, which is not very useful from the point of view of audience measurement.

2. Next, the pages with an invalid status code are eliminated. That is, those that generate error codes, 400s and 500s, or any other message that indicates that the files were not served to the user.

3. It is also necessary to eliminate the page requests generated by the site's own internal traffic. Website managers and the employees of the companies in charge of them usually generate traffic on the server, and that traffic cannot be counted as audience generated traffic. The identification of internal traffic is usually done by comparing the IP addresses in the log-files with the IP addresses of the computers of the company managing the website.

4. Pages requested by 'spiders' and 'robots' also have to be eliminated. 'Spiders' and 'robots' are automatic browsing agents used by search engines, price-comparison engines, and other large-scale search tools. Since they are automatic systems in which there is no specific request on the part of the users, the records generated by such agents need to be identified and eliminated.[5] There are listings, such as the one created by the Interactive Advertising Bureau (IAB), with the names of the most common 'spiders' and 'robots,' that can be used as an aid in the log-files' cleaning process.

5. Next it is necessary to eliminate all the pages that do not generate HTML, such as images, multimedia files, style sheets, etc. These are files with the extensions .jpg, .class, .gif, .mp3, etc.

6. Blank pages are also eliminated. Often empty HTML files are added to the design of webpages, but these files do not add anything to the content of the page.

7. It is also necessary to eliminate redirection pages. A redirection action is an automatic action that takes the user to an address, URL, that is different from the one on which she typed or clicked. Redirection pages usually appear when the URL requested by the user has been changed and the user is not aware of that change.

8. Administrative and test pages are eliminated as well. These are pages used by the managers of the website without adding anything to its content.

9. Error pages need to be eliminated too. These are not entries with error codes, which were mentioned above, but pages created by the website, usually with the graphic style of the site, in order to communicate to users that an error has taken place and that they cannot receive the files they requested because, for example, the access is restricted.

10. In log-files there are sometimes entries of files requested that cannot be viewed by a web browser because, for example, they are designed to be viewed using wireless devices. Such entries also need to be eliminated.

11. Often, more than one HTML frame is used in order to create a single webpage. These multiple frames need to be reduced to one.

12. It is also necessary to eliminate pages that are part of interstitial advertisements, pop-ups, and pop-unders; that is, pages that are sent to the client without an explicit request from her. These are pages, often with commercial content, that appear before the requested page (interstitial pages), above the requested page (pop-ups), or below the requested page (pop-unders).

13. WAP and PDA pages need to be eliminated too. They are pages that are designed for wireless devices, even though they can be viewed by a web browser.

14. Other types of error pages have to be eliminated, such as, for example, search errors (because a search format is not correct or does not produce any results) or errors in the use of forms (fields not completed, inappropriate formatting of the typed information, etc.).

15. Include files are also eliminated; that is, files, usually text files, that are called by other webpages, usually dynamic pages. The use of this type of files is habitual when information common to all the webpages of a site needs to be shown: headings, navigational icons, addresses, telephone numbers, etc.

16. If the analysis wants to distinguish between requested pages and served pages, it is also necessary to eliminate, to the degree that it is possible, refresh pages. These are webpages that are designed so that the browser will make an automatic request of the same page in a predetermined time interval—this is a very common tool in, for example, pages that display the score of certain sports events and that are updated frequently.

17. Once this process is over, it is possible to offer information about the number of pages served, the number of pages requested, the number of visits, the duration of the visits, and the number of unique browsers—until very recently, it was common to talk about 'unique users,' and some organizations still do, but that metric, as we will soon see, presents many problems.

It is clear that the process of cleaning log-files is rather complex. Each of the steps mentioned could have a great influence on the final result of the measurement, and it is therefore necessary to know in detail how the cleaning is carried out in order to evaluate the final results of the analysis. There are many software packages that can help in the cleaning and analysis of log-files. However, each has its own peculiarities and specificities. In addition, there are important steps in the cleaning process that are difficult to make automatically and require a detailed knowledge of how the site was programmed in order to allow decisions about what counts as a page and which entries need to be eliminated from the log-files. Issues such as the identification of 'spiders' and 'robots,' interstitial windows, pop-ups, pop-unders, or the distinction between pages generated by auto-refresh and pages requested explicitly by the users are difficult to resolve.

Metrics and Results

Due to the huge quantity of information contained in log-files, it is possible to derive a great number of metrics from them. However, I am going to focus on those metrics that are most often used when presenting the results of website log-files analysis: pages, visits, and unique users.

The cleaning process I have described above leads directly to the basic metric in log-files analysis, that is the page. A page is a set of hypertext files that are sent to a user as a result of a specific request that is registered in the server's log-files. In theory, it is possible to distinguish between pages served (sent from the server), pages displayed (pages viewed in the browser), and pages requested (pages explicitly requested by the user). Regardless of the type of pages we would like to measure, in order to quantify them it is necessary, as we have seen, to go through a complex cleaning process that eliminates the irrelevant pages and that reduces to a single entry all the different files that make up a page and generate independent entries in the log-files. Even though hits, the entries generated in the log-files by each of the different files that make up a page, were at some point considered the elementary metric in the web, the page has taken that place. In essence, the page has become the equivalent of the OTSs (Opportunities to See), which are the basic metric for advertising in traditional media.

The next metric used in log-files analysis is the visit. The visit is a metric specific to the web, and it is not directly comparable with other metrics used in other media. In fact, the use of the visit as a metric seems to respond to that hybrid character of the web mentioned above, neither a flow nor a closed product, since the visit has a temporal component, characteristic of broadcast audience measurement, and at the same time refers to pages, a concept taken from print media. The visit is defined as a series of page requests from a single user to a single website. A visit starts when a user requests a page from a website, and continues while new page requests are made, until a predetermined period of time lapses in which no new request is made. In order to measure visits it is necessary to identify the successive page requests and make sure that they come from the same user or, at least, the same browser. This is done through cookies and other identification tools that will be discussed below. It is also necessary to define very clearly how many minutes of inactivity, without requests to the site, are required before the visit is considered finished and a new visit begins to be counted. Different auditing organizations and companies have used different thresholds: 10, 20, or 30 minutes. The total time of the visit is calculated comparing the time stamp of the first page request registered in the log-files and the time stamp of the last request, to which often an arbitrary number of minutes is added, since it is impossible to know how much time the user spent viewing the last page that was delivered. Regardless of the difficulties or arbitrariness of its calculation, or of the popularity it has achieved as a metric, the truth is that the estimation of the number of visits to a website has limited usefulness from the point of view of online advertising activity.

However, the real test of every audience measurement method is the ability of the method to quantify the audience and, if possible, to offer a profile (demographic, geographic, etc.) of that audience. It is in this area in which the analysis of log-files presents obvious limitations.

In order to quantify the audience of a website through the analysis of log-files, it is necessary to link the activity generated in the server with the individuals that make the page requests. If the website requires users to register and introduce some kind of personal identification, and if we suppose that only one individual uses that identification, then it would be possible to quantify the audience of that website. If, on top of that, the process of user identification requires the disclosure of users' personal information, and if we assume that that information is truthful, then it would be possible to offer a profile of the audience of the website. However, I have included the analysis of log-files among the category of passive measurement methods precisely because such cases are rare. Most websites do not require an access password every time some information is requested from the server and, therefore, the audience measurement derived from log-files must quantify the number of users based on the information collected without users' intervention.

The process of identifying individual users through log-files takes as a starting point three items of information: (1) the user agent (i.e., the information regarding the browser and the operating system on which it runs), (2) the IP address of the computer from which the request was made (i.e., the number that identifies all computers connected to the Internet), and (3) cookies (i.e., the identification files that web servers store in the user's browser when the latter establishes a connection). From these three sources it is possible to try to quantify the number of users of a website. But each of these sources presents certain problems that complicate the quantification.

The first source of information is the user agent. The user agent, usually the web browser through which the connection is established, can only be used as a complementary piece of information to distinguish, for instance, between two connections established from the same IP address. Since there is a limited number of browser types and versions, the information on the user agent through which the connection is established cannot identify individual users because a large number of users may use the same type of browser, the same version of that browser, and on the same operating system.

The second source of information, the IP address, can be one of two types: permanent and dynamic. Permanent IP addresses are always assigned to the same computer when it connects to the Internet, and it is therefore possible to know that a specific computer is connected. Dynamic IP addresses are assigned to a group of computers randomly each time they connect to the Internet, and thus the same computer may establish online connections using more than one IP address, and one IP address may be used by different computers in successive connections. Such dynamic addresses are very common in connections established through ISPs. Also, it is not unusual for individuals who work in the same organization to share a single IP address when they connect to the Internet using different computers. This often makes it impossible to establish with any certainty the computer from which a page is being requested. In addition, IP addresses can identify computers, but not the users of those computers. The most IP addresses can say about users is the geographic region from which the requests were made, since there exist databases that show the IP addresses assigned to different parts of the world. However, this is not an easy task, and often many IP addresses—around 40%, according to Coffey (2001); between 25% and 40%, according to Shaw (2003)—cannot be linked to any particular geographical region.

The third source of information is cookies. Cookies are text files that the web server sends to the browser and are stored in the user's computer. If the same browser establishes another connection with the website that sent the cookie, this website is able to read the cookie that was sent and can, therefore, follow the trace of the different connections established through the same browser. Cookies can be of two types: session cookies and persistent cookies. Session cookies expire within a short period of time, usually a visit to a website, and are commonly used, for example, to allow the server to memorize the different product selections made by a user when visiting an online store so that they can all be included in the same order—if the server did not use a cookie, it would often be unable to know that the same user has placed different products in the shopping cart, for example. This kind of cookie is, obviously, not very useful when the goal is to measure the audience of a website, since different cookies will be assigned to the same user in subsequent visits. This makes it necessary to use persistent cookies, those that do not expire within a short period of time. However, using persistent cookies does not allow the identification of individual users, since the same user might access the website from different browsers or computers, and the same browser and computer might be used by different users to access the same site. On top of this, the acceptance of cookies by the user is not necessarily automatic, since it is possible to reject a cookie that is sent by a website (though some sites will not allow access if cookies are rejected), and the deletion of cookies (a process that is rather fastidious if it is done manually) has become a rather simple process; thanks to certain software tools and new browsers.

None of the three sources of information described above is able to offer a precise quantification of the audience of a website. Considering the limitations I have mentioned, log-files analysis has to make do with approximations of the number of unique users of a website based on estimations of the number of unique browsers that access that website. In order to produce these estimations of the number of unique browsers there are five different procedures that can be followed, each of which generates different results. I will briefly describe each of these procedures (Bennett et al., 2002):

1. *Quantification of the number of unique cookies*: Once the log-files have been cleaned it is possible to count the number of unique cookies registered. This procedure might produce lower counts, since it ignores those browsers that do not accept cookies and browsers that have visited the site only once and therefore do not yet have a stored cookie.

2. *Quantification of the unique combinations of IP addresses associated with a particular user agent*: Each unique combination of IP address and user agent is counted as a unique browser. This procedure generates errors due to the possibility that the same browser might access the same website with different IP addresses (i.e., dynamic IP addresses) or, on the contrary, due to the possibility that several browsers may share the same IP address and generate the same user agent information, as is often the case in companies or other organizations.

3. *Quantification of unique cookies plus the unique combination of IP address with user agent*: This procedure combines the previous two. The log-files are divided into two different files, one with those entries that contain cookies and the other with those that only contain IP addresses and user-agent information. The first procedure is applied to the cookies file. The second procedure is applied to the file with IP addresses and user-agent information, and this application produces the same errors that were described above. In addition, there is a risk that information items generated by the same browser may end up appearing in both of the files into which the log-files are separated. For example, a browser that visits a website for the first time will generate an entry that has no cookie, and it will therefore end up in the second file. In subsequent visits, because it will probably have a cookie, its entries will be saved in the first file and, therefore, will be counted twice as a unique browser.

4. *Quantification of unique cookies plus unique and non-duplicated combinations of IP addresses with user agent information*: This procedure is similar to the previous one, but in this case those combinations of IP address plus user-agent that are present in both the file with cookies and the file without cookies are eliminated from this latter file, which avoids double counting. The analysis of the file containing entries with only IP addresses and user-agent information can generate errors similar to the ones described in procedure number

2, but they are in this case reduced to those entries in which there are no cookies.

5. *Quantification of unique cookies plus projection*: Similar to what is done in the third procedure, log-files are divided into two files, one with the entries with cookies and the other with entries without cookies. With the first file, the average number of pages requested by each unique cookie is calculated. In the second file, the number of entries is divided by the average number of pages requested by a unique cookie, with the ultimate goal of projecting the number of unique browsers without cookies. The result is added to the number of unique cookies in order to calculate the total number of unique browsers. One weakness of this approach is that it assumes that the behavior, number of pages requested, of browsers without cookies is similar to that of browsers with cookies. However, as some research done by the Audit Bureau of Circulations Interactive (ABCi) seems to show, among the browsers without cookies there are many who do not have them because they only requested a single page from the website, which makes the average number of pages requested by browsers without cookies smaller than the average number of pages requested by browsers with cookies. However, the exact quantification of this difference is rather problematic.

The last two procedures (i.e., 4 and 5) are the ones that seem to offer better results.[6] Nonetheless, they all share an assumption that seems increasingly difficult to maintain, that cookies are really permanent, that they are not deleted. If we take into consideration cookie deletion, these quantifications become even more problematic.

But, regardless of whether users delete cookies or not and of how the different procedures compare to each other, in the end the most they can achieve is an estimation of the number of browsers that have made requests to a website. Even though for several years the results of such estimates were presented as the number of unique users of a site, nowadays there is a tendency to refer to them as estimates of the number of browsers, or browser profiles, that have visited a website, without reference to the number of users. Supposing that the number of browsers that have visited a website could be calculated with precision, we would be able to estimate the number of visitors to or users of that site only if we were able to calculate the number of browsers used by each user or, inversely, the number of users that use the same browser. However, as FitzGerald (2002: 53) asserts:

> It is not possible to determine the extent or nature of this multi-person-per-PC impact from site-centric measures.

Or, as Shaw (2003: 124) explains in a more generic way:

> It has been shown that there is no known method today for measuring or calculating DPV (Devices per Visitor), and further that this value may indeed be indeterminable, meaning it may never be possible to measure it in the future. Even if DPV could be calculated, the issue of Population Identification remains.

Thus, the analysis of website log-files shows obvious limitations when it is used as an audience measurement method for the web. It allows us to estimate, without much precision, the number of browsers that have exchanged information with a website, but it cannot calculate the number of users, or their demographic characteristics, not even their geographic location, or the place from which they connect to the Internet (home, work, etc.).

Advertisement Server Log-Files Analysis

The analysis of log-files from ad-servers is a method that presents many similarities to the analysis of website log-files and, therefore, I will not repeat here those characteristics that are common to both methods. But the analysis of ad-server log-files also presents certain peculiarities, such as the object of the measurement or the data gathering possibilities, which require a specific examination. Since web advertisements can be managed independently from the content it is possible to gather information for measurement not from the server where the website's information is located, but from the servers in charge of managing the delivery of the advertisements themselves. In this sense, we can describe it as a passive method that is based on the information provided by the exchanges among the machines that constitute the net.

Depending on the specific model used to manage the advertisements and on where the data needed to perform the measurement is gathered, the analysis of ad-server log-files can be carried out by the managers of the website or by the managers of ad-server networks—networks of ad-servers in charge of managing the advertisements to be inserted in different websites. When a website manages its own advertising, the usual situation is for it to have a server on which the advertising content is stored and from which it is served. There is also the possibility of transferring the responsibility of managing the advertising to an ad network, so that the advertising is served from the ad network servers. Thus, both the managers of websites and the managers of ad networks may perform specific measurements of the advertising content of the web. The truth is that on some occasions both organizations may carry out measurements of the same advertisements. It is not uncommon to find obvious disparities between the two measurements.

We can consider the analysis of ad-server log-files to be a census-like method, since it collects all the activity generated by ad servers. Obviously, as is also the case with website log-files, coverage is reduced to those advertisements that are managed by ad servers on which the analysis is performed and, therefore, it does not offer a general view of web advertising. However, compared with the analysis of website log-files, the analysis of ad-server log-files does present one advantage. Most advertising providers use cache busting; that is, techniques that through the insertion of random numbers or time stamps do not allow the use of cache memory and, therefore, they are able to obtain a more precise measurement of the number of times an ad has been viewed (PriceWaterhouseCoopers/IAB, 2001).

Regarding data gathering, the data could be collected from different points in the exchange process between users' web browsers and ad servers. The many different ways in which content, advertising, and other kinds of servers can be combined make it possible to collect the information to be analyzed from many different points and at very different moments. For example, the information might be gathered from the ad server of a website before the different elements that form the advertisement are served to users. Or, to mention another possibility, the information could also be gathered from the servers of an ad network once the ad server of a website has redirected the user's request to the ad network.[7] The collected log-files have to be subjected to a cleaning process similar to the one applied to website log-files.

Regarding the possibility of gathering information about users' behavior, it is necessary to mention the ability that ad networks have to create user profiles, since they can examine the cookies placed in users' browsers by different websites whose advertising is managed by the network. When a cookie is sent to a user's computer, that cookie can only be read by the website that sent the cookie, but that website cannot read the cookies sent by other websites. Since ad networks manage the advertising for different websites, such networks can read the cookies sent during visits to all these websites and can therefore register the activity of a browser in successive visits to the websites whose advertising is managed by the network. With this information it is possible to create user profiles, with their interests and favorite sites. However, the issue of user identity remains unresolved. Some networks, such as DoubleClick, have tried to obtain user identification through the purchase of databases with personal information that is later combined with the user profiles obtained through cookies (Campbell & Carlson, 2002).

In the analysis of ad-server log-files, as is the case with website log-files, it is possible to use many different metrics. However, the most relevant ones and the ones more commonly used are those referring to the number of impressions of an advertisement (the basic metric) and to clicks (both in terms of total clicks and in terms of click-through rates). The measurement of advertisement impressions refers to the number of responses from an ad-serving system to the request for an advertisement by a user's browser. In order to get to this number, it is necessary to carry out a cleaning process of log-files similar to the one described above for website log-files. It is advisable that the quantification be performed using information collected from a point as close as possible to the final viewing of the advertisement by the user's browser (PriceWaterhouseCoopers/IAB, 2001).

Regarding clicks, these are a metric used to express the number of times a user clicks on an advertisement and is redirected to another webpage. Click-through rates are calculated by dividing the actual number of clicks on an advertisement over the number of impressions of that particular advertisement. It is a metric that goes beyond the mere exposure to advertising content and aims at measuring the attractiveness of particular advertisements, a piece of information of relevance in the management of advertising campaigns.

Analysis of Log-Files Generated Through the Use of Tags

Another variant of passive methods involves the use of tags, and it is referred to by some authors as a browser-centric method. Tags receive different names: pixel tags, web bugs, web beacons, or clear GIFs. They are miniscule images, 1 by 1 pixel, usually transparent, that are inserted into webpages with the aim of establishing the number of times the pages are visualized by a browser. When a page that contains a tag is viewed through a web browser in a user's computer, the browser requests the tag image from the server that stores them and that serves as a counting device. This process is invisible to web users. In a sense, what the tag does is to force the browser to generate a log-file in a server other than the one storing the requested page. The information supplied to the counting server is similar to that which appears in regular log-files, but the data gathering and analysis process has, as we will see below, certain advantages compared with the same process in the analysis of website log-files.

The initiative in the development and application of this method has been taken, for the most part, by private companies, such as RedSheriff, Weborama, and Websidestory. These companies receive a fee in exchange for managing the counting servers and performing the analysis of the data generated by the use of tags. This methodology is also used by some Joint Industry Committees (JICs).[8] In any event, the application of this methodology requires the cooperation of the website's managers so that tags may be inserted in the different pages that are to be measured.

We can describe measurement through tags as a census-like method since it is possible to count each and every time a webpage is viewed by a browser. At the same time, the measurement is not affected by the use of cache memory in proxys or browsers, since tags generate a record in the counting server regardless of where the visualized page is stored. However, the coverage of this method depends on the ability of those organizations that carry out the measurement to obtain as many clients or collaborating websites as possible. Depending on the specific characteristics of each country (such as the time since this method has been available, the organizations in charge of doing the measurement, or the prevalence of other methods) the amount of coverage is very diverse.

The data-gathering process takes place automatically in the counting servers of the organizations performing the measurement. In this sense, in contrast to the other passive methods analyzed above, the measurement is centralized and out of reach for website or ad-server managers, which contributes to its credibility. The analysis of the data is easier than in other passive methods, since there is only one tag per page and the cleaning process becomes simpler and is focused on the quantification of the number of times a tag appears in the counter and on information about the client computer that is associated with the tag. In addition, the system does not collect information produced by the activity of 'spiders' and 'robots,' and, therefore, avoids the danger of inflating the numbers when such activity cannot be distinguished from the activity generated by human users.

In spite of the advantages presented by the use of tags for the collecting and managing of the data, the metrics and the results obtained by using these measurement methods are essentially the same as those provided by the analysis of website log-files, with all the same limitations when it comes to quantifying and qualifying users. Therefore, we should still refer to passive measurement methods as methods for the measurement of circulation, but not as methods for the measurement of the audience, since in the end this type of analysis offers very little information regarding the actual size and profile of the audience.

In summary, the measurement of the audience through passive methods presents a series of obvious limitations that prevent them from performing some of the essential functions of any audience measurement process; that is, quantifying the audience and offering information about its composition. If this is the case, we might wonder why so much attention is paid to this type of methods when we talk about web audience measurement. The reason seems to lie not so much in the present state of web audience measurement as in its past and its future. When the need to measure the audience of the web first became apparent, the fact that the transactions between client and server computers left a detailed record of the activity led many people to think that the web would be an easily measurable medium and that, thanks to log-files and other activity records, it would be possible to obtain exact measurements of the audience of the web. However, as soon as the measurement of the web audience began, researchers became aware of the fact that, in spite of the huge amounts of information recorded about computer exchanges, in the end it did not offer the possibility of connecting the recorded activity to the individuals generating it, that is, to the members of the audience.

On the other hand, and in spite of the limitations currently shown by passive methods as a tool for measuring the web audience, it seems clear that any attempt to develop new methods that might offer better results will need to take advantage of the detailed information offered by the activity records of those machines that make up the web. It is not possible to neglect passive methods if we want to understand how the World Wide Web audience is and will be measured.

CHAPTER 7

Active Methods

Active methods are those methods exclusively based on the information provided by web users. Over time social research has developed a panoply of tools for the gathering of information from researched subjects: interviews, focus groups, surveys, panels, etc. However, since my goal here is to study the tools that can provide measurements of the online activities of researched subjects, only quantitative tools are relevant to my purpose. In particular, surveys are the most common tool used to obtain measurements of the web audience.

Panels can also be used as a measurement method. However, panels that exclusively rely on the information provided by users, as would be the case with 'browsing diaries,' have never been implemented as a way of measuring the web audience. The panels that are commonly used, which I will examine below, are the ones that combine information provided by users with information provided by the record left by the exchanges among computers. For this reason they will be included here within the mixed methods category. My analysis of active methods will focus on the survey.

The survey is the social research, quantitative technique *par excellence*. It is based on the drawing of a sample which represents a larger population or universe. It uses standardized questioning procedures with the goal of obtaining quantitative measures on a series of variables. These variables can offer information on any issue considered relevant for advertising planning (age, gender, income, address, technology access and use, hobbies, lifestyles, brand consumption, etc.).

Surveys can be classified according to many different criteria depending on the concrete applications of the technique. However, with the goal of allowing for a clearer analysis of the different issues that are relevant to a study of the survey as a method for measuring the web audience, I have chosen here to divide surveys into only two types. The classification used here is based on whether the data collection process takes place over the web itself (i.e., online surveys) [1] or, as it has traditionally been done, that process is carried out through other means (i.e., offline surveys).

Online Surveys

Surveys can be carried out over the phone, face to face, by mail and, most recently, online. The web offers the possibility of programming an online questionnaire to be answered by the audience. It is a relatively simple procedure and, often, cheaper than telephone, face-to-face, and even mail surveys. This is especially the case if the goal is to interview web users. When someone wants to obtain information on web users using traditional offline data collection procedures, one of the problems that may arise is the limited penetration of the medium. With offline surveys, it may be necessary to contact many non-users in order to interview web users. As the AIMC (2003) mentions in its methodological discussion of Internet surveys in Spain,

> a statistically representative sample of Internet users is usually obtained through a probability research of the total population. That implies a strong inefficiency factor, due to the as of yet not too high penetration of Internet use.

This problem disappears with online surveys since, by definition, all the people that are contacted are Internet or web users. It is probably this element of efficiency that has made the use of online surveys a favored method. However, as we will soon see, it is precisely this element that makes online surveys an inappropriate method for measuring the web audience.

Measuring Organizations

One of the most important characteristics of surveys, and especially of online surveys, is the simplicity and flexibility of their implementation. Any website can place online a survey with very little prior programming or even without any programming if specific online survey tools are used. Such tools allow users to create online questionnaires in a user-friendly environment and without requiring any previous programming experience. However, if the goal is to measure the web audience or the audience of a series of websites, organizations with the capacity to carry out complex and wide-ranging surveys are necessary. In any event, the attempt to quantify the web audience through online surveys seems, as we will see, like a rather futile effort.

Sampling Issues

Surveys basically consist in the collection of information from a sample representative of a larger universe to which the results are later projected. One of the problems posed by online surveys as a tool for audience measurement is the impossibility of sizing the universe through them. Since the web itself becomes the instrument for data collection, it is impossible to know how many individuals are not web users or do not visit a specific website. In a sense, the same issue that makes of the web an efficient tool for the gathering of information on web users (i.e., that it only collects information from users and does not waste resources contacting or interviewing non-users) is the one that introduces fundamental problems when the aim is to quantify the size of the audience. Even if it were possible to obtain a measurement of the universe through other means, such as a telephone survey, it still would not be possible to have a sample frame from which to draw a representative sample that could be contacted and asked to take the online questionnaire. As Best and Krueger (2004: 15) put it, "developing sampling frames for the Internet is considerably more difficult than for conventional communication mediums." In a situation like this, the chances a member of the universe has of becoming a member of the sample depends on how likely it is that the user will visit one of the pages or sites that have links or banners to the questionnaire. And since there is no comprehensive map of the web through which links or banners could be distributed randomly, it is not possible to consider such a sample a random one. Notably, it is the frequency and the intensity of web use that determine to a great extent the chances a user has of running into the links and banners leading to the questionnaire. The bias already detected in this kind of survey produces an over-representation of those people who use the web more intensely. Finally, only those people who have found the questionnaire on the web and have decided to take it become members of the sample, creating in this manner a self-selected sample (Lamas, 2000). So far the experience with this type of survey shows that the response rates tend to be very low, making it rather difficult to extract valid conclusions from the data. All these problems constitute an insurmountable obstacle for the measurement of the web audience through online surveys.

Data Gathering and Analysis

Data collection in online surveys is relatively simple and cheap. All that is required is a certain number of links or banners leading to the HTML questionnaire with the survey questions. Since the questionnaire is programmed in computer language, it is quite easy to include in it consistency controls and routing (Lamas, 1997) (i.e., it is possible to determine specific questions received by each respondent depending on the answers given to previous questions), it is also possible to add visual elements (from logos to images from other webpages), and it is even possible to insert audio and video files. Responses are stored automatically in a database, a spreadsheet, or any other format that allows for their easy transfer to statistical software packages for cleaning and analysis.

Metrics and Results

As we have seen, it is not possible to perform a measurement of the web audience, or of the audience of specific websites, by using online surveys. In spite of this, it is possible to find online surveys offering data on the particular websites visited by the survey's respondents. But, considering the problems with the representational validity of online samples we have just discussed, the results obtained from online surveys can only be viewed as simple research exercises without any statistical validity. Not even huge samples, as the ones often used in this type of survey, can overcome the limitations that this method presents. This is why traditional ways of realizing surveys (in particular face-to-face and telephone interviewing), with their proven techniques, seem more appropriate as a tool for measuring the web audience.

Offline Surveys

The use of telephone or face-to-face interviewing in surveys aimed at measuring the web audience takes advantage of the know-how accumulated by experts, organizations, and companies over the decades in which these techniques have been in use. Since there is already a large body of literature that deals with surveys as a research method, here I will only pay attention to the way in which this method is applied to the measurement of the web audience, and I will not delve into more general methodological considerations that will distance me from my objective. I will focus on the advantages and limitations of applying telephone and face-to-face interviews to conduct surveys aimed at measuring the web audience.

Measuring Organizations

Almost any organization, any company, or any website can use offline surveys to conduct measurements of the web audience, due to the flexibility of the method and the large number of social and market research organizations with the logistic and technical capabilities to conduct them. However, and as we will see below, the use of offline surveys for measuring the web audience requires the use of rather large samples and many resources. This is why the organizations in charge of carrying out these large surveys aimed at measuring the web audience are either large companies specialized in social and market research—as is the case of Scarborough Research in the United States—or Joint Industry Committees (JICs)—as is common in Europe.

Sampling Issues

Often, the surveys used to measure the web audience are national surveys and that allows for the use of census data in order to define the universe to be measured. However, this procedure eliminates from the measurement the audience members that live abroad and it tends, therefore, to under-represent the audience of websites that have visitors residing in other countries.

There are many different types of samples that can be used when surveying the web audience (i.e., random sample, systematic random sample, stratified sample, cluster sample). Regardless of the type of sample used, offline surveys aimed at measuring the web audience pose a problem of efficiency. The reach of the Internet and of web use in many countries is still limited. As a consequence, in order to interview the number of people required by the sample design, it is necessary to contact large numbers of people, many of whom are not web or Internet users, which increases the cost of the survey.

In addition, the level of fragmentation of the medium also has a significant influence on the sample size when the goal is to offer valid results on the audience of specific media vehicles. The web is a very fragmented medium, with millions of outlets, and there are endless websites with small or very small audiences that are very difficult to measure with any degree of precision with manageable sample sizes. The results are always unstable and have huge errors.

On top of this, there is another issue that needs to be considered. In order to calculate the required sample size for a survey, it is necessary to take several issues into account, such as, the size of the population, the confidence interval and confidence level required, and the variance of the population. But it is also necessary to take into account the degree of disaggregation of the data that will be required. If what we want to know is not only the size of the audience of a website—which in itself, as has just been explained, may require huge sample sizes—but also the composition of that audience, then we will need to have in our sample a significant number of people who have visited that website. And that is basically impossible for the vast majority of websites.

Thus, because the web presents such a large number of vehicles, if we want to know the audience of those vehicles, it is necessary to use very large samples to reach a certain degree of statistical validity in the quantification. This issue, together with others that I will soon mention, explains why most offline surveys only cover a relatively limited number of websites.

Data Gathering and Analysis

Surveys allow for adapting data collection and analysis to specific measurement needs. Through them, it is possible to collect comprehensive information about web users on everything from demographic variables to lifestyle ones, from specific behaviors to attitudes. More specifically, it is possible to collect information on web browsing patterns, ways of establishing connections and the places from which they are established, websites visited, the use of other online communication tools, etc.

However, collecting information about the audience through offline surveys presents a series of problems and limitations which, in some cases, are accentuated when the audience in question is the web audience. First, surveys need to limit the number of websites whose audience is to be measured, and not just because of the issues about sample size that were discussed above, but also because of time/space constraints and because of limitations in the user's memory and in their willingness to collaborate. It is not possible to include in a telephone or face-to-face interview a list of even a fraction of all websites available online, since such a list would be endless. And it is not possible to demand that users spontaneously remember each and every website they have visited or ask them to review an endless list with hundreds or thousands of websites. In this sense, face-to-face interviewing has certain advantages over telephone interviewing, since the former allows for the inclusion of visual aids (such as website logos, page examples, etc.) which can be a great help in such a visual and complex medium as the web.

Regardless of the specific interviewing technique, offline surveys implemented to measure the web audience can only include a listing of a limited number of websites, usually the most popular. But even the selection of those sites is not an easy task, since in order to decide which sites are the most popular it is necessary to rely on previous measurements. The specific method used for those measurements and the criteria used to include or exclude sites from the list may easily be put in question.

The use of surveys for measuring the web audience also poses a series of problems that, though present when surveys are used to measure the audience of other media, become even more relevant when the audience to be measured is that of the World Wide Web. For instance, the lack of sincerity in responses or the bias in favor of what seems to be socially acceptable responses are problems with which many surveys have to deal. But when the goal of the survey is to measure the Internet audience, that problem can take on new proportions. In a much more ample and obvious way than is the case with other popular communication media, the web offers its users the possibility of accessing socially questionable contents and services. This can easily lead web users, when they are interviewed for a survey, to hide certain behaviors that take place during their online activities—an obvious example of this would be the use of pornography—and even add some new ones that may be considered socially appropriate.

Regardless of the degree of sincerity of interviewees, another problem that surveys need to confront is the limited memory of human beings. Surveys rely on people's memory, and with such a complex and fragmented medium as the web, it is extremely complicated to remember in detail certain activities, such as, for instance, all the websites visited during the previous week. Considering the multiplicity and complexity of the vehicles available online, interviewees tend to privilege the most popular and well-known websites and brand names. This problem can become even worse if we take into account the often slight differences between websites, which make it difficult for users to know exactly which website they are visiting. This memory problem, though it may also be present when the audience of other media is measured, acquires a new dimension when the audience being measured is the web audience.

Metrics and Results

Offline surveys have the advantage of allowing for the collection of information on the audience of several media at once and in a homogeneous way. This in turn allows researchers to establish comparisons among different media offerings, and the results of the web audience measurement can easily be integrated with the results of the measurement of other media, thus facilitating the planning of multimedia advertising campaigns (Agulló, 2000; Coffey, 2001; Lamas, 2002; Lavilla, 2002). But, from the point of view of the results yielded, the major strength of offline surveys when it comes to measuring the web audience is their ability to offer a general view of the web's usage. That is, their ability to measure the audience of the medium as a whole within the population from which the sample was drawn, along with its general characteristics and relevant information about, for instance, the different uses to which the web is put, the types of connections used, the frequency of use, the places from which the connections are established, the tools most often used, the relevance of electronic commerce, etc.

Regarding specific vehicles or websites, offline surveys are able to yield information on the particular sites that have been visited by interviewees. However, apart from the issues regarding sincerity and the ability to remember online behavior that were mentioned above and that cannot be disregarded, the truth is that this type of study does not offer a general panoramic view of the different websites available to users, and they end up restricting their coverage to the sites considered to be the most popular. Finally, and even though surveys allow for the collection of detailed information about respondents, it is almost impossible for them to give precise information on issues such as the number of pages viewed, the time spent on a particular site, the advertisements seen, the advertisements clicked, etc. In this sense, surveys offer opposite and complementary information to that offered by the passive methods described above.

In summary, we can say about the active methods for measuring the web audience that online surveys present a series of obvious methodological limitations that make them a non-viable measurement method, while offline surveys can serve as a useful tool if what is needed is a quantification and description of the web audience as a whole. Offline surveys can even be used, in spite of the problems that have been mentioned, to measure the audience of a limited number of websites. But what no survey seems able to offer is a complete panoramic view of the audience of the different websites that make up the web, or a minimally precise measurement of the specific activities of user on the websites being measured.

CHAPTER 8

Mixed Methods

Under the category of mixed methods, I have included those methods that combine the information collected passively (from the traces left by communication among computers) with the information collected actively (from the collaboration of the researched subjects). Since these methods feed from two complementary information sources, they open the possibility of overcoming the respective limitations of passive and active methods. However, these methods have their own problems and limitations as well.

Currently, the mixed method par excellence is the electronic measurement panel that uses representative samples in order to measure the web audience. In recent years, however, new types of panels have been implemented that stress the size and global nature of their samples rather than their representational power. It seems difficult to decide whether these new types of *macro*-panels truly constitute a different method from the panels that use representative samples, or if they are simply a variation on the same method. Regardless of what the answer might be, and considering the importance that these macro-panels seem to be gaining, I will devote a brief section to their analysis. The main focus of this section, however, will be those panels that use more traditional sample procedures.

Electronic Measurement Panels

Electronic measurement panels are large-scale studies that collect information on Internet users through surveys, select a representative sample of users, install a measuring software in their computers in order to electronically and passively record the use of those computers and the Internet connections established through them, and automatically transmit the information to a center where it is tabulated and projected to the population being measured. This method for measuring the web audience is perhaps the best known, and it combines traditional research techniques (such as the survey and the panel) with the new possibilities opened by the advent of the Internet (the use of the trace left by the computers participating in communication processes over the web). Based on the structure of the traditional audimeter panels used to produce broadcasting ratings, this method also uses the new developments in software and hardware to measure the behavior of the audience.

The measurement process using electronic panels needs to follow a series of steps before the required information is obtained:

1. *Definition of the population being measured and behaviors that are to be measured*: The first step is to define the universe from which the sample will be drawn and to which the results will be projected, and to define what exactly— which behaviors and activities—is going to be measured. For instance, the minimum age required, the use or lack of use of the Internet during a certain period of time, or the possibility of accessing the web from home and/or work are definition criteria of the population that need to be specified beforehand.

2. *Measurement of the defined population*: In order to measure the universe to which the panel refers, and since the population census cannot be used as such, it is necessary to carry out a representative survey—usually national and, if possible, using Random Digital Dialing (RDD)—that will yield information about the size and structure of the population to which the panel refers and of any possible sub-universes that might be interesting to measure. This survey, usually referred to as an enumeration survey, gives information on Internet use and on the characteristics of the users which will then be taken into account in the selection of the panel members and in the weighting of the final results. If the size and composition of the population tend to change quickly, it is recommended that this enumeration survey be carried out relatively frequently, at least monthly (Coffey, 2001). The specific procedure through which these surveys are carried out—telephone or personal interviewing, the minimum age of interviewees, the number of

times contact is attempted, etc.—have varied from country to country and from study to study. The weighting mechanism used to offer results is also very varied. Besides measuring the population, these surveys are also used as a first attempt at gauging the interest of interviewees in becoming panelists (Haering, 2002; Lamas, 2002).

3. *Drawing a representative sample of the population to be measured*: A representative sample is designed taking into account the information gathered through the enumeration survey. This sample can be drawn randomly or, as is more common, using quotas based on certain characteristics of the population, such as demographics, types of connection, or the date of one's first Internet access. Even though the enumeration survey collects information on Internet and web use from any locale (i.e., home, work, public place), the truth is that, due to implementation limitations, the representative sample usually only takes into account Internet use from the home and, only occasionally, from the workplace. This means that those individuals who access the Internet from public places (i.e., libraries, cybercafes, etc.) and often also those who access the Internet from work are excluded from the population being measured and, therefore, from the sample being drawn. Regarding collaboration rates, the number of people willing to become panelists, there is not much precise information about them, but it is possible to say that they appear to be rather low in spite of the use of incentives, such as free magazine subscriptions, cash, etc. Regarding the rotation of panelists, it is standard not to allow any member of the sample to stay on for more than four years (Lamas, 2002).

4. *Installation of the measurement software (i.e., the meter) in the computers used by the panelists*: Since Internet communication takes place via digital devices, it allows for the implementation of information collection devices that are based in software rather than hardware. Apart from being much cheaper, these software meters allow for an easy installation process that does not require the presence of specialized technicians and can be carried out by the panelists themselves. The

software can either be downloaded from the web or can be mailed in some digital storage device to the home of the panelists. The software is installed in all the computers in the home that is part of the sample and it collects information on the online activities of all household members—in order to do this, it asks at the beginning of each session for the identity of the user. The information is collected second by second, stored in the users' computers, and securely transferred to the measuring organization while the computers are idle—which is a much cheaper option than the one used by television panels—without affecting browsing speed—as the contrary could introduce biases in the results.

5. *Development of a series of norms for managing and cleaning the data generated by the measuring software*: Meters have a tremendous capacity to collect and generate raw data. This information has then to be cleaned and analyzed, and in order to do this it is necessary to establish a series of very specific criteria. It is necessary, for instance, to assign each of the Uniform Resource Locators (URLs) collected by the meter to a specific website. We should say, however, that the organizations implementing these electronic measurement panels have so far not been very explicit when it comes to explaining what types of specific criteria are being used in order to transform the raw data generated by meters into data that can be used in the audience measurement business.

6. *Weighting the results to avoid biases and projecting them to the population*: Even when the sample used to create the panel has been designed with the utmost rigor in order to represent the population being measured, it is often necessary to weight the results from that sample to adapt it to a constantly changing universe and to compensate for any problems in the data collection process. The weighting criteria can be very different (demographic variables, Internet-use variables, etc.) and they can also produce different types of biases in the results. Also, the different ways in which the universe is measured in order to inform the weighting process may produce undesired distortions in the results (Haering, 2002). In any event, since the fi-

nal goal is to obtain a measurement that is representative of the population as a whole, once the sample has been weighted the results can be projected to that population.

Measuring Organizations

The implementation of electronic measurement panels is an expensive and difficult process that requires abundant resources and qualified staff. This is why these panels, together with the technology needed to make them work, have been developed by companies with sufficient financial, technological, and human capital. In particular, we could mention three companies who have had the largest impact on the development of this method: Media Metrix, NetRatings, and NetValue. These three companies—the first two American and the latter French—can be pointed out as the most relevant organizations to an examination of the implementation over the past decade of electronic measurement panels for web audience measurement.

Sampling Issues

The definition of the universe to be measured with the electronic measurement panels poses some very important issues. First a decision is to be made whether the universe to be measured is that of people with Internet access or that of people who have used the Internet over a specific period of time, usually taken to be of one month. The former option poses the problem of defining in an unambiguous and homogeneous way what is meant by 'having Internet access,' since, at least in theory, any person living in a developed country has access to the Internet—a different issue would be to determine how difficult it is for that theoretical access to become effective use. To leave in the hands of interviewees the decision over what they understand by 'having access to the Internet' can introduce important biases in the panel. The other option, that is, defining the universe as 'those people who have used the Internet over some determined period of time' poses the problem of the instability of the universe. Since the population that makes effective use of the Internet in a specific month is rather volatile and changes rapidly, the panel needs to be constantly readjusted or weighted to adapt to such a changing universe (Coffey, 2001).

Another issue to be considered is the geographic range of the panel. Since most electronic measurement panels take a specific country as their universe, this method leaves out of the measurement all those members of the web audience that reside abroad, as is often the case when offline surveys are used to measure the web audience. The companies that implement electronic panels have tried to solve this limitation by using two different strategies. The first strategy is the creation in different countries of national panels with similar specifications so that the results of those panels can be added up. This strategy has demanded huge financial and organizational efforts. In spite of these efforts, and although it has been possible to measure a significant portion of the global web audience, there remain many countries in the world that do not have any electronic panels measuring their web audience.[1] The second strategy that has been used to overcome the geographic limitations of panels is the creation of global macro-panels. I will devote a specific section below to such macro-panels, and I will examine how they also display significant methodological problems when trying to solve this particular issue.

Another relevant issue is the difficulty of measuring online activity generated in places other than the home. A significant portion of online activities takes place in such alternative locations (i.e., schools and universities, companies, libraries, etc.) which often may offer higher connection speed than the one available from homes. The use generated from such locations can represent a very significant part of the audience of certain websites (such as educational sites, sites that offer information for specific professional groups, etc.) and not measuring such activity could mean leaving out significant population groups (such as students who rely on public access and do not have Internet connections at home). Some attempts have been made to measure web usage in places other than the home, but the truth is that it is not an easy task, to say the least. First, it is relatively complicated to obtain a sample frame that would allow for the drawing of a representative sample of companies or educational centers with Internet access. Second, even though panelists for the workplace sample could be contacted through the enumeration survey—as Nielsen NetRatings does—most companies, educational institutions, and organizations of every kind prohibit the installation of meters in their computers for security reasons—possible leaks of sensitive information, viruses, spyware, etc. In fact, the lack of representational value of workplace panels is perhaps an insolvable problem (Haering, 2002). The issue of measuring web usage in public spaces, such as cybercafes or libraries, seems even more complicated.

Another relevant question is what happens with people who access the web using devices other than computers. Since electronic measurement panels are based on the installation of the meter software in users' computers, those users who access the web via other access platforms (i.e., cell phones, PDAs, web television, etc.) would not be measured by this method.

Finally, with regard to the issue of sample size, electronic measurement panels confront the same problem faced by surveys when it comes to measuring the web audience. Even though electronic panels often use samples several times larger than the ones used for measuring the television audience, and they often reach several tens of thousands of panellists, the data are only statistically significant for a limited number of sites. This is why even though the meters collect information on visits to any website, these panels only report data on the most visited sites. Electronic panels can yield statistically significant results for a larger number of websites than most surveys, but they cannot measure with any validity the audience of most of the websites available online.

Data Gathering and Analysis

Since data collection in electronic measurement panels does not rely on people's memory, it avoids the problems associated with faulty recall that are so common in surveys. On top of that, and since the usage data come from the computers used to browse the web, these data are very rich and precise. However, the behavior of the subjects being measured may change because they are being observed, and this reactivity can distort the measurement. Even if we assumed that the individuals being measured do not alter their behavior as a result of the measurement, there a few issues regarding data collection in electronic panels that need to be examined.

Data collection in the panels is done automatically; thanks to the installed meters. The type of data collected depends to a great extent on how those meters are configured. However, the exact functioning of such data-gathering software has not been subjected to any detailed examination by any independent organization. Even so, it is possible to mention some of the essential characteristics of the different meters developed in the 1990s by the companies that have used this method (Haering, 2002). The system that was developed by Media Metrix was installed in the operating system of the computers. The advantage of this type of meter is that it gathers information on all computer activities and can, therefore, measure things such as when a user goes from reading a webpage to opening a window with another program and permits a more precise measurement of the time spent on any particular page. The main limitation of this meter is that it cannot detect many elements within webpages, such as banner ads. The meter developed by NetValue was installed at the level of the TCP/IP, and allowed the identification of any other online communication protocol being used (i.e., instant messaging, e-mail, etc.). This type of meter was able to collect information on any kind of advertisement encountered while browsing—from static banners to animations, audio, or video. On the other hand, this meter did not allow for any measurement of the time spent on the last page that was viewed in the browser, since it only computed as the end of the time spent the moment when a new page request was placed. The meter developed by Nielsen/Netratings, was installed at the browser level, and it allowed for the collection of information on the banners inserted on the webpages but it did not offer information about tools such as instant messaging or e-mail. This meter did not measure the duration of the time spent on the last page requested. In summary, as we can see, the richness and precision of the data collected by electronic-measurement panels depend to a great extent on the type of software used to gather them.

Once the data collected by the meters have been sent to their destination, they need to be subjected to a cleaning-and-analysis process similar to the one applied in the case of log-files analysis. Some of the issues that need to be carefully examined, apart from the elimination of all non-HTML files, are as follows:

- Whether the pages were delivered because of an explicit request from the user or they are passive pages—pop-under, pop-up, etc. This distinction is not always easy to make.
- Whether the pages have a valid status code.
- Whether the pages are made up of more than one frame. In the case that there are more than one, they have to be reduced to one. It is necessary to determine whether they come from the same site or from different sites. If they come from different sites it is necessary to decide to which of them the page is attributed.
- Whether or not redirection pages are counted.
- Whether pages with self-refresh are counted only once or are counted every time they refresh.

Furthermore, once the data have been cleaned to obtain a count of pages, it is necessary to assign those pages to a category, a specific vehicle, website, company, or whatever unit is chosen. While this assignment process is simple and almost automatic in television, with the web the issue turns out to be much more complicated. The web is a very flexible medium, without emission frequencies (as opposed to broadcasting media) and without closed issues (as print media) and the assignment of pages to one vehicle or another turns out to be a rather controversial and complex issue (Parker, 2001). This is why the companies that run these panels have come up with a series of specific criteria for the assignment of pages to larger units. They speak of websites, unique websites, domains, channels, properties, parents, brands, etc. The particular cases can be endless and complicated, the assignment process is not self-evident at all, and it can be open to manipulation.

Metrics and Results

The use of electronic measurement panels allows for the collection of a huge amount of detailed information on all the online activities of the panelists that can be combined with a demographic profile obtained by questioning them. With regard to web usage in general, the panel yields global data on time spent using the web, number of sessions, days on which it is used, etc. With respect to specific websites, panels yield data on the number of unique users—reach—the demographic profile of visitors, migrations between sites, where the users come from and where they go to after visiting a site, repeat visits, time spent on the site, audience duplication between sites, most visited pages, etc. Some panels can also offer the reach of an advertisement or banner throughout all the sites in which it is inserted, the profile of the contacts, the distribution curve for those contacts, the click-through rates, etc. (Lamas, 2002).

Compared to the analysis of log-files, panels have the advantage of applying the same measurement procedure to all websites, allowing for direct comparisons between sites and avoiding interested manipulations. Furthermore, since they assign an identification code to each member of the panel, panels capture information on individual users, not on machines, browsers, or cookies, which produces a much more precise estimate and profile of the audience.

However, there is an obvious limitation due to the fragmentation of the medium. If in television-audience measurement it is already rather difficult to measure those channels that have very specific targets and attract small audiences, in the web that problem is much larger considering the endless number of options available to users. This is why the results of the panel are more valid when they refer to websites that are popular. But, since the audience is so fragmented for so many different websites, the number of panelists that visit most of those websites is so small that the results tend to be quite unstable. In any event, the number of sites about which electronic panels can offer audience data with statistical rigor is usually larger than the one provided by surveys.

Apart from the limitations that electronic panels present in terms of their ability to offer valid data about a significant number of websites, their inability to measure the online activity generated outside the home, or any of the other problems described so far, there is one additional issue that deserves to be pointed out. At the time when in several countries there were more than one electronic panel measuring the web audience, the results from those panels were, for the most part, remarkably dissimilar. This led Lamas (2002) to say that "the differences among the estimates provided by the different electronic measurements are of such a magnitude that they cannot be explained neither by their respective measuring techniques nor by sample errors." Or, as Haering (2002: 39) mentioned after an analysis of the different electronic measurement panels functioning in France, "for universes that on the face of it appear to be comparable, the results obtained by the various operators, as much in the number of Internet users as in the classification of sites, once again reveal disturbing disparities."

Global Macro-panels

A new variation in the panel methodology has also been implemented for measuring the web audience. These are the global macro-panels, which attempt to overcome the limitations that the electronic measurement panels have when it comes to measuring the global audience of the web, and the audience of less popular sites. The global macro-panels are panels that sacrifice the representational value of the sample in favor of global and very large international samples.

Perhaps the most interesting of these panels is the one implemented by the American company ComScore.[2] The panel implemented by ComScore has over 1.5 million panelists, around 1 million in the United States and 500,000 in the rest of the world.[3] Panelists are recruited through banners inserted in websites that collaborate with ComScore, and they are promised higher speed in their browsing—which in itself can introduce a bias in the measurement (ARF, 2001)—an antivirus service and participation in a sweepstakes (Fulgoni, 2003). The individuals who decide to become part of the panel have to answer a series of questions about the people and computers in their household. After this, the panelists install a computer application that redirects the web traffic generated from their computers to the hundreds of proxy servers owned by ComScore. This initial questionnaire is the only collaboration required from panelists. Since from then on the different users of the computer do not need to identify themselves when they use it, we can say that ComScore takes as its reference a universe of computers, not of individual persons (Lamas, 2001).

The errors and biases introduced by non-probabilistic samples are somewhat compensated through the use of two major sources of information. One is the use of enumeration surveys using RDD. The other is the implementation of a smaller panel with a probabilistic sample. The information gathered from these two sources is later used to weight the results of the huge non-probabilistic sample. However, there is no evidence to show that the weighting of the data leads to valid results. In addition, these two sources of information are only used for the US population and, therefore, the results of the portion of the sample that comes from outside the United States are not weighted, and its errors and biases are not corrected to any extent.

In summary, global macro-panels are a novel approach that poses serious questions about the future of web audience measurement. Many of these questions will appear in the next section, when I examine the industry dynamics in web audience measurement and the attempts to obtain a common currency.

Conclusions to Section III

I started this section talking about how in the mid-1990s the World Wide Web already possessed the general characteristics that define traditional mass media and that allow us to talk of a web audience. I also mentioned how the constitution of the web audience, as is the case with the audience of traditional mass media, required the use of certain measurement methods, and that those methods need to adjust to the specific characteristics of the new medium and to the needs of the advertising market. In this sense, it seemed necessary to carry out an analysis of the different methods used to measure the web audience, of their limits and possibilities. And even though I have developed such an analysis throughout this chapter, it seems a good idea to retake the issue of the general characteristics of the web as an object of measurement and of the needs of online advertising when it comes to carrying out the measurement. I will not be very detailed here, since I hope to have provided in the analysis of each of the web audience measurement methods all the information required to make an assessment of their validity and rigor. But I am going to summarize the ability of each of the three types of methods to adapt to the specific characteristics of the web and to the special relationship of the web with advertising. In particular, I am going to refer here to the following issues:

- Capacity of the different methods to measure the total size of the web audience.
- Capacity of the different methods to measure the audience of specific websites.
- Capacity of the different methods to measure the audience of specific parts (sections, pages, etc.) of specific websites.
- Capacity of the different methods to measure the audience of specific web advertisements.

- Capacity of the different methods to produce a profile of the audience, that is demographics, etc.
- Statistical validity of the results produced by the different measurement methods.
- Capacity of the different methods to measure the global audience of the web, without country or region restrictions.
- Capacity of the different methods to measure the audience that accesses the web from different locales (i.e., homes, workplaces, schools, etc.).
- Capacity of the different methods to take advantage of the trace left by the computers that participate in web communication.
- Capacity of the different methods to measure the audience of a significant number of specific websites.
- Capacity of the different methods to measure the audience that accesses the web by using machines other than computers (i.e., Web television, PDAs, WAPs, etc.).
- Capacity of the different methods to measure issues that go beyond the simple exposure to a specific advertising form, such as clicks, sales, etc.

Table 4. Limits and possibilities of the methods used to measure
the web audience

	Passive methods: log-files, tags	Active methods: surveys	Mixed methods: panels
Size of the total audience of the medium	No, measurement of a limited number of vehicles. Problems calculating the number of users, except in those sites that require login and password.	Yes, but only in the geographic area covered by the survey, usually a country. There are initiatives to harmonize surveys across different countries.	Yes, thanks to enumeration surveys, but only in the geographic area covered by the survey, usually a country. There exists the possibility of adding the results from different national panels and of creating global non-probabilistic samples.

	Passive methods: log-files, tags	Active methods: surveys	Mixed methods: panels
Size of the audience of specific websites	Problems calculating the number of users, except in those sites that require login and password.	Yes, but only of a limited number of vehicles and subject to statistical validity issues and to trust in the good memory and sincerity of respondents.	Only the audience that accesses the web from certain locations and only of a limited number of sites, since huge samples would be required to cover most of the websites available.
Size of the audience of parts of specific websites	In spite of their gathering detailed information, there are problems calculating the number of users, except in those sites that require login and password.	No, since the limitations of respondents' memory and the need for very large samples make it impossible to get into such precise measurement.	Even though for the audience that accesses the web from certain locations—such as the home—there exists the option, huge samples would be required for statistical validity.
Size of the audience of specific advertisement	Problems calculating the number of users—except in those sites that require login and password. Problems also measuring the number of impressions of an advertisement that is inserted in more than one website—except for advertisement networks log-files.	No, since the limitations of respondents' memory and the need for very large samples make it impossible to get into such precise measurement.	It depends on the kind of meter being used. But even though for the audience that accesses the web from certain locations—such as the home—there exists the option, huge samples would be required for statistical validity.
Profile of the audience	No, except in those sites that require login and password, and request additional information during the registration process.	Yes, by gathering information on demographics, lifestyle variables, other media consumption, etc.	Yes, by gathering through questionnaires information on demographics, lifestyle variables, other media consumption, etc.

	Passive methods: log-files, tags	Active methods: surveys	Mixed methods: panels
Statistical validity	Census-like method—except, in certain occasions, for pages stored in cache.	Yes, but only for the most visited websites.	Yes, but only for the most visited websites.
Global audience	Records all server activity, regardless of where the requests come from, but has problems quantifying the number of users.	Measurement restricted to the geographic area covered by the survey, usually a country. There are initiatives to harmonize surveys across different countries and to carry out international surveys, but they are never totally 'global.'	Even though panels usually have a national reach, it is possible to add the audiences from different national panels if identical procedures are followed. In any event, there are always countries that are not measured. There also exists the possibility of creating global panels with non-probabilistic samples.
Access from any location	Records all server activity, regardless of where the requests come from, but has problems quantifying the number of users.	Yes, since the information is provided by users, it can refer to online access from any location.	No, most panels only cover the online activity generated from the home. Those panels that also cover the online activity generated from the workplace have problems representing the universe. Online access from public locations remains outside of the measurement.
Use of the trace left by computers	Yes, it constitutes the only source of information.	No, the information is provided by the respondents.	Yes, but it is combined with the information provided by panelists.

	Passive methods: log-files, tags	Active methods: surveys	Mixed methods: panels
Coverage of a significant number of available websites	The extent of the coverage varies from country to country, but it only covers a small fraction of all available websites.	The measurement refers only to a limited number of websites.	Information on every single website visited by panelists is gathered. However, and due to sample size issues, they only provide statistically valid information on a certain number of sites, the most visited.
Multiple access technologies	It is possible to measure the online activity generated from machines other than computers, but there are problems calculating the number of users.	It is possible to measure the online activity generated from machines other than computers.	The measurement is performed through software installed in computers and does not take into account web access through other devices.
Beyond exposure	Yes, it allows researchers to follow the trail of users' online activity, from clicks to purchases.	Not in any precise way due to the memory limitations of respondents.	Yes, it allows researchers to follow the trail of users' online activity, though it depends on the type of meter used.

As we can see, each of the three types of methods used to measure the web audience possesses a series of strengths, but also significant limitations. It should be noted that this analysis has assumed throughout the willingness of researched subjects to collaborate, and has not taken into account the different measurement-resistance and privacy-protection tactics available to web users—such as the elimination or rejection of cookies, the use of software that allows for the automatic elimination of web advertising, the use of multiple-browsing software that makes it impossible to distinguish automatic browsing activity from human generated browsing activity, the lack of sincerity when filling out questionnaires and registration forms, the change of behavior when the subject is aware of being observed, etc. I have also assumed that the measurement methods are applied with the utmost rigor at every step, from the design and recruitment of the sample to the analysis and presentation of the results, including the collection and cleaning of the data.

Perhaps the limitations of the different methods that have been analyzed are due to the fact that they are tools from traditional communication media that are being applied to a completely new medium. It seems very easy to see the parallels between the methods used for measuring the web audience and the methods used for measuring the audience of other communication media. It is possible to observe a clear parallel between passive methods and the control of the circulation of print media. Obviously, the concrete form of the methods—the analysis of the trace left by the activity of computers and the auditing of print outs and sales—are very different. But the model and the results show obvious similarities. In fact, the organizations in charge of auditing the circulation of print publications have been the ones that have usually taken the initiative in the application of passive methods for measuring the web audience.

Regarding active methods, there has been no significant change in the way a method such as the survey, which has been used for decades to measure the audience of traditional media, has been applied in the measurement of the web audience. Even the specific tools designed for collecting information on the web audience "use aided recall techniques combined with a question about the moment of the last visit, following the methodology most commonly used for the study of the audience of print media" (Lamas, 2002).

With regard to mixed methods, the panels used in the measurement of the web audience, irrespective of the different technologies in which television meters and computer meters are based, present clear similarities with the panels used in the measurement of television audiences, even in terms of the measuring organizations involved, usually large companies specializing in market research. These similarities were also perceived by the Media Ratings Council (MCR), the organization in charge of supervising the rigor of audience measurement in the United States. The MCR soon understood that its standards could also be applied to the electronic measurement panels used to measure the web audience, "as the process closely resembled the current television measurement" (Ivie & Terlizzi, 2001: 138). In spite of the specificity of the web's technology and use, the panels used to measure its audience are clearly based on the broadcasting model, and as Ejdys et al. (2003: 83) assert:

> There is no theoretical difference between such an approach and television audience measurement or radio audience measurement where such panel-based methodologies have been employed for many years. However, the nature of the Internet-using population differs fundamentally from television and radio, leading to practical difficulties in implementing such a methodology.

The use of methods taken from traditional mass media turns web audience measurement into a sort of small blanket, which when trying to cover the head leaves the feet out in the cold. Passive methods leave aside the main object of study, the audience, and focus exclusively on machines. Active methods have the opposite problem, since they can offer lots of information on the audience members, but can say very little about what they do online. And mixed methods, the ones that could conceivably overcome both problems by combining different types of information, can cover neither all audience activity nor the full array of available websites.

The limitations of the methods described above for measuring the web audience have become apparent in recent years. As Lamas (2002) commented, "perhaps we are facing a new medium so technologically complex and with so many possibilities that we will never have a single measurement system, since only a combination of methodologies will be able to provide a just and precise vision of the Internet's reality." And even though the possibility of combining different methods to improve the accuracy of the data in measuring the web audience was already contemplated in CASIE's (1995) *Guiding Principles of Interactive Media Audience Measurement*, this path has gained momentum only in recent years. The study carried out by MacEvoy and Kalyanam in 1999 for Future of Advertising Stakeholders (FAST) called the *Data Reconciliation Study*[1] might be considered the first step in this direction (Goosey, 2005) The Australian company RedSheriff has been one of the pioneers in the combination of methods for measuring the web audience. RedSheriff combined panel-based measurement (a mixed method) with tags (a passive method) in

2000 in Australia, and it also combined in New Zealand the tag method (passive) with online surveys (active) (Goosey, 2005). It was actually the purchase of RedSheriff by Nielsen NetRatings in early 2004 that clearly pointed in the direction of method combination as a significant development in the evolution of web audience measurement methods. But it is probably in Europe where the use of multiple methods to obtain a single measurement of the web audience has been most deeply explored.

Since, as we have seen in this section, the measurement of the web audience seems to allow for many different methodological approaches, the possible combinations of methods are numerous and they can achieve high degrees of complexity. I will mention here some of the possibilities that are already being tested and used. It seems that the most common combination mixes panels with tags. The ultimate goal is to mix the demographic information provided by panels with the census-like nature of passive methods in measuring web traffic. In this sense, Nielsen NetRatings proposes the combination of its orthodox electronic measurement panel, with the tag method used by RedSheriff plus the use of online surveys. What is interesting about this approach is that Nielsen NetRatings, the leader in panel methodology (mixed method), considers that "at the very heart of this approach is the browser centric [passive] measurement for estimating page impressions and unique browsers" (Goosey, 2005: 39). Online intercept surveys are used to offer sociodemographic data about visitors. The panel, which up until now was the core of the company's methodology, is used as a tool for converting the unique browser estimate derived from the use of tags into an estimation of unique users through the provision of the parameters required to correct for cookie deletion, multiple users per browser, and multiple browser use. The panel data is also used to weight online survey results for any nonresponse bias (Goosey, 2005).

But the combination of tags and panels also allows for a new development: the use of login pages instead of meters to create electronic panels. This variation is already in use or in development in some European markets, such as the Netherlands,[2] and it solves a significant problem of panels that use meters. Since most samples used in panels with meters are representative of home Internet use only because the installation of meters outside the home has faced significant hurdles due to the opposition of companies, educational institutions, and other organizations—mostly because of security and privacy concerns—some measuring organizations have opted for the substitution of login pages for meters. Login pages require no software installation and they are simply the entry page, or the portal, to the web. In this way, when a panel member wants to use the web, regardless of where she is, she starts at this login page, where she needs to identify herself. The page assigns the panelist a session cookie that will expire at the end of the browsing session and that will be used to identify her once the log-files produced by the tags of participating websites are analyzed. This approach is able to account for web use generated from any location, not only from the home. In this sense, it may become an improved version of electronic panels. However, there are also some possible problems that need to be pointed out. One is the fact that the panel will only measure those websites that install the measurement tags in their pages—as opposed to meter panels, which are able to measure all the web activity of panelists. Another one is the increased need for panelists' collaboration, since every single browser they use needs to be set up to start at the login page, and they need to identify themselves every time they use any of these browsers.

Other European initiatives are using slightly different combinations of methods.[3] In Germany, tags are combined with online and offline surveys (Noller et al., 2005). In Sweden, offline surveys are being combined with a panel that uses cookies instead of meters, and the analysis of log-files (Callius et al., 2005). In Belgium, tags, unique cookies, and online surveys are also being used. All these combinations of different methods for measuring the web audience have generated an increasing interest in data integration techniques. [4] The ARF (2003: 4) defines data integration as "a formal process to combine information from two or more separate data sources, making sense of information in the databases for the purpose of accurately estimating certain values that are not available in any single data source." In that same document, the ARF (2003: 3) mentions the fragmentation of the audience of different media and, in the specific case of the Internet, points out the need to integrate "consumer survey data with traffic and server data."[5] Data integration techniques might help resolve some of the obvious problems that single-source measurement has when it comes to measuring the web audience. However, as the ARF (2003:3) reminds us, "the quality of the integrated data is limited by the quality of the individual elements" and, as we have seen in this section, the quality of the data produced by some of the methods used to measure the web audience is often questionable.

In summary, we can conclude that, indeed, as was said at the outset, the methods currently used to measure the web audience present important limitations, cannot account for the specific characteristics of the World Wide Web as a communication medium, and do not seem able to satisfy the needs of the advertising market. If we take all these limitations into account, the creation of a common currency for advertising exchanges on the web seems to be still very far away. However, the establishment of a common currency can be achieved in spite of the limitations that have been described if the different agents interested in the measurement accept those limitations and commit to assume and adopt a standard that, even if not perfect, allows the audience market of the web to function.[6] The following section of this book focuses precisely on those dynamics in the web audience measurement industry that move in that direction.

The Audience Measurement Industry

In Section II, I showed how the evolution of the Internet reaches a turning point in the mid-1990s—due to a great extent to the advent of the World Wide Web—from which it starts showing some of the essential traits that allow us to talk about mass communication media, audiences, and audience measurement. In Section III, I showed how web audience measurement has developed over the last decade a series of methods, techniques, and procedures, and I analyzed each of these in order to expose their limitations in terms of their ability to account for the peculiarities of the web and to serve the needs of the advertising market. However, analyzing the origins of Internet audience measurement and exposing the limitations of the methods used to do that measurement does not offer a complete view of the object of study. If we want to really understand web audience measurement, it is necessary to recognize that the measurement does not respond to scientific or academic interests. Rather, it responds to interests and needs linked to the commercialization of the medium and to advertising, as was mentioned. In this sense, audience measurement has the goal of facilitating economic exchanges. Thus, we cannot simply dismiss the methods analyzed because of their flaws. Instead, we need to frame them within the larger process in which they are deployed so that we can see how methodological limitations can be ignored as long as those methods allow audience measurement to perform the institutional role that gives reason to its existence.

Therefore, in order to analyze web audience measurement, it is also necessary to pay attention to the dynamics generated within the audience measurement industry, to the different agents involved and to their interests. It is not simply an issue of examining how the implementation of certain measurement methods produces audiences, but also of examining how the different agents involved in the measurement produce data. As Meehan (1984: 221) states:

> ratings per se must no longer be treated as reports of human behavior, but rather as products—as commodities shaped by business exigencies and corporate strategies.

That is, we should widen our perspective in order to show not just how the audience becomes a commodity that can be traded due to the use of more or less precise measurement methods, but also to analyze the production process of the audience data that fuels the advertising market.

The measurement of the audience of traditional mass media has existed for decades and it is a relatively consolidated activity, with more stable characteristics. But web audience measurement is a quite recent phenomenon, with barely a decade of existence. The lack of a historical perspective that would allow for the study of long-term fundamental trends makes the analysis more difficult. It is the lack of that historical perspective that led us to combine an analysis of the documents produced by the different agents and organizations involved in measurement with an analysis of periodicals that are closer to the industry's current developments. With this approach I hope to add a new point of view and obtain a more comprehensive perspective of the object of study.

Web audience measurement has certain peculiarities that were spelled out in the previous chapters. The complexity and fragmentation of the medium, the use of very different methods to measure its audience, and the specificities of online advertising are issues that can influence the development of online audience measurement. An analysis of the measurement industry's dynamics, even if it is only for a decade, will allow us to see to which extent web audience measurement displays similar dynamics to those that define audience measurement in other media, and to which extent the peculiar characteristics of the web as a medium introduce specific and different dynamics.

In summary, my goal here is to analyze the development of an online audience measurement industry. I aim to show the basic tendencies that have shaped the industry. My starting point is the idea that, in the same way that happens with audience measurement in traditional mass media, the need for rationalization of economic exchanges leads to the need for a common currency, for a single source of reference for the measurement. And that need shapes in a fundamental way the development of the industry. In order to examine this issue, I will look at the interests, both common and particular, of the different agents involved in the measurement process, and we will see how these interests may influence the development of the industry. I will then examine the role that these different agents have played in the development of web audience measurement. On the one hand, I will examine the influence of advertisers, agencies, and content providers in shaping measurement. On the other hand, I will examine the role of the organizations that carry out the measurement and their strategies in order to establish their position within the web audience measurement market. As a whole, I will be offering a view of World Wide Web audience measurement that will complement and enrich the perspective taken in the two previous sections.

CHAPTER 9

Interests and Standardization

The Agents and Their Interests

When we examined the birth of web audience measurement, we saw how that birth was closely linked to the commercialization of the medium and, in particular, to the interests of the advertising market. We also saw how, once the measurement was started, it was used by different companies as a self-promotional tool and by the stock market as a way of estimating the value of online companies. Obviously, the existence of different uses for audience measurement might contribute to shaping the specific dynamics of the measurement industry. But the truth is that the origins of web audience measurement are clearly influenced, as is the case for the audience measurement of other media, by advertising interests.

During the mid-1990s, the advertising industry became aware of the speed at which interactive media in general, and the Internet in particular, were spreading and attracting a significant number of users. Those users had a valuable profile for advertisers—young men with high-income levels—and here they were spending time using a medium that had no advertising content. If advertisers use ads as a tool for managing mass consumption, seeing the spread of interactive media with no advertising content must have seemed to them as a dangerous development. It is at this juncture that Procter & Gamble's president warned the advertising industry and asked them to turn interactive media into vehicles for advertising (Turow, 1997). The goal was to make sure that those interactive media did not evolve in a direction that did not match their interests. As an article in the *New York Times* mentioned after a conference at which many big advertisers were present,

Indeed, big-spending marketers including P&G, General Motors Corp. and AT&T said they're no longer content to just have a presence in new media. They want to control the future of media and marketing. (Donaton & Sloan, 1995)

Once it has been decided to insert advertisements in the web, it is necessary to determine where exactly they will be placed and how much it will cost. That is, it is necessary to establish a market with a system for setting prices. And that only seems possible if a measurement system is set in place to give information about who is reached by the different advertising vehicles on the web. As one of the founders of the electronic measurement panel Relevant Knowledge explained,

the large package-goods companies are not going on the Web right now because there is no reliable standard [for measuring Web usage]. (Maddox & Riedman, 1997)

As the mechanism to measure and set prices did not exist at the time when advertising entered the web, advertisers used to say that they were only running 'experiments' with limited investments, since there was no way of knowing what worked and what did not work, what was a fair price and what was not (Elsworth, 1997). The precarious state of the mechanism for setting the price of online advertising in 1995 was described by the vice president of an advertising agency as follows:

Today, you come up with a number that seems reasonable and then keep raising the price as long as people are willing to pay for it. (Flynn, 1995)

In this environment it seemed impossible to promote the sale of advertising space. That is why when the Coalition for Advertising Supported Information and Entertainment (CASIE)—the working group created by the advertising industry as a response to the speech by Procter & Gamble's president—started functioning, it set as one of its priorities the promotion of the creation of a mechanism for measuring the web audience. A mechanism was needed that would rationalize the online advertising market and serve to determine prices. Thus, advertisers had a clear interest in initiating the measurement of the web audience, since they wanted to insert advertisements but believed that this was not possible until measurement could offer some warranty regarding their advertising expenditure.

Since advertising agencies depend on the existence of advertising campaigns and these in turn seemed to depend on the existence of a measuring mechanism that could serve as a price-setting system, the agencies were also interested in the development of web audience measurement. The first agencies to become interested in Internet advertising were small agencies specialized in interactive advertising, with fresh ideas and innovation ability (Williamson, 1995). However, the larger advertising agencies soon reacted and got deeply involved in the development of an audience measurement mechanism, as they were afraid those small specialized agencies would end up with the lion's share of the new field of expansion for the advertising market, that is the interactive advertising market (Turow, 1997). In this way, from the start the advertisers that showed the most interest in the development of web audience measurement were large corporations who were producers of consumer goods, and used, therefore, to paying for large advertising campaigns in traditional mass media. And the agencies that ended up taking the lead in supporting the development of web audience measurement were also large agencies used to working in those large campaigns in mass media. Both these elements help explain why the development of web audience measurement ended up leaning toward a model that was similar to that used to measure the audience of traditional mass media.

Regarding content providers, for them advertising seemed to constitute a promising source of income. In the Internet environment, where the libertarian and communitarian logics contributed to reject pay-per-content, where it was difficult to develop payment methods and techniques adapted to the new medium, and where other business models had not yet proven their viability, audience measurement opened the door to an interesting source of revenue, that is advertising. In addition, traditional mass media, accustomed to having advertising as an essential source of revenue, began to enter the web. This meant that there were a significant number of websites managed by large communication corporations that were used to advertising and to whom audience measurement was no novelty.

Thus, the different agents involved in the advertising market had a common interest in developing an online audience measurement system. All of them expected to obtain some benefit from the web's advertising market, and all seemed to be aware of the need for an audience measuring system in order to develop that market. As the president of one of the companies doing web audience measurement commented about online electronic panels, "this is the type of technology that will enable advertising on the Web to be a viable business" (Maddox, 1997).

However, in the same way that there are common interests, there is also a discontinuity in interests among the different agents that take part in the advertising and audience measurement markets. On the one hand, the advertisers and advertising agencies that plan advertising campaigns are the ones who pay for the product generated through measurement. Their goal is for the measurement to allow them to obtain a good price when it comes to buying advertising space or audiences. In this sense, they are more interested in obtaining measurements that are precise or, better yet, undercount the number of individuals who are exposed to advertising content. On the other hand, the managers of websites are the ones who receive the payment from advertisers and are, therefore, interested in avoiding an undercount of the number of individuals exposed to advertising. That is, the size of the audience, the result of the measurement, becomes a disputed element among the different agents involved in the advertising market. In fact, as the material analyzed for this chapter shows, it seems that the most common role for content providers in the field of web audience measurement has been that of protesting when they considered that their websites were under-represented in the measurement results and that, therefore, they were receiving too low a price for their audience (Hansell, 1998).

Since the different agents that participate in the advertising trade cannot blindly trust each other, there is a need for the measurement to be performed by independent third parties or to be audited when they are performed by non-independent agents. This leads to the need for measuring or auditing companies or organizations with the role of reconciling the differing interests of advertisers and content providers. This explains, for example, the fact that the first website to include advertising on its pages, HotWired, immediately hired the services of Nielsen Media Research to certify that the data that were being given to advertisers were correct (Cleland, 1995). This need for independent measurements clearly appears in the documents that were created through the years by different organizations to promote web audience measurement.[1] But the need for independent, third-party measurement is especially manifest in the large number of measuring organizations that popped up in the first years of web audience measurement. They were, on the one hand, private companies with the ability to innovate (both in terms of methods and in terms of technology) and to mobilize the resources needed to take advantage of a new business opportunity. On the other hand, they were organizations that had been involved in the measurement of previous mass media and that included in some form all the different agents that participate in the advertising market.

The development of electronic measurement panels for measuring the web audience was from its inception almost exclusively in the hands of private measurement companies. But, as we saw in the previous chapter, some of the most valuable sources of information for web measurement are the files generated by the computers participating in online communication, and that information is usually in the hands of website managers. It is, therefore, easy for these managers to produce reports with information about the traffic of a website, reports that can be used to lure advertisers. However, such reports have a credibility problem similar to that of custom research projects paid for by a particular media organization (Miller, 1994). This, again, is why they need to use external auditors. We find then that, alongside the companies managing electronic measurement panels, there appeared a series of companies (such as I/PRO) or independent organizations traditionally in charge of monitoring press circulation (such as the Audit Bureau of Circulations in the United States) that offered to produce estimations of the web audience by using log-files analysis, or to audit the measurements performed by the companies managing the different websites.

We thus witness the birth of a new agent involved in web audience measurement, the third-party independent organizations in charge of conferring credibility to that measurement. However, the measurement is not given credibility simply because it is performed or supervised by an organization without an interest in the specific measurement results. The measurement also has to comply with a series of requirements; it has to be of a minimum quality before it can perform the institutional role for which it is created. In a sense, independent measuring organizations become arbiters in the measurement business, but their role as arbiters also needs to be supervised by those agents who pay them and who fuel the audience market.

In the United States, since the 1960s there has existed an organization, the Media Rating Council (MRC), whose specific role is to guarantee the quality of audience measurement. This not-for-profit organization, whose members are media companies, advertising agencies, and professional organizations within the media and advertising sectors, was created with the mission of improving the quality standards of audience measurement after the troubled period undergone by the industry in the 1960s. In particular, the MRC has the following three main goals:

1. To secure for the industry and related users audience measurement services that are valid, reliable, and effective.
2. To evolve and determine minimum disclosure and ethical criteria for media audience measurement services.
3. To provide and administer an audit system designed to inform users as to whether such audience measurements are conducted in conformance with the criteria and procedures developed.

The MRC carries out periodic audits of different audience measurement systems for different media in the United States. Ever since the birth of web audience measurement, the MRC has understood that its standards and procedures, as well as its auditing system, could perfectly be applied to electronic measurement panels, as the measurement method used was substantially similar to the one used to measure the television audience. From 2000 onward, after the analysis of web audience measurement based on the use of log-files, the MRC decided that those same principles and their corresponding auditing system could be applied to the methods I have here called passive (Ivie & Terlizzi, 2001). [2]

Apart from conferring accreditations that certify the quality of web audience measurement with respect to a series of more or less generic criteria, the field that has to be evaluated needs to be constituted. Before giving away quality stamps, it is necessary to shape the industry's practices, rationalize its functioning, and establish standards, principles, and directives that determine the concrete shape of web audience measurement. And these, as Donaton (1996) mentioned, did not exist in the mid-1990s:

> the lack of Internet standards is currently the single greatest impediment to the Web's emergence as a viable long-term advertising medium. The void impacts everything from definitions to audience measurement to ad sizes and pricing.

In the audience measurement of traditional mass media, with their established routines after several decades of functioning, those standards, norms, and principles are just a more or less implicit frame in the background of the industry. But in web audience measurement, a recent phenomenon still in formation, those standards acquire a shaping power that explicitly determines the development of the industry. If one carefully analyzes the short history of web audience measurement, it is possible to see how the attempts to standardize that measurement are at the core of the evolution of the industry. The need to rationalize a field still in formation is understood and appreciated by all the agents involved. As an example, the president of Media Metrix commented:

> The industry—including agencies, advertisers and publishers—has been focusing on the need for a standard audience-measurement service to help propel the growth of the medium. (Maddox, 1998b)

In this formative process, all the agents involved in the measurement participate. However, the different agents do not play the same role in this process. On the one hand, the clients of measuring organizations, namely advertisers, agencies, and advertising vehicles—since they are in the end the ones paying for the measurement—can influence the way in which the measurement is carried out individually, by deciding whether or not they want to become clients of and spend their money in a measuring organization. But they can also work as a group and develop a series of minimum standards in order to protect their interests and decide how the measurement should be carried out. On the other hand, the measuring organizations themselves participate in the process of configuring the measurement through their business practices, the implementation of certain methods, and the market strategies that allow for their establishment as organizations with enough credibility to lure clients. In what follows, I will analyze the role played by the different agents in the process of standardization of web audience measurement. First, the role of media, advertisers, and agencies will be examined. The role of measuring organizations will be discussed in the following chapter.

Media, Advertisers, and Agencies: Toward Standardization

In the audience measurement industry, media, advertisers, and advertising agencies become clients of measuring organizations. Since in the end they finance the measuring process, they exert a great deal of power over the form of that process. As mentioned before, they have the power to decide to which measuring service they will give their money. On an individual basis, however, this kind of decision does not have major repercussions, since measuring organizations can always find their source of income in other clients. Besides, the value of audience measurement resides to a great extent in its ability to become a common currency in the advertising market, which is made up of many organizations. That is why it is for the most part irrelevant whether or not a particular organization, be it medium, advertiser, or agency, decides to give its support to a specific measurement service. What is truly relevant, both from a financial point of view and from the point of view of the value of the measurement as a coin of exchange, is whether a critical mass of clients decides that certain measurements deserve to be trusted or do not deserve to be trusted. That is why the influence of these agents (media, advertisers, agencies) on the audience measurement process always stems from agreements and organizations that involve a significant number of the potential clients of measuring services.

Media, advertisers, and agencies have clearly understood the need for standardizing web audience measurement in order for it to play its role as a coin of exchange in the advertising market. And they have also been aware of their ability to influence that standardization process. But if the evolution of the web audience measurement industry is examined, it is possible to observe that the leadership role in the standardization process has been played for the most part by advertisers and advertising agencies (Donaton & Sloan, 1995).

The secondary role played by content providers in the process of standardization of web audience measurement seems rather obvious. But the reasons behind the limited influence of content providers in this process are not that clear. Nonetheless, we could point to some possible explanations. On the one hand, the World Wide Web, as a communication medium, is highly fragmented, with thousands of vehicles of a very diverse nature. And while in media presenting a structure closer to oligopoly it is relatively simple for the different vehicles to join forces, among the thousands or millions of websites the task of reaching agreements and producing common strategies to favor the standardization of audience measurement is basically an impossible feat. Apart from the huge number of websites, it is also necessary to point out their very different natures, from new online ventures to the giants of offline communication, each with their peculiar strategies and approaches. In fact, the only notable effort by content providers in the attempt to standardize web audience measurement is the document elaborated by the *Magazine Publishers of America* (MPA) in 1995, titled *Proposed Standards for Internet Advertising Measurement*. This document was a result of the work of the *Advertising Measurement Task Force* within MPA, and it described some of the basic principles that an acceptable measurement system should follow. It proposed that this measurement system should be centered on people, use and visits, considered websites to be the appropriate source from which the information needed for the measurement should be collected, acknowledged the role of independent third parties in order to audit and validate the results published by the websites, called for all websites with advertising space to follow a common measurement standard, and stated that the development of measurement methods that could allow comparisons between the Internet and other mass media was not a necessary requisite for the development of the Internet as an advertising medium (Kelly, 1995). In sum, it was a series of principles developed from the point of view of content providers that considered the analysis of website log-files to be the source of data for the measurement. I will come back to some of these issues below, but what I would like to point out here is that this is in fact a single effort, without continuity, and that it was carried out by an association that represents American offline magazines, which constitute a very limited number of vehicles in the online world.

Apart from the issue of fragmentation and multiplicity of content providers on the web, there are other factors that may contribute to explaining the limited role played by these content providers in the process of standardization of web audience measurement. As I discussed in Section II, from its origin web audience measurement was used by many websites as a self-promotional tool and by the stock market as a way of estimating the value of the companies involved in the new online economy. In this context, standardization was not only less relevant than it is when the measurement is used to set the prices in the advertising market, but also the lack of it could actually have been beneficial for some market players. The lack of standardization allowed websites to obtain audience data from different sources, to choose from the different measurements those that were more favorable, and to use the results for self-promotional purposes or, what was often much more lucrative, to multiply the value of their shares in the stock market (Maddox, 1998a). Therefore, if the business goal behind the measurement is the rationalization of the advertising market, standardization can be beneficial. But when the measurement is used for other goals, also business goals but of a different nature, standardization is by no means a necessary development. This phenomenon might help us explain the lack of participation of content providers in the efforts to create the standards that would shape web audience measurement in the first years of its existence.

In contrast with content providers, the advertising industry did carry out a clear effort to shape web audience measurement. Not only did the largest advertiser in the world, Procter & Gamble, participate from the start in the development of online advertising and its measurement methods (Maddox, 1999), but also the whole industry took a leading role in shaping web audience measurement through the work of different organizations and the publication of directives, principles, and standards on different issues. The most prominent professional organizations of the advertising industry in the United States have been behind all the most significant initiatives aimed at standardizing web audience measurement. These organizations are as follows:

- *Association of National Advertisers (ANA)*: Founded in 1910, it represents more than 300 companies that spend as a whole more than 100 billion dollars annually on marketing and advertising.
- *American Association of Advertising Agencies (AAAA)*: Founded in 1917, it is the main professional organization of advertising agencies in the United States, and its members manage around 75% of the total advertising expenditure of the country.
- *Advertising Research Foundation (ARF)*: Founded in 1936 by the AAAA and the ANA, it is a not-for-profit regarded as the most prominent organization in the fields of marketing, advertising, and media research. Its members represent more than four-hundred advertisers, advertising agencies, media, research organizations, and educational institutions. Its main goal is to improve the research on advertising, marketing, and communication media in order to increase the effectiveness of marketing and advertising. To achieve this, ARF has carried out large research projects throughout its history, projects that have had a great impact on audience measurement in all media.[3]

These three organizations, together with Procter & Gamble, have exerted the most influence in the standardization process of web audience measurement, and in order to channel that influence they have promoted or participated in different *ad hoc* organizations whose specific goal has been the development of Internet advertising in general, and audience measurement in particular. And even though in some of these organizations there were representatives of web content providers, the truth is that they remained in the back seat of these initiatives.

In what follows I will briefly review the organizations created by the advertising industry with the explicit goal of promoting online advertising. These organizations have held a leading position in the attempts to standardize web audience measurement. I will also briefly discuss some of the most relevant documents produced by these organizations in their attempt to shape audience measurement.

Coalition for Advertising Supported Information and Entertainment (CASIE)

Organization created in May 1994 by the ANA and the AAAA, with the support of the ARF. In October 1995, with the collaboration of ARF, CASIE (1995) published its first document aimed at influencing the standardization process of web and other interactive media audience measurement, *CASIE Guiding Principles of Interactive Media Audience Measurement*. The introduction of the document explicitly mentioned the need to develop web audience measurement:

> An important way to ensure that substantial advertising revenues can flow to these new media is to provide for the types of value measurements acceptable to advertisers and agencies [...] Both buyers and sellers of these new media share a common interest in supporting the most reliable, quality measurement of these media.

The document focused on the measurement of the exposure to the different advertising vehicles, and it neglected issues such as the exposure to specific advertising items, or the measurement of other variables that could lead to the sale of the advertised products. That is, though acknowledging the peculiar characteristics of interactive media, it sought the application to this media of the measurement model used for traditional mass media. In particular, the document proposed eleven principles:

1. *Best media practices*: Audience measurement in interactive media should follow the criteria developed for the audience measurement of other communication media in the previous eight decades—with the only exception of those that are clearly impossible to apply—in order to obtain accurate, precise, and reliable estimates.

2. *Third-party measurement/auditing*: The measurement should be done by independent organizations, and not by the media being measured. In the event that the information provided by the computers taking part in the communication

process is used in the measurement process, this information should be audited by an objective third party. It would also be beneficial to audit third-party audience measurement.

3. *Full disclosure*: The users of the results of the measurement should receive complete information about the research methods and practices used, and all the data collected should be accessible to these users.

4. *Comparability*: It is highly desirable that audience data referred to a particular interactive medium be comparable to estimates about other interactive vehicles.

5. *Methodological experimentation encouraged*: Research organizations are encouraged to innovate, but they have to prove the validity of the measurement and of the conclusions derived from the innovation.

6. *Privacy*: The identity of consumers should not be revealed by the audience measurement providers, unless it is required for auditing purposes.

7. *User information preferable*: Advertisers need to know the number of different users that access a particular vehicle and the number of times they access it over a given period of time. These two measures provide data that can be compared with the audience measurement results for other media.

8. *Use of census and samples*: Though the advantages of using census instead of samples are acknowledged, the need for the measurement of individual users should not be compromised in order to achieve these advantages. The possibility of combining a census of visits with a sample of users is considered to be a viable approach to maximize accuracy.

9. *Non-intrusiveness*: Those methods that are the least visible to and require the least effort on the part of the consumer are to be preferred.

10. *Total medium measurement*: It is highly desirable that audience estimates be provided within the context of a total medium measurement in order to allow for comparisons among vehicles and for their evaluation against the entire medium.

11. *Industry consensus*: Research standards for interactive media should be set by a broad representation of the advertising in-

dustry, including advertisers, agencies, media, research companies, and industry bodies.

In October 1996, CASIE launched the first initiative for the standardization of the shapes and sizes of web advertising spaces in order to reduce production costs, simplify the creative process, and facilitate the comparison of advertising rates.

Interactive Advertising Bureau (IAB)

Created in 1996, it is the largest professional association focused on Internet advertising.[4] Its activities include the evaluation and recommendation of standards and practices, the elaboration of studies aimed at documenting the effectiveness of the Internet as an advertising medium, and the promotion within the advertising industry of the use of online advertising. Among its members figure more than a hundred companies that sell advertising space online plus several dozens of advertising agencies, measuring organizations, market research providers, and technology companies. The IAB, which has a European chapter and more than twenty offices worldwide, has been, and still is, one of the most influential organizations in the development and standardization of online advertising and web audience measurement. Its work has had the support of the online advertising industry as a whole, and of the other organizations described here. Even though it would be too lengthy to mention all the documents produced by the IAB that have to do with web audience measurement, I will at least describe some of the most relevant ones. The work of IAB toward the standardization of online advertising forms has been quite productive. It started with the review of the principles put forward by CASIE in 1996 (Williamson, 1996). In February 2001, IAB made public its *Interactive Marketing Units*. The goal of this document was to create a series of standard measures for online advertisements that would rationalize the process of buying advertising space and creating advertisements. Another effort by IAB in the search for more standardized online advertising formats dates back to August 2002, with the document *Universal Ad Package*, in which the IAB proposes to reduce to four the number of formats used for the insertion of banners. This effort to standardize online advertising received new impulses with the *Rich Media Guidelines*, which attempted a similar rationalization process with advertisements of more complex formats, and with the *Pop-Up Guidelines* and *Broadband Ad Creative Guidelines*. The first example of the efforts of the IAB toward the standardization of the field of web audience measurement dates back to 1997. The IAB published, with the support of CASIE and as a result of the *Media Measurement Task Force*, the document *Metrics and Methodology*. This document explained how advertisers and content providers should measure the web's traffic with the goal of managing online advertising. The central goal of the document was the establishment of a series of voluntary directives for the measurement of online advertising in order to make the different measures comparable. The information obtained from log-files was the focus of attention. The document also presented a glossary of basic terms, including the main metrics, commonly used in the measurement of website traffic and a description of the methods applied to obtain the data (Williamson, 1997). In January 2002, with the collaboration of the MRC, the ARF, and the ABCi (Audit Bureau of Circulations Interactive), plus the support of the AAAA and the ANA, IAB made public a new document focused on web audience measurement, *Interactive Audience Measurement and Advertising Campaign Reporting and Audit Guidelines*. The document was based on a research project carried out by PriceWaterhouseCoopers for the IAB (PriceWaterhouseCoopers/IAB, 2001) that contained an analysis of the different ways of collecting the data from the trace left by computers in order to measure web advertising, an explanation of the different metrics used for web advertising and a reflection on the problems and limitations of this type of measurement. The document elaborated by the IAB (2002) started by acknowledging the importance of measurement: "Consistent and accurate measurement of Internet advertising is critical for acceptance of the Internet and is an important factor in the growth of Internet advertising spending." It followed with a detailed definition of some of the most relevant metrics (ad impression, click, visit, unique browsers, unique users, page impressions, etc.), recommended some techniques to solve the problems generated by the use of cache memory and proposed some guidelines for the filtration of log-files, the realization of audits, the ways of reporting data, and the transparency of the measurement process. This document was updated in late 2004 (IAB, 2004a, b) with the aim of achieving two main goals. First, developing for the first time a measurement standard that measures the advertisement itself, instead of measuring the programming or content. And second, making of the Internet the first medium to launch a global measurement standard accepted by the key stakeholder organizations in the United States, Europe, Asia, and Latin America.

Future of Advertising Stakeholders (FAST)

In August 1998, Procter & Gamble organized in Colorado a summit of the different agents involved in interactive advertising, that is advertisers, content providers, advertising agencies, and technology companies. As a result of that summit, FAST was created with the aim of continuing the work carried out by CASIE, promoting voluntary and uniform standards for audience measurement, and rationalizing the different advertising forms in the web. A European chapter of FAST was later created, Future of European Advertising Stakeholders. It was also, for the most part, an initiative of advertisers and agencies, and it had similar objectives to the US chapter, but the emphasis was on the European reality (Wentz, 1999).

In March 1999, FAST made public its standardization principles for web advertising forms, *Interactive Standard Advertising Units* (ISAUs). Besides grouping all the possible forms of web advertising into five main types—banners, banners with sister windows, pop-ups, transition pop-ups, and interstitials, each of them with their subcategories—the document elaborated by FAST included some general principles, such as the goal of minimizing the impact of advertising on the user's connection quality and speed, the proposal of creating simple advertisements that could be delivered when the user's system was not able to handle more complex ones, the setting of a 5–6-second threshold as the maximum download time for advertisements, etc. In sum, the document's purpose was the classification of online advertising forms and the setting of some principles aimed at preventing the user from seeing online advertisements as a nuisance. Also in March 1999 FAST presented a study, carried out with the collaboration of the ARF and the IAB, in which the results obtained from the application of different methods for measuring the web audience were compared. The goals of the study were to inform the web industry on audience measurement issues, to evaluate the discrepancy between traffic estimates based on log-files and audience estimates based on the use of electronic panels, to identify the most relevant sources of discrepancy in the results of the measurement, and to recommend solutions and next steps to be taken by the industry. The study was based on the comparison of log-files from 35 websites audited by I/PRO and the ABCi, and the data obtained from Media Metrix and NetRatings panels. The results of the study showed huge discrepancies in the data, especially in those referred to smaller websites, but also significant in the case of larger websites. For example:

- For the traffic of a particular day, the discrepancy between the data obtained from panels and from log-files ranged from 0% to 425%.
- In the case of monthly audience, the discrepancy ranged from 15% to 300%.
- Regarding monthly rankings, log-files and panel results showed discrepancies starting from the second or third position.

The authors of the study, Kalyanam and MacEvoy, tried to identify the reasons that could explain these discrepancies and proceeded to offer some recommendations:

1. To establish a series of directives that would allow for a homogenization of the ways in which websites organize their content, with the aim of avoiding errors in the ways of treating and analyzing data.
2. To make public and audit the methodological process that leads to the creation of electronic panels for measuring the web audience.
3. To establish a permanent industry mechanism for the constant and periodic evaluation of the discrepancies in the data obtained through the different measurement methods.

4. To improve the representativeness of the samples of electronic panels by increasing their size to reach a million panelists and weighting the data based on activity variables.

In September 1999, FAST published its *Audit Metrics and Methodology*, a new step in its attempt to establish a series of definitions and metrics to be used in auditing website traffic. A few months later that document would be complemented with another one, *Audit Guidelines*, in which a series of principles for the realization of audits were proposed, such as following the established standards, public access, lack of self-interest in the audit results, the frequency of the audits, etc.

In January 2000 FAST, in collaboration with the ARF, made public a new document that has had a wide repercussion in the development of web audience measurement, *Principles of Online Media Audience Measurement*. The main goal of the document was

> to further the quality and comparability of all online media measurement, through their subscription to a common set of principles [...] The central purpose is to direct the industry toward audience measures that are comparable in quality and nature to those employed for other commercial media. (FAST/ARF, 2000)

The document was articulated in four parts. First, the description of three types of online media measurement methods: site centric, ad centric, and user centric. Second, the proposal of a series of fundamental principles that should guide the application of these methods. Third, a glossary of common terms used in web audience measurement. And fourth, the identification of those areas that required basic research in order to establish valid methods for web audience measurement. Of these four points, perhaps the most relevant, and the one to which the most space was devoted, was the proposal of principles to guide web audience measurement. These principles showed obvious continuities with the ones proposed by CASIE. They were divided into two groups: ethical principles and methodological principles. The ethical principles were the following:

1. *Post and practice privacy policies*: Researchers must respect the rights of the individual to anonymity and privacy.

2. *Fully disclose methodology*: Complete information on the research practices and methods that have been used, as well as on the data gathered, must be made available to clients.

3. *Use third-party measurement and established industry audit practices*: Audience measurements should be taken by objective third-party research suppliers and not by the media vehicles being measured. When the media self-measure, the results should be audited.

4. *Take steps to ensure that data are used responsibly*: Research companies, online media, and advertisement serving networks must take steps to ensure the responsible use of their data in the public domain—among clients, the press, and others likely to cite their results in public contexts.

5. *Support global harmonization*: Online media usage around the world should be measured under the guidance of the same principles to ensure global comparability of measurement.

6. *Encourage methodological experimentation*: Research organizations are encouraged to be innovative in method and practice. However, the burden of proof of the validity of the measurement and of conclusions based on the measurement is on the research company.

7. *Participate in industry development of best practices seeking industry consensus*: Online media research standards ought to be set by a broad representation of the advertising industry, including advertisers, agencies, media, research companies, and industry bodies.

Regarding the methodological principles, they can be summarized as follows:

1. *The foundations for measurement of online media should be laid so as to maximize comparability to other existing media*: Marketing plans require the ability to compare different media.

2. *More advanced measurements that 'go beyond the basics' should reflect the unique capabilities of online media*: This development should be encouraged as a means of fully valuing online media. However, these more diverse measures should

still relate back to established models for cross-media comparison and forward to marketing objectives to ensure their validity.

3. *All measurement systems should use best media research practices*: Audience measurement of online media should follow the quality criteria developed for other types of media research over the last eight decades, except where these are clearly not applicable, to ensure estimates that are accurate, precise, and reliable.

4. *All measurement systems should use standard industry definitions*: Measures that are comparable must begin with common definitions.

5. *All measurement systems should use a clearly defined universe*: A clearly defined universe provides the basis for relating online media audiences to other media audiences as well as to brand marketing objectives.

6. *All measurement systems should accurately measure the behavior they claim to measure.*

7. *All measurement systems should employ measurement that is non-intrusive*: Audience behavior should be measured as passively as possible.

8. *All measurements must be comparable across measurement systems*: If online audience measurement is to be the currency of online media, it is essential that all measurement systems of the same viewing event indicate the same audience size and composition; more broadly, the same media value.

The work carried out by FAST, which was dissolved in August 2000, has been continued on the other side of the Atlantic by FAST Europe. This organization adopted in June 2000 the principles proposed by FAST with minor adaptations to the European reality, and it has contributed with some of its own proposals to the standardization of web audience measurement.

As we can see, the advertising industry has made a big effort in terms of proposing principles, standards, and directives in order to structure web audience measurement. Since their proposals had the support of a broad section of the advertising industry, represented in the organizations mentioned above, they acquired a force and an importance they would not have had if they had been the proposals of individual players in the field of audience measurement. This effort to standardize web audience measurement, led by the advertising industry, decisively contributed to shape that measurement. Since it was a field under construction, and in order for it to play the institutional role it is supposed to play, the standardization process had to delve into essential issues of great relevance. The proposal for the standardization of measurement coming from the advertising world had to set the bases of the field and, in order to do that, had to touch upon such basic issues as the definition of advertising forms on the web or the creation of an essential vocabulary that could be accepted and understood by all the players in the measurement process. Once the bases were set it became possible to study the process of methodological standardization, the process of reconciliation of the different methods in use, and the issue of comparing the methods and results of web audience measurement with the methods and results of audience measurement in traditional communication media, with the ultimate goal of including the web in the mix of advertising vehicles available to the industry and measured by it.

Observing on hindsight the role of the advertising industry in this whole process, it is possible to see how the final goal is to obtain a stable enough measurement to become the currency in the web advertising market. As a member of CASIE said, "we can't have five different measurement systems out there" (Elliot, 1995). But, in addition, the advertising market can be considered a single market in which the different vehicles, the different media, are options that have to be evaluated and compared each time a campaign is planned. Thus, creating a common currency for the web is not enough. It has to be a currency comparable with the ones used for other media. When the *MPA* published the document aimed at the standardization of web measurement, it explicitly stated that it was not necessary for the measurement of the web to be comparable with the measurement of other media. For magazine editors, the web was a new and different business. But for the advertising industry, the web is just one more vehicle that has to be integrated and compared to other media, and therefore its measurement has to follow similar lines to the ones followed in the measurement of other media. It is necessary to take away from the web its differentiating characteristics and turn it into just another medium. Thus, web audience measurement ends up being based on measures of exposure, on *Opportunities to See* (OTS), whose final goal is the production of two essential measures of the audience measurement of traditional media, that is reach and frequency. The increasing importance of the reach and frequency measures in web audience measurement is evidence of the success of this strategy (Coffey & Mazumdar, 2002; Collins & Bhatia, 2001).

However, as we saw in the previous section, the web is not so easy to measure, and that allows measuring organizations, with their ability to innovate and their market strategies, to acquire a huge influence in the development of web audience measurement, since it is difficult to follow the script written by the advertising industry.

CHAPTER 10

Embodying the Standard

The recommendations put forward by the advertising industry constitute the framework for the development of web audience measurement. But the concrete form of that measurement is created by the different measuring organizations. As we saw in the previous chapter, both the advertising industry and the media are aware of the need for independent third parties to carry out the measurement in order for this measurement to have credibility. From the birth of web audience measurement all kinds of companies and organizations jumped into the measurement market.

For advertisers and agencies it is irrelevant who carries out the measurement as long as it adapts to their needs, and it is credible enough to play its role as a currency; but for measuring organizations it is not irrelevant at all, since their survival depends on their ability to find a niche in the audience measurement market. If we add to this the obvious monopolistic tendencies within the measurement market, since the existence of a single measurement system is more efficient in terms of the use of resources and in terms of the credibility the measurement obtains, it is understandable that measuring organizations have to struggle hard with their competitors in order to survive. This struggle seems to be a defining trait of the audience measurement market, but the nature of the measuring organizations and the strategies they follow to establish themselves in the market depends to a great extent on the measurement method used and on the structure of the audience measurement market of traditional media.

When surveys are used to measure the web audience, measuring organizations are dealing with a method that has evolved and developed over decades with a series of practices, rules, and concepts that can be applied without much variation to the measurement of the web audience—regardless of the limitations that were analyzed in the previous section. Thus, it is natural for the same organizations in charge of measuring the audience of the other communication media to broaden their field of study and include the web. Although in the United States this type of measurement has traditionally been carried out by individual companies, in Europe it is common for Joint Industry Committees (JICs) to take the lead in the use of surveys to measure the web audience. These are non-profit organizations with representation from the media, advertisers, and agencies, and they carry out, supervise, or promote media and audience research. For example, in Spain among the different surveys that collect information on Internet use and on the web audience, the Estudio General de Medios (EGM) is the most established, best known, and most used. The organization in charge of the EGM is the Asociación para la Investigación de los Medios de Comunicación (AIMC), a JIC.

While it is true that surveys can be easily applied to web audience measurement, it is also true that they offer little room for improvement in order to solve the problems encountered when measuring such a complex, global, and fragmented medium. One of the available options is to increase the sample size in order to measure with some precision a larger number of websites. This strategy favors those measuring organizations with a consolidated market position, since it is rather difficult for newcomers to gather the necessary resources for carrying out large-scale surveys—especially in a relatively new market, in which for many years there was much to lose and little to gain. The other obvious option to improve the value of surveys that measure the web audience is to implement international surveys. Again, this is an option that favors those organizations with an established position in the market, and it also requires huge resources. In fact, the most significant initiative aimed at the implementation of international surveys to measure the web audience has been taken by European organizations that are already established in the field of audience measurement in their respective countries. The name of this initiative is Euro JICs, and it was started in June 2000. Several European JICs belong to it, and it is also open to neutral and not-for-profit Media Owner Contracts (MOCs). So far, seven countries have contributed to this effort: Austria, Belgium, France, Germany, Spain, Switzerland, and United Kingdom. The main goal of Euro-JICs is the harmonization of the research about the Internet and other electronic and/or digital media, and the auditing of this research. In addition, it seeks to standardize the definitions,[1] methods, and reports of the different research projects, and to provide comparable data about Internet use at the European level. In order for these data to be representative, Euro-JICs favors the collection of data from large random samples. The collection process takes place either face to face or on the phone, and one of the first agreements of the initiative was the elaboration of a standard questionnaire to be used by all participant organizations. However, this effort has only contributed a couple of brief reports with generic data about Internet use in the participating countries, and it has not delved into the measurement of the most visited sites or domains in Europe.[2]

Although the application of the survey methodology has been relatively straightforward, the dynamics of the other measurement methods have been more complex. In the case of the use of passive methods, based on the trace left by computers, there is a mix of organizations already established in the market for auditing the circulation of print publications and newly minted companies that aspire at entering the web audience measurement market. The obvious parallels between the monitoring of the circulation of publications and the measurement of the traffic of websites soon led the different organizations in charge of monitoring print-press circulation to enter the new web market. Since the data needed to carry out this type of passive measurement are usually in the hands of the different websites, and these websites can conduct the measurement themselves, the market of passive methods for measuring the web audience has evolved for the most part as a market of audits, in which participating organizations take advantage of their credibility as established auditors or try to build that credibility. In this sense, attaining enough credibility to find a niche in this market becomes the main goal for such organizations.

At the international level, the organizations in charge of auditing the circulation of the print press in different countries, grouped under the International Federation of Audits Bureaus of Circulation (IFABC), put forward a series of standards in 1997 aimed at establishing the credibility of these organizations to facilitate their entering the web traffic measurement market, and at offering advertisers comparable international data. These standards, which were updated in 2001, were focused on the definition of a series of metrics and on the proposal of a series of directives for managing the gathered data. At the presentation of these standards, the Secretary General of the IFABC (1997) stated:

> Establishing international reporting and measurement standards serves each of the bureau members and fosters growth in the Web as an international advertising medium. As each of our members extends their brand to the Internet, we, as organisations representing advertisers, their agencies, and publishers, are extending our audit services to serve their needs.

In the case of the United States, which has a more competitive situation than most countries, the market was rather complex, and it was, at the end of the 1990s, divided between organizations traditionally in charge of auditing press circulation (such as the Audit Bureau of Circulations or BPA) and recently created companies specialized in web audits (such as I/PRO) plus some other minor players. While established organizations can use their history and prestige to enter the web audits market, newcomers have to build that credibility. For example, I/PRO, pioneer and leader in the field of web traffic measurement and in the audits of that traffic, has been very active in order to find a comfortable position within this market. One of its first initiatives was the closing of an agreement with Nielsen Media Research—leader in the field of television audience measurement in the United States—that included the purchase of part of I/PRO by Nielsen. This agreement was understood as a way of reinforcing I/PRO's credibility and increasing its popularity (Marx, 1996). Later I/PRO reached collaboration agreements with companies such as DoubleClick—leader in the advertisement server networks field—Netgravity, Firefly, and iChat, and bought its rival NetCount in 1997 (Elliot, 1997). In spite of these alliances which allowed I/PRO to control a large share of the web audits market, the company's survival was in danger until, in 1999, it was bought by CMGI—a large investment group—and reached a collaboration agreement with a direct rival, BPA. The goal of I/PRO has been to become the standard for web audits, which is evident in the company's tagline *Set the Standard*, and in the creation of some significant documents, such as *A Standard for Auditing Web Site Traffic* (I/PRO, 2002)—perhaps the most complete description ever published about the log-file analysis process—and *Measuring Web Site Traffic: Panel vs. Audit*—an attempt to show the superiority of the passive methods used by I/PRO over the methods based on electronic panels. These two documents illustrate a very common strategy, which also appears when the dynamics generated among electronic panels are analyzed, in the struggle for a privileged position in the audience measurement market. That strategy consists of, on the one hand, trying to show that what one does is the standard toward which everyone should aim, and, on the other hand, criticizing the defects of rival methodologies. Following this strategy has allowed I/PRO to remain a leading organization in the market of web audits, a market that has undergone a consolidation process.[3] This process of consolidation has no doubt responded to three fundamental phenomena: first, the maturation of a market with only a few years of existence; second, the crisis that followed the burst of the Internet bubble in 2000 with the ensuing shrinking of the market; and third, the need for the standardization of web audit procedures.

But that consolidation process was altered with the advent of new competitors that wanted to take advantage of the developments in the passive measurement methods, mostly the use of tags, to compete with already established auditors. Over the last few years, some companies with a global outlook (such as the Australian RedSheriff,[4] the French Weborama, and the American WebSideStory) have started using for measurement the analysis of the information generated by the tags read by users' browsers.[5] This method presents, as we saw in the previous section, some advantages over the methods based on the analysis of website log-files. On the one hand, it guarantees the credibility of the measurement since the data is directly collected by the measuring organizations without the intervention of websites, making almost irrelevant the need for audits. On the other hand, tags have the methodological advantage of eliminating the problems generated by the use of cache memory and robots, since they count the number of pages actually viewed by the browser, not the number served by the website. In addition, they simplify the data cleaning process, allowing a faster turnaround and avoiding distortions and manipulations. All these advantages are strategically pointed out by the companies that use this method to penetrate the web audience measurement market

(Webb et al., 2003). The arrival of these companies has generated an increasing instability in the measurement market of passive-method users. But it is in the area of companies that use electronic measurement panels where the instability has been constant from the beginning.

The use of electronic measurement panels for measuring the web audience has been the development that has generated the most interest in the industry due to its ability to combine the information gathered from web users with the information gathered from computers. The similarity of this method to the one commonly used for measuring the television audience has also contributed to generating high expectations for these panels.[6]

Examining the brief history of electronic measurement panels, it is possible to observe how there is an evolution toward a single source of measurement, while, in the process, a series of very interesting strategies and dynamics are revealed. In what follows, I present a summary of the complex history of electronic measurement panels:

- In 1995, the NPD Group created PC-Meter, a panel with a 500-home sample. PC-Meter offered free information on the most visited websites, until 1997, when it changed its name to Media Metrix.
- In 1997, two new panels were launched. In June, two former executives from Turner Broadcasting founded Relevant Knowledge, and, by year's end, the electronics giant Hitachi created NetRatings.
- In March 1998, NetValue was launched in France, the first significant competitor in this market to be created outside the United States.
- In October 1998, Media Metrix and Relevant Knowledge merged under the Media Metrix name.
- That same month, Nielsen Media Research, the giant of television audience measurement, finally entered the web audience measurement market through an agreement with NetRatings, which changed its name to Nielsen NetRatings.
- In April 1999, PC Data, a company specialized in the marketing and sale of computers, decided to launch its own measurement panel.

- In May 1999, Media Metrix went public and separated from the NPD Group.
- In June 1999, NetValue reached an agreement with Taylor Nelson Sofres for the global expansion of the panel.
- In September 1999, AC Nielsen, a giant in market research, bought 10% of NetRatings for 12.5 million dollars. The goal was the creation of the Erating.com service to measure the web audience in Europe, Asia, Latin America, the Middle East, and Africa. AC Nielsen controlled 80% of Eratings.com and Net-Ratings the remaining 20%.
- In the fall of 1999, VNU, a large Dutch group with companies in the market research, marketing, and print publications markets, bought Nielsen Media Research. The participation of Nielsen Media Research in NetRatings was explicitly mentioned as one of the reasons behind the purchase.
- In December 1999, Nielsen Media Research went from controlling 11% of NetRatings to controlling 54% in exchange for 246 million dollars. That same month, NetRatings started the process to go public.
- In February 2000, NetValue went public in Paris and a month later started its expansion in Asia.
- In April 2000, NetValue disembarked in the United States.
- In mid-2000, Media Metrix bought Jupiter Communications, a leading company in the field of Internet market research. The purchase would end up being a disappointment, and it would become a heavy burden for Media Metrix's future.
- In September 2000, Jupiter Media Metrix took PC Data to court because of issues related to the use of measurement technology patented by the former.
- In January 2001, ComScore launched a new panel based on large non-probabilistic samples.
- At the beginning of 2001, VNU bought AC Nielsen.
- In March 2001, PC Data ceased measuring operations after losing the legal battle that Jupiter Media Metrix had started against it. PC Data was sliced and passed onto its competitors. NetValue kept the panelists and sold PC Data's client relationships and website to ComScore. Jupiter Media Metrix kept PC

Data software and related technologies following a court agreement. A few days later Jupiter Media Metrix decided to take Nielsen NetRatings and NetValue to court because of alleged infringement of measuring patents owned by Jupiter Media Metrix.

- In October 2001, NetRatings reached an agreement to purchase for 71 million dollars a Jupiter Media Metrix with financial problems.
- In November 2001, NetValue and ComScore reached a collaboration agreement.
- In February 2002, NetRatings and Jupiter Media Metrix had to suspend their purchase agreement because of the opposition of the Federal Trade Commission (FTC). Considering the situation, and due to financial problems, Jupiter Media Metrix decided to sell its assets to its competitors.
- In June 2002, ComScore bought the Media Metrix panel for 1.5 million dollars and integrated it with its non-probabilistic panel.
- In August 2002, Nielsen NetRatings bought NetValue.

It is possible to see how the field of electronic measurement panels has undergone important transformations since its inception in 1995. It has gone from a market with one pioneering company (PC-Meter) to a market with multiple competitors (Media Metrix, NetRatings, Relevant Knowledge, PC Data, NetValue, ComScore) and ultimately to a market dominated by Nielsen NetRatings with the only competition from ComScore. Throughout this process, it is possible to observe a series of dynamics and strategies that show how a field takes shape. On the one hand, and in spite of the proliferation of competitors, the whole industry is aware of the fact that the struggle for survival will be hard and that most of the competitors will disappear in the process. For example, a Jupiter analyst commented when NetRatings was launched that "there's room because there's no winner yet" (Maddox, 1997). That is, it is a game in which the winner takes all but in which, as long as the market has not designated a winner, anyone can enter and fight for the victory. And in order to achieve that victory, competitors use all the weapons at their disposal.

Since the launch of a measurement operation is rather costly, one of the main needs for these organizations is capital. In order to obtain that capital, the measuring companies went to the stock market—companies like Media Metrix, NetValue, or NetRatings went public—or reached agreements with larger companies that had enough resources to build the panels—Media Metrix signed agreements with Ipsos and GfK for its European expansion, NetRatings signed with Nielsen Media Research and AC Nielsen, NetValue with Taylor Nelson Sofres, etc. To a great extent the need for resources is determined by the global character of the web. In order to obtain precise measures of websites with a global appeal, or to offer large international brands the possibility of launching global campaigns, measurement panels cannot be restricted to national borders. All the major players in the area, such as Media Metrix, NetValue, and NetRatings, launched panels in several countries with the goal of covering with their measurement most of the world's population of web users. Media Metrix built alliances in Sweden, France (Ipsos), Germany (GfK), and the United Kingdom (Ipsos), and already offered results in these countries by December 1999; NetRatings joined forces for its international expansion with AC Nielsen in September 1999; NetValue, started in France in 1999, already had results for France, Germany, the United Kingdom, and the United States by February 2000.

As the measurement through electronic panels has a clear technological component, obtaining a patent over the technology also became a weapon to be used in the market struggle. Since Media Metrix was the pioneer company in the implementation of electronic panels, it got patents over the meter technology, and later used these patents to expel one of its competitors, PC Data, from the market, and to take the others to court (Thompson, 2001). The existence of this pending court case about patents was one of the main reasons why Nielsen NetRatings decided to reach a buyout agreement with Jupiter Media Metrix that would close the conflict in an amicable way, instead of waiting for Jupiter Media Metrix to go out of business after using up all its resources (Hansell, 2002b). Since the buyout had to be suspended because of the opposition of the FTC, NetRatings ended up buying the patents from an almost defunct Media Metrix (Hansell, 2002a).

The bursting of the Internet bubble, with the ensuing disappearance of many online companies and the financial problems of many others, clearly reduced the number of clients available to measuring companies. At the same time, the flight of many investors to more consolidated industries caused a drastic reduction in the capital available to measuring companies (Thompson, 2001). This situation ended up favoring the concentration process in the electronic panels market, with mergers, buyouts, and alliances. This process began with the merge of Media Metrix and Relevant Knowledge, continued with the dismantling of PC Data, went on with the frustrated buyout turned into dismembering of Media Metrix, and finalized with NetRatings' buyout of NetValue.

But next to these dynamics and processes of a purely business nature, there is also a methodological discourse that attempts to show the scientific and practical value of the measurement performed by the different companies while at the same time criticizing the methods used by competitors.[7] As Hansell (1998) explained,

> because no Web rating has yet emerged as the industry standard-bearer, disputes about measurement methods give the various services ground for distinguishing themselves from the competitors.

Thus, for instance, NetValue's founder asserted: "Our methodology is on par with Nielsen, superior to Media Metrix. Our technology is certainly superior to both" (Lawrence, 2000). Issues such as the frequency in which data are offered (monthly, weekly, daily), the size of the panels (from a few thousands panelists to millions of them), the way in which panelists are recruited (mail, random digital dialing, online), the ability to offer results referring to local and global markets, the possibility of offering measures of reach and frequency, the ability to measure the audience of specific advertisements, and the exact configuration of the software used in the meter, are all issues that are often used to promote one's own company and to criticize its rivals. Thus,

> over the years, the firms have debated which service provides the most accurate ratings, uses the best recruiting techniques and delivers the best client service. (Thompson, 2001)

However, all these methodological discussions among the different panels were superceded by the market's own dynamics, which seemed to have made Nielsen NetRatings the global panel of reference for the measurement of the web audience.[8] It became the standard by default, due to the disappearance of the rivals that employed the same methodology. The company's motto, *The Global Standard for Internet Audience Measurement and Analysis*, refers to this perception. But it is not advisable to follow these types of statements blindly, since almost all companies involved in web audience measurement at some point or other have promoted the idea that they were the ones embodying the measurement standard. In fact, the consolidation of Nielsen NetRatings as the standard and reference in the field of panels for measuring the web audience has been threatened by ComScore, who uses a different version of measurement panels (Riedman, 2002), and also by recent developments in the measurement initiatives in Europe.

First, the rivalry between Nielsen NetRatings and ComScore in the field of electronic panels goes beyond the simple market competitors' struggle, since each of them represents a very different vision of how audience measurement should be. Behind the appearance of very similar methodologies actually hides a very important issue for web audience measurement and for audience measurement in general. On the one hand, Nielsen NetRatings has absorbed or expelled from the market all those companies that managed traditional panels for measuring the web audience. Furthermore, it has behind it the weight of a brand like Nielsen, with a distinguished and long history in audience measurement, and currently in charge of the main measurement operation of the medium of reference in the country of reference—the television panel in the United States. Finally, it uses an orthodox measurement system, since it applies to the web the same procedures it applies to its television panel. All this allows Nielsen NetRatings to claim for itself the name of *Golden Standard*, as it did in the ARF/ESOMAR conference that took place in Los Angeles in June 2003, using Future of Advertising Stakeholders (FAST) standards as evidence (Goosey, 2003). On the other hand, ComScore entered the market without any pedigree—besides having purchased the pioneer panel of Media Metrix—and with a heterodox methodology—huge samples recruited on the web or via e-mail. ComScore concentrates on two fundamental issues, that the web is a global medium and that it is very fragmented, and claims that in order to account for these two characteristics of the web purely probabilistic samples have to be forgotten. In order to reinforce its position, ComScore requested of the ARF a methodological evaluation (ARF, 2001). The results of this evaluation were quite positive for ComScore since the ARF left the door open to the possibility of correcting the biases in non-probabilistic samples by using a calibration panel and statistical techniques like the ones used by ComScore. To this needs to be added, the work done by Harris Interactive (Terhanian et al., 2001), one of the leaders in web surveys, and its initiative to correct the biases of non-probabilistic online recruited samples through the use of what is called the Propensity Score Adjustment—a variable that estimates the probability a particular individual has of becoming a member of an online recruited sample.[9] With all this, ComScore went to the same ARF/ESOMAR conference in Los Angeles and asserted that, if the web audience is to be measured adequately, a revolution in audience measurement was necessary. The outcome of this confrontation between Nielsen NetRatings and ComScore is bound to have a major impact on the future of web audience measurement.

Each methodology shows obvious weaknesses but, as we have seen in this chapter, methodological issues are not the only ones that influence the evolution of audience measurement, they are, rather, the weapons that different players use to create room for themselves in the measurement market. And both competitors have been using these weapons even in the pages of trade publications. For instance, a senior vice president of Nielsen NetRatings (Bhatia, 2004) sent a letter to the editor of Advertising Age stating:

> Since 1999, NetRatings has created and maintained the industry's highest quality media-research panel based on methodologies accepted and used by other major media, including TV and print. Our Netview panel is 100% recruited via rigorous RDD (random digital dialing) methodology [...] Other recruitment and incentive schemes, such as online recruitment combined with offers of increased access speeds are inherently biased towards heavy users, thereby resulting in higher estimates. A biased panel, no matter how large, will provide inaccurate estimates.

And while the dispute between the rivals is settled, the advertising industry has to put up with the uncertainty of two sources of data. As the president of the Internet Advertising Bureau lamented, "the online advertising industry could reach $15 billion someday, but discrepancies and inconsistency in the data could hinder our ability to get there" (quoted in Fitzgerald, 2004).

But Nielsen NetRatings' position as the global standard for online audience measurement has not only been threatened by US competition. Recent developments in the European web audience measurement industry have put in question Nielsen NetRatings' idea of a standard. Nielsen NetRatings, aware of the methodological limitations of electronic panels (described in detail in the previous section), bought in early 2004 the Australian company RedSheriff, whose methodology was based on passive methods, in particular the use of tags. The purchase seemed to point toward a new strategy: the combination of passive and mixed methods in order to overcome the limitations of these two types of measurement. However, it seems that in several European countries other stakeholders, most of them the local JICs, are taking the lead in the combination of methods for measuring the web audience with the aim of becoming the source of reference. In Belgium, for example, the local JIC (CIM, Centre d'Information sur les Media) is combining passive and active methods by using tags, unique cookies, and online surveys that are later weighted and projected to the population. In the Netherlands, Stichting Internet Reclame (STIR), an initiative promoted by eight major Dutch Internet operators, has developed the Webmeter, a panel based on the use of unique cookies that are later counted in the servers of participating websites. In Sweden, the ORVESTO Internet initiative combines a multimedia postal survey with a panel that uses cookies and the analysis of these cookies at the server level, where the traffic information is combined with the demographic information obtained in the survey and the panel recruitment process. In Germany, AGOF combines passive methods with online surveys and a representative telephone survey. In Italy, the Audiweb initiative aims at combining offline surveys with passive methods and panels. In Portugal, a similar project is underway. Most of these initiatives involve the local JICs and often major players in the market research arena—such as, for instance, Taylor Nelson Sofres or Intomart GfK. They are, without a doubt, formidable competitors for Nielsen NetRatings, which has operating panels in some of these countries.[10]

In the end, the goal of these methodological innovations—the ComScore non-representative macro-panel, Nielsen NetRatings' goal of combining passive and mixed methods, or the already existing method combinations in Europe—seems to be the creation of better, or more 'scientific,' measurement operations. The hope is that the improvement of the existing operations will lead to a more stable industry in which the best measurement will become the source of reference. However, these methodological innovations are making the measurement process much more complex, less intuitive, and closer to statistical abstractions and models. This tendency could make clients more suspicious about the validity of the measurement and more reluctant about getting involved in this market. It could also ease the introduction of constant variations or improvements in the measurement process. And none of these developments seems to lead to what is the final goal of the industry: a single respected measurement operation.

Conclusions to Section IV

When the relation between audience measurement and advertising is discussed, it is often mentioned that audience measurement plays the role of proving to advertisers that they are actually getting what they are paying for. This proof is achieved through audience measurement and, thus, only when a basic agreement has been reached among the different agents involved regarding how the measurement process should be carried out can the process of trading the audience be started with an accepted price structure. Since measurement is a necessary step for the development of the audience market, all the agents involved in this market are interested in the existence of measurement. But while all the agents are interested in the existence of measurement, the truth is that each of them finds themselves in a different position and their specific interests are not necessarily coincidental. Depending on the results of the measurement, some agents—the ones selling audiences, the media—will earn more or less money, while others—the ones buying audiences, the advertisers—will pay more or less money. This leads to the need for a neutral third party who, though interested in the existence of measurement, will not be benefited or hurt by the concrete results of that measurement. The need for these third-party entities able to be neutral and reconcile the different interests at stake is manifested in the creation of independent companies devoted to audience measurement, in the creation of organizations with representatives of the different agents involved, such as Joint Industry Committees, for instance, and in the use of auditing organizations when the data comes from the media whose audience is to be measured. All these forms play a similar institutional role, to give credibility to the measurement by certifying its validity independently from the other agents involved in the audience trade.

However, the fact that audience data are produced by third parties who have no interest in the concrete results of the measurement does not mean that the measurement will be automatically accepted by the market. The measurement has to allow for the determination of the price of the audience and to do this, it has to comply with a series of minimum quality standards. It is the different agents involved in the process who decide what those minimum standards are. But even when the measurement responds to those minimum standards, it is difficult for it to achieve enough credibility when its results depend on who handles the measurement process and how it is handled. If the audience measurement results are to play their institutional role as currency, the measurement process has to undergo a process of standardization, a rationalization that leads to ignoring certain information and obviating certain methodological problems. As we saw at the beginning of the book, business and advertising demands lead to privileging quantitative methods that produce data that are easily manageable and traded. Even though qualitative research may offer deeper and more detailed information on the audience of a medium, it is difficult for it to become a currency of exchange, since it cannot be reduced to units and standard measures that are essential for economic exchanges. This same logic is the one that pushes toward the standardization of quantitative audience research, of audience measurement. If the measurement methods are applied differently and they produce different results, they will no doubt create conflicts and disputes among the different players in the market, and fluid trade will be impossible. We can say that the scientific validity of the data is sacrificed to privilege their reliability, so they can be sufficiently credible and allow all the players in the industry to continue with their trade.

Thus, in order for audience measurement to become an articulating mechanism for the advertising industry, it must constantly stay at an equilibrium point in which the measurement is not so blunt and unsophisticated as not to reflect at all what it is supposed to measure, but also in which it is not so elaborate and detailed as to impede its becoming the industry's currency. But that sought after equilibrium is always an unstable equilibrium. As the history of audience measurement shows (Beville, 1988), the monopolistic tendencies in the audience measurement market lead to the privileging of one source as the valid and reliable one, but this position of privilege is constantly challenged by new measurement operations, new companies, new initiatives that aspire to dethrone the established ones. Sometimes they succeed, sometimes they fail, but by following these attempts we can uncover the strategies and dynamics that underlie the industry. Traditionally, as Meehan (1984) mentions, the most common strategy has been to introduce modifications in the measurement methods in order to make them 'more scientific' and then trying to capture more clients and step by step obtaining the trust of the different players in the market. The ability of the measurement to serve the needs of the industry in terms of advertising planning and business exchanges without altering consolidated routines has also been used as a tool for defending the superiority of certain measurement operations over others (Miller, 1994).

All these issues I have mentioned—the existence of audience measurement as a requisite for fueling advertising expenditure, the existence of coincidental and opposed interests among the different agents, the need for some minimum quality standards, the search for a common currency, the monopolistic tendencies in the market, the specific strategies followed by the players in order to become a reference in the market—have usually been discussed in the context of the audience measurement of traditional mass media. But, as we have seen in this section, all these phenomena also take place in web audience measurement. We can say, therefore, that there is no great difference in terms of logic and dynamics between web audience measurement and traditional media audience measurement. Nonetheless, it is possible to perceive in the short history of web audience measurement some specific dynamics that should be pointed out here.

First, the development of web audience measurement, though supported by all the agents involved in the advertising trade, has clearly been led by the buyers—advertisers and agencies. That leadership, articulated through the different organizations and documents analyzed in this chapter, has decisively contributed to setting the bases for the industry. It has contributed to giving structure to all the different advertising formats on the web and to the definition of a basic vocabulary for web audience measurement. It has also contributed to defining a framework for the development of measurement based on a series of general principles aimed at sustaining the credibility of that measurement—the need for independent third parties, respect for people's privacy, need for a consensus within the industry, etc. And, in a significant way, the leadership of advertisers and agencies has contributed to shaping web audience measurement in a line of continuity with audience measurement in other media. This has been achieved by insisting on taking advantage of the audience measurement practices developed over eight decades in other media and, especially, by insisting on the need for users' exposure measures comparable with the measures obtained in traditional mass communication media. In this sense, we can say that for the advertisers and agencies that participated in this effort, the web is just one more advertising vehicle that needs to be rationalized, structured, measured, and integrated in the set of preceding advertising vehicles. Of course, lots of information and variety is lost in the process but, as an advertiser puts it, "it will help media buyers and advertisers alike once we can truly compare different media to each other and have it make sense. I'm willing to sacrifice accuracy for consistency" (Cleland, 1998).

Second, if we examine the evolution of measuring organizations, we can see how the structuration process remains open. There is no doubt that a consolidation process has taken place, due for the most part to the general crisis that followed the bubble, with the double consequence of limiting the business opportunities of measuring organizations and of minimizing the role of audience measurement as a tool for estimating the value of online businesses in the stock market. But, on the other hand, this consolidation process becomes more complicated due to the application of very different measurement methods, which make it more difficult to find a common source of reference for the measurement. And, besides this, the deficiencies and limitations of each of the different methods open the door to the proposal of new methods, variations on the ones already in use, or combinations of them, with the ensuing instability that this introduces in the industry. It is difficult to determine at this point whether the difficulties in the way of establishing a common currency in the web audience market are due to the youth of the industry, about a decade old, or if they derive from the peculiarities of the medium. But it seems obvious that issues such as the global nature of the audience or the fragmentation of the medium make more difficult the consolidation process and have a significant impact in the industry's dynamics. In any event, the panorama of the web audience measurement industry seems much more varied and complex than that of the audience measurement industry of other media.

Even though the developmental logic of and the interests behind web audience measurement push toward the constitution of a single currency, recognized and used by all the agents involved and able to facilitate a fluid trade in the advertising market (Cormier & Haering, 2003), that currency does not yet exist, and it is possible that it might not ever exist. As Lamas (2002) commented, "it is clear we are still far from a measurement standard [...] Or perhaps that moment will never arrive."

Conclusions

Through the course of this book I have examined each of the three statements that were put forward as a way of articulating my endeavor:

1. The birth of Internet audience measurement coincides with the historical moment in the development of the medium in which it starts showing some of the essential characteristics that define previous mass media.

2. The audience measurement methods applied to the World Wide Web show obvious limitations in taking into account the peculiarities of the medium, and they also show obvious similarities to the methods used for measuring the audience of traditional mass media.

3. In a fashion similar to that of the audience measurement of traditional mass media, business interests lead web audience measurement to seek audience data that can become the 'coin of exchange' for the economic transactions involving the medium and advertisers.

Since I have offered specific conclusions for each of these statements at the end of the sections devoted to them, I will simply, and by way of summarizing, say that the three statements have been proved correct. Therefore, we can assert that Internet audience measurement as a mechanism for the production of the audience has its origin in the moment when the Internet and, in particular, the World Wide Web showed those defining characteristics of mass media that allow us to start talking of the existence of an audience—asymmetry in communication processes, popularization to the point of reaching a significant number of users, and the presence of business and, in particular, advertising interests. Secondly, we can assert that the methods currently used to measure the web audience present clear limitations when they try to take into account the peculiarities of the medium, and that, therefore, web audience measurement has difficulties in playing an institutional role in the process of audience manufacture and sale. Finally, we can assert that the dynamics of the web audience measurement industry—standardization processes, monopolistic tendencies, the need for independent measuring organizations, competition among those organizations, etc.—are manifestations of the same logic that drives the audience measurement process in traditional mass media: the search for a common currency to allow and facilitate the commercialization of the audience and the exchanges involved. Therefore, in this final section I would like to go beyond what has already been discussed in order to put in context the conclusions I have elaborated throughout the book and to discuss some issues with far reaching implications related to my topic and to the statements I had proposed to study it.

Regarding the birth of Internet audience measurement and the corresponding advent of the process of audience manufacturing, it should be pointed out that it is not a necessary or unavoidable development. Rather, it is a historical configuration with a specific reach and a limited field of application.

The concrete form that a medium might take depends on many different factors. A crucial one is the role of political power. In spite of all the libertarian rhetoric surrounding the Internet,[1] of the influence of the hacker culture (Himanen, 2001), and of the role played by altruistic and communitarian values (Castells, 2001), the truth is that the Internet was born in the womb of the American military and government. It was political power that financed and promoted the creation and development of the web, and that decided at the beginning of the 1990s to transfer it to the corporate realm (Kahn, 1994). It is true that there existed alternative or countercultural movements that promoted online connections, movements that in an ingenious way and without the intervention of any political or economic power used the technology to allow citizens to enjoy the communication tools created around the Internet infrastructure. But this should not lead us to think that the Internet is in itself and in essence a 'technology of freedom.' As the analysis of the development of the Internet in countries with authoritarian regimes shows (Kalathil & Boas, 2003), the evolution of the medium is conditioned in a fundamental way by the political decisions surrounding it. Nonetheless, in the case on which I have focused throughout the book, that of the United States, the Internet was released from government control in the mid-1990s, and this same pattern was followed in other countries with democratic regimes and capitalist economies. From that moment onward, the Internet started, thanks to a great extent to the World Wide Web, to penetrate all the layers of economic, cultural, and political activity, to become a transforming force in many fields, making its control or regression very difficult, if not impossible. Thus, the configuration of the Internet as a mass medium through which the manufacture of the audience takes place is limited to a series of countries in which political power has left the initiative to private hands, and it is centered on the World Wide Web, the tool that transformed the nature of the communication processes established over the Internet.

However, the possibility of controlling a medium, such as the Internet or the web, is not unique to political power. For some authors it is the very privatization of the Internet and its opening to commercial interests (Lessig, 2000) and large corporations (McChesney, 2000) that constitute a significant danger for online freedom. A danger that becomes even larger when political power and economic interests go hand in hand (McChesney, 1996). The history of mass media and, in particular, of radio (Barnouw, 1967; Smulyan, 1994) offer enough evidence to take seriously the power of business interests to transform and control the evolution of media that seem essentially free and to convert them into media that are controlled by a few large corporations. In this manner, the media are reduced to a limited offering managed by companies seeking profits. As Neuman asserts (1991: 165), "when new media technologies conductive to increasingly diverse and smaller-scale mass communications emerge, commercial market forces and deeply ingrained media habits pull back hard in the other direction." As we have seen before, the penetration of advertising interests in the Internet constitutes a conscious effort by the advertising industry aimed at controlling the development of the Internet, and in this effort the implementation of audience measurement systems becomes a necessary tool for achieving that goal. Therefore, it is conceivable to think that the World Wide Web will end up following the model of other media and that it will go from being controlled by the government to becoming a medium controlled by large corporations, and that in such a situation the measurement of the audience will become an essential tool for that control.

Not all media are the same, however. Private media, in general, operate in a dual market. On the one hand, they participate in a market of products: programs, issues of print publications, etc., that can be sold at a specific price. On the other hand, they participate in a market of audiences to the extent that they present advertisements paid by advertisers in order to reach with their messages the potential customers exposed to the medium (Napoli, 2003). The specific situation that leads a communication medium to focus on one or the other market depends on economic and technological issues. In addition, within each of the different media there can be specific vehicles that opt for a particular model—there are free newspapers and pay newspapers, broadcasting television channels that carry commercials and pay television without them. Since payment models have not been very successful on the web, advertising—and therefore audience measurement as an indispensable mechanism for the functioning of the advertising market—could become an essential element of the medium's reality, as happens with other privatized mass communication media that do not use the pay model—and even with some public service media (Ang, 1991). We would then be facing another case of a medium that would have gone from government control to being controlled by the advertising logic and the manufacture of the audience through its measurement and exchange. However, the issue is far from simple, since we can observe how many different business models coexist on the web. We have vehicles based on payment in exchange for content (few), vehicles based on mixed model with advertising and payment (few), vehicles based exclusively on advertising (prominent), but also vehicles based on commerce (not of 'content,' but of products or services), and, what is even more interesting, vehicles that are not based on business interests at all, but that may have tremendous repercussion and audiences of a significant size. Thus, the World Wide Web in Western countries is, as a whole, a medium no longer controlled by the government, a medium in which commercial interests have penetrated, a medium in which pay-for-content as an alternative to advertising business models has a limited presence, but also a medium in which, as opposed to traditional mass media, advertising has not completely penetrated the logic of the medium and, hence, a medium in which audience measurement does not constitute as essential an element as it does with other media when it comes to explaining their institutional logic.

The reasons behind all this undoubtedly are complex, and it will not be possible here to delve in detail into them. However, it is possible to point out at least some of the issues that may help us understand this situation. As was mentioned in the first section of this book, according to Schramm and Roberts (1971), mass communication media are characterized by establishing a complex organizational fabric in order to carry out their communicational activities and goals. However, the organizational fabric required to create a communication vehicle on the web and to make it function is much more simple and cheap than in other media. In addition, since there are no government limitations (no licenses or permits are required) or technical limitations (the problem with scarce frequencies or, in this case, scarce IP addresses is not really an issue on the web) it is very easy to create an online communication vehicle. Since they are vehicles that do not require large resources to function, they can subsist without having to follow commercial logics. Besides this, they are vehicles that, once they have been created, are available to any user from anywhere in the world (all websites are basically at the same distance from a user's computer), are easily located (search systems allow it), and offer content that remains available over time (as opposed to, for instance, radio or television).

In such a large and complex environment as the web, where there are millions of pages and sites, it is extremely difficult to estimate the importance of such vehicles that do not follow commercial logics or have a complex institutional structure. The predominant image of the web nowadays is that of a fragmented medium, but in which most of the audience is concentrated in a limited number of websites that are based on commercial logics, that usually carry advertising, and that usually show up in the audience measurement results and, therefore, participate in the process of manufacturing the audience. However, there is a small detail in the results of web audience measurement that seems to signal that those large advertising-supported websites are only the tip of an iceberg that remains for the most part under water. In the results of television audience measurement panels there is always an 'other' category that sums up the audience of small channels. The inclusion of this category makes it possible to calculate the share of the different channels. However, if one examines the results of web audience measurement panels it is possible to see how that 'other' category is not present. Considering ,the way, in which these panels measure the audience, to calculate the 'other' category is extremely easy, since the only operation required is to add up the audience of all those websites for which the number of panelists that visit them is too small to yield a statistically significant audience size. The fact that this information has been absent from the reports that measuring organizations give to their clients leads me to suspect that the audience of the 'other' category is probably larger than the audience of the websites that actually appear in those reports.

Therefore, and regarding the first of the statements, it is true that the birth of Internet audience measurement in the mid-1990s coincides with the moment in which, due to the advent of the World Wide Web, there existed the necessary conditions to begin the process of audience manufacturing. However, it is necessary to put that conclusion in perspective, and to remember that this is a specific development of certain countries with a particular political and economical system—democracy and free market capitalism—and that this development does not seem to affect the medium as a whole, nor to acquire the institutional relevance that it has in other media in which audience measurement becomes an essential element for their institutional functioning.

Regarding the second statement, the one referring to the limitations of the measurement methods, it seems difficult to predict the evolution of these methods considering the constantly evolving environment of the web. However, it is possible to mention a few issues that may be relevant for an understanding of the future development of these methods.

As we saw before, the web, due to its specific technological structure, makes it possible to obtain huge amounts of information regarding the communication processes established through it. It is this capability to produce and store detailed information about communication exchanges that led to the belief that the web would be the medium with the easiest and simplest audience measurement process. However, this belief was soon shattered by a fundamental issue: the inability to link the collected information with individual users. When the web was starting to become a popular medium it seemed that this issue would be easily solved, it would just require asking users to register before entering a site. However, it was soon clear that forcing users to identify themselves and to use access passwords was a way of keeping them away from the site—problems remembering passwords and user names, refusal to share personal information, etc.—and registration before access slowly disappeared from many websites. The use of persistent cookies became a sort of substitute. But, as we saw before, such cookies are not the best solution when the goal is to measure the web audience. Furthermore, the masking of one's own identity on the web can be done in many different ways, and the complexity and variety of connections to the web makes it even more difficult to link online activity with specific individuals. In this way, the possibility of carrying out a census-like measurement of users' online activities is clearly limited by the lack of a link between activity and user. This limitation can only be overcome if a general identification system is established, a system that tags users individually. And even though there are authors who think that the arrival of such a system is just an issue of time, the truth is that the issue of privacy seems to be, for the moment, an insurmountable barrier for the implementation of that kind of system.[2]

If the methods named here as passive have linking problems, mixed methods, or panels, have problems representing the universe they try to measure. In spite of the information they offer about the number and the profile of web users, the truth is that the fragmentation of the medium, its global character, and the proliferation of access points pose a serious hurdle when using methods that are based on the representational nature of the samples. The development of panels in countries where most of the online population is concentrated with the aim of adding the results of the different national panels, seeking businesses collaboration in order to implement workplace panels with a certain degree of significance, or the attempts at increasing the size of the samples, are different ways of trying to solve the shortcomings of this type of method. However, it seems that such efforts have not been able, so far, to overcome the limitations of electronic panels with respect to web audience measurement. In fact, the initiatives that try to overcome the limitations of this method by using samples that do not aim to represent the universe, but that are then weighted, constitute an evidence of the persistence of those limitations. Even though the use of these samples present serious methodological problems, they point to an interesting development in audience measurement (Fulgoni, 2003). As we saw in the first section of this book, when discussing the origins of audience measurement, around 1930 a fundamental change in measurement methods took place due to the development of the statistical rudiments that would allow for the measurement of a large, disperse audience, such as that of radio, by using samples that represented the universe (Beniger, 1986). In a sense, audience measurement based on samples and not on census means a concession to imprecision, since it implies a series of measurement errors. However, this imprecision and these errors have been fully assumed by those who use the data produced through measurement, to the point that they are very rarely mentioned. Perhaps we are witnessing the beginning of another fundamental change in the evolution of measurement methods that will lead to the overcoming, or ignoring, of the problems posed by the use of representative samples to measure the web audience. In the same way that samples have been used to study or measure certain populations, it is possible that in the future representative samples will be used to weight other non-representative samples and obtain in this manner some knowledge about populations that would otherwise not be captured by the measurement (Terhanian et al., 2001).[3] No doubt, the error levels would increase. But if a certain level of error has already been assumed in order to obtain useful measurements, it is possible that an increase in the error levels could also be assumed. To a great extent, it will depend on the importance of the interests at stake.

The difficulty of establishing valid measurement methods also has an influence on the issue examined through the third statement, which referred to the dynamics of the industry and to the search for a common currency that can be accepted by all the agents participating in the trading of the audience. Since there is no method or combination of methods that is accepted by the market as a whole, it is difficult to create a common currency that might bestow the business exchanges around the audience with credibility and stability. Web audience measurement has a short history, and this makes it necessary to consider the hypothesis that it is the youth of the medium that explains the lack of standardization. However, it is also possible that, in fact, the problems with web audience measurement have to do with issues that go beyond the short life of the medium and its audience measurement industry, issues related to the distinctive nature of the medium, not only from a purely technological point of view, but also from the social, economic, and cultural points of view. If this is the case, we might then be witnessing a useless effort in which the 'institutionalization forces' of the medium apply obsolete models to new circumstances.

This attempt at applying models derived from traditional mass media is manifest not only in the use of measurement methods taken from the audience measurement of those media, but also in the ultimate goal in the development of web audience measurement over the past decade. This goal is to integrate the web into the media system with the aim of facilitating advertising planning. Since the development of web audience measurement is a result of the needs of the advertising market, there is an attempt to reduce the peculiarities of the web, to channel them through a process of standardization and rationalization of the measurement to the point of turning the web into just another medium. In this manner, the search for a common currency does not only refer to the need to establish a standardized and trusted system for measuring the web in order to compare the data on the different online vehicles, but also refers to the need for a common currency that will allow for comparisons between the web and other communication media. The process of searching for a common currency carries with it the elimination from the measuring process of those traits that make of the web a different medium. However, as Cormier and Haering (2003: 204) point out, "a very important part of Internet advertising tends to produce direct response, which doesn't need any other currency than response itself." Thus, it is not just that the measurement methods have problems adapting to a new reality like the web, but also that the very dynamic of searching for a common currency seems to go against the reality of the medium. Perhaps the path to the rationalization of the web as an advertising vehicle that would allow business interests to exploit its commercial value will not take place through the establishment of a common currency based on audience measurement but through the analysis of the huge amounts of information generated by online communication exchanges and the use of new sets of measures. In fact, it seems that the commercial use of data on user's online activities depends more on the development of what Gandy (1993) calls the "panoptic sort" than on the development of audience measurement.[4] That panoptic sort is constituted by a complex set of technologies that collect, process, and share information on individuals and groups; information generated by their daily activities as citizens, workers, and consumers; and information used for coordinating and controlling their access to the goods and services that define our lives in a capitalist economy. It is indeed a whole fabric that uses information from, for instance, our credit card purchases, our telephone bills, our communications with the administration, our health insurances, etc., with the goal of optimizing the consuming potential of individuals and groups. The advent of the Internet has increased the capabilities of this system to obtain the information it requires for its functioning, and the system itself is in turn used to optimize the business opportunities of the web and of its users' activities (Campbell & Carlson, 2002).

But, apart from the problems or developments that web audience measurement faces, it also seems necessary to examine what that measurement says about the medium itself, since, as Bill Harvey, president of a consulting firm that worked with CASIE in the development of measurement standards, said, "the medium is the measurement to some extent" (quoted in Cleland, 1995). On the one hand, audience measurement has an explicit influence on the perception of the medium, even if only because of its ability to bestow with reality such an ethereal entity as the audience. In this way, and since the measurement focuses on a reduced number of websites, with large audiences, and based more or less explicitly on an advertising business model, the results of the measurement tend to portray the web as a medium not very different from traditional mass media.[5]

Besides this, Web audience measurement is usually presented in reference to specific websites. In this manner we talk of the audience of Yahoo.com, the audience of AOL.com, etc. This kind of presentation leads to clear parallelisms with traditional mass media. However, it is not the same thing to say that, for instance, five million people read a publication or watch a television channel as it is to say that five million people visited a specific website. In fact, a website can turn out to be much more complex and diffuse than a newspaper or a television channel. We can say that most readers of a newspaper are exposed to the same content. We can say that viewers of a television channel must have been exposed to different content depending on the time they watched. But the users of a website, even if they visit at the same time, can be exposed to very different types of content, or they can even be exposed to no content at all if their goal is to buy, chat, search, etc. A visit to any prominent website can give us an idea of how much is behind the word 'website.' However, the presentation of the audience as the audience of a specific website contributes to give it a cohesion that does not exist on the web, at least not to the extent that it exists when we refer to the audience of traditional mass media.

On the other hand, the development, methods, and dynamics of the measurement, with their peculiarities and problems, also help us understand the nature of the medium. That is, on the one hand, the measurement yields a view of the medium; on the other hand, an examination of the measurement through which that image is obtained helps us construct a perception of the medium that goes beyond what we can derive from the results of the measurement. Throughout the book, as the origins and development of web audience measurement have been examined, an image of what type of communication medium is the web has also been drawn. It is, no doubt, a special kind of medium: essentially global, very fragmented, with interactive capabilities that are not present in traditional media, intrinsically flexible, in constant evolution, with the possibility of subsuming all other media in its own structure, and, what perhaps encompasses all the mentioned features, very complex. The history of the medium that was sketched in the second section of this book, the difficulty of developing measurement methods that adapt to the characteristics of the medium, or the problems finding a measurement system that would rationalize the economic exchanges in the medium, all point to concluding that we are actually dealing with a medium of a different nature.

If we consider that the web is a peculiar medium and, on top of that, we realize that it is not so popular in many countries as other media are, this can lead us to conclude that in reality we should not give much importance to its specific developments. If audience measurement has problems dealing with the web, that is not going to cause any significant change in a consolidated media system where the web is just a late and not that relevant addition. However, issues such as the fragmentation of the offer and of the audience, the increasing ability of the user to control the circumstances of media consumption, the presence of different access platforms to the medium, or the increasing flexibility of space/time in media use, have also been acquiring increasing importance in the traditional media system and, by extension, on the audience measurement of those media (Napoli, 2003). Therefore, and regardless of the relevance that the existence of a medium such as the web may have for the advertising market or for the mass communication media system, the truth is that the issues and problems faced by web audience measurement allow us to foresee some of the attributes that will define the media system and its audience measurement in the future.

Regarding the 'audience' concept itself, it is a concept with a very long tradition in communication research, a concept that has become over time an essential pillar for the analysis of the impact of mass communication (Allor, 1988). However, it is necessary to point out that its use in communication research derives from its use in commercial audience research. As Mosco and Kaye (2000: 35) explain,

> it was not until broadcasters needed to determine the actual size of the unknown audience that the analytical objectification of the audience began. [...] This was to have important consequences, fundamentally transforming a common word into an institutional term, and eventually bequeathing to the field of mass communications an analytical category loaded with meaning.

Thus, the use of the 'audience' concept in communication research is historically linked to commercial interests and to the development of processes to measure it. In this sense, to the extent that commercial audience measurement undergoes a transformation due to the advent of new communication realities such as the Internet or the web, the concept of the 'audience' itself, and its use in communication research, will necessarily be affected. As we mentioned at the beginning of this book, work on the reception and use of the Internet has leaned toward the use of concepts such as 'community' that seem to offer a more adequate characterization of the communication processes that are established over the Internet. Since we are talking about communication processes in which it is not easy to distinguish between senders and receivers, in which there is not a large number of people involved, and in which there are often no commercial interests associated with them, it does not seem very appropriate to apply the concept of the 'audience' to the Internet. On the other hand, and as we have seen throughout the book, the World Wide Web has a series of general characteristics that allow us to apply to it the 'audience' concept. But since the measurement that makes that audience manifest and gives that audience a profile faces serious problems and shows obvious limitations, we should also question its appropriateness or, at least, its generic application to the web. Perhaps we should, paraphrasing Dayan (2001), talk of 'the peculiar audience of the web.'

Notes

Chapter 1

1. The generic title of the book refers to the Internet audience. However, and for reasons that I will detail below, I will progressively focus on the audience of the World Wide Web, which is just one of the many tools available over the Internet, though perhaps the most relevant one. For the moment, I will not make an explicit distinction between both audiences, but throughout the book I will examine the reasons that lead me to focus on the World Wide Web.

2. IP addresses consist of a series of digits that identify the machines connected to the Internet.

3. Actually, it would be audience labor or audience attention, not the audience itself, that is traded by the media and advertising industries. As Jhally and Livant (1986: 130) explain, the answer to the commodity question "seems obvious and straightforward: Media sell audiences to advertisers. We need, however, to pin down specifically what about audiences is important for the mass media. [...] What the media sell (because they own the means of communication) is what they control—the watching-time of the audience." And, from a Marxist point of view, "watching is a form of labor" (1986: 135). Or, as Napoli (2003: 5) reminds us, "in selling audiences to advertisers, media firms essentially deal in human attention." For more on this issue, see Gandy (1990).

Chapter 2

1. The concept of 'control' used by Beniger is taken from Cybernetics and Systems Theory, and is defined as "purposive influence toward a predetermined goal." It has two essential elements: information processing and reciprocal communication. His concept of 'control' lacks, therefore, the political connotations found in Foucault's work.

2. To the extent that the commodity produced by the media is manufactured through research, through the search for a certain knowledge linked to specific interests, Foucault's work and his reflections on the relationships between knowledge and power, discourse and subject, have entered the theoretical background of institutional analysis of audience research (see Ang, 1991; Gandy, 1993).

3. As Wimmer and Dominick (1987: 51) assert, "the idea behind measurement is a simple one: a researcher assigns numerals to objects, events, or properties

according to certain rules." Therefore, when we talk about measurement we are talking about certain fundamental concepts: "numerals," "assignment," "object of the measurement," and "rules." The numerals mean nothing unless they have been assigned to the object of measurement. The object to which the numerals are to be applied needs to be specified. And this assignment or attribution of numerals to the object being measured cannot be random or arbitrary, it needs to follow certain rules and patterns that indicate how the assignment is to be realized.

4. This development was described with a certain degree of sarcasm by Leo Bogart (1988: 11) when he said: "Now all of a sudden a genius in England has discovered that television sets don't watch television but that people watch television."

5. This is the case because, as Napoli (2003: 20–21) points out,

> the audience marketplace illustrates two countervailing forces. On the one hand, the desire for better quality in audience measurement persists, because better measurement means a higher-quality audience product (something generally desired by both advertisers and media organizations). On the other hand, the audience marketplace wants a single parsimonious currency, something achievable only when the provider of audience data is a monopoly.

Section II

1. In order to properly analyze the different elements that converge in the efforts to measure the Internet audience, it is necessary to carry out an analysis of the historical evolution of the medium. However, I do not intend here to tell a detailed history of the Internet, of which there are good examples both in books published in the recent years and on the web itself. Rather, my goal is to examine the evolution of the medium in order to contextualize and understand the origins of Internet audience measurement. Among the books we can point out those by Abbate (1999), Berners-Lee (1999), Gillies and Cailliau (2000), Hafner and Lyon (1998), and Naughton (2000). We will be drawing profusely from these works to describe the evolution of the Internet and the constitution of its audience. The resources available online are countless, and we will refer to some of these through the course of this section.

Chapter 3

1. ARPA was created under the tenure of Neil McElroy as secretary of defense in Eisenhower's administration. Interestingly, McElroy is credited as the inventor of soap opera while he was a marketing executive at Procter & Gamble (Hafner & Lyon, 1998).

2. For a detailed study of BBN's work in the creation of the embryo of the Internet, see Hafner and Lyon (1998).

3. The delay in the development of protocols for the connection to hosts meant that the IMP network, though ready by late 1969, had no effective use for some time.

4. I will analyze in detail this process of privatization and commercialization in the next chapter.

5. The website of the World Wide Web Consortium (http://www.w3.org) contains huge amounts of information on the web's history, design, and technology, including Berners-Lee's original proposal at http://www.w3.org/History/ 1989/proposal.html

6. Later renamed, in spite of Berners-Lee's opposition, as URL. Berners-Lee proposes the use of an intermediate solution: Universal Resource Identifier (URI) (Berners-Lee, 1999).

7. Gopher: a system based on hierarchical menus created by the University of Minnesota that allowed users to browse the information available on the Internet. WAIS: a system for searching indexed content on the net.

8. The addition of the <IMG> (image) tag to the HTML language was criticized by the creator of the language, Berners-Lee (Naughton, 2000). The first browser developed by Berners-Lee could not display images and text in the same window, since

it was a system designed for scientists and scientists often have graphs and diagrams that they refer to throughout a long piece of text. With the NeXT browser, there were no images in-line with the text as is the case with most of today's browsers. Instead there would be a hypertext link that would open up another window with the image in it. That meant that you could keep the image on the screen whilst you scrolled through the text in another window. With a modern browser, you would have to keep scrolling up and down between text and image. They are designed to make Web pages look like the magazines we are all used to. (Gillies & Cailliau, 2000: 193)

Chapter 4

1. I will not mention here each and every communication tool available on the Internet. For a more detailed listing of these tools and of the general properties of the communication processes that they facilitate, see Long and Baecker (1997). For a clear technical description of these tools, see Gralla (2004).

2. The Bulletin Board System (BBS) functions in a way similar to that of newsgroups, and they produce similar communication processes. Therefore, we will not devote a specific section here to BBS.

3. For a detailed analysis, see Almirón (2001) and Rheingold (1985).

4. Emphasis in the original.

5. This is an exclusively textual browser that reads documents line by line. The first browser developed by Berners-Lee, only compatible with NeXT computers, functioned in a graphic environment that allowed the user to move throughout the screen and to click on any point.

6. For a more detailed description of the different browsers created at various institutions at the beginning of the 1990s, see Berners-Lee (1999), and Gillies and Cailliau (2000).

7. Even though the quote is rather long I include it here because it shows very clearly what Berners-Lee's original intention was, how his original conception was transformed, and the possible reasons behind that transformation.

8. Berners-Lee (1999) has pursued in his work within the World Wide Web Consortium (W3C) his idea of developing browser–editors.

9. Programming language developed by Sun Microsystems that allows the execution of programs (applets) through the web browser without needing to have those programs installed in the user computer where the browser is installed. Viola, one of the first web browsers, already had the option of executing programs (Berners-Lee, 1999) but it was the integration of Java within Netscape Navigator 2.0 in 1995 that made this kind of application very popular on the web (Clark, 2000).

10. These data are included here to illustrate my point, and I will not get into an analysis of their origin or of the method used for gathering the data. The different measurement methods will be the focus of the following section.

11. In fact, the US Geological Service used the services of Telenet ever since the mid-1970s (Abbate, 1999).

12. Among these online services, Prodigy, in January 1995, was the first to offer Internet access (Meeker, 1997).

13. The text of this message can be found at http://www.templetons.com/brad/spamreact.html

14. The IPO of Netscape in August 1995 can be considered the beginning of the bubble. For an analysis of the different elements that contributed to the advent of this bubble and its subsequent explosion, see Cassidy (2003), and Perkins and Perkins (1999).

15. See, for example, the works by Demers and Lev (2001), Hand (2001), Rajgopal et al. (2000), and Trueman et al. (2000).

16. This phenomenon was not exclusive to the United States. In Spain, for example, Ballestero (2002: 49) describes a similar situation:

> They thought that the fact that thousands of users visited their websites would put their companies in the center of interest of the advertising industry and generate relevant revenues from advertisements. With this argument, these new .com businessmen estimated the value of their companies in terms of their real and potential visitors, dragging both private and institutional investors into this illusion.

Section III

1. As we also saw in the previous section, the World Wide Web is just a piece of the Internet. It is probably the most relevant one, but just one of many. The manufacturing of the audience takes place, for the most part, in the World Wide

Web. But we cannot forget that the World Wide Web is an immense and complex communication environment, and that even though we can generically apply to it the traits that we analyzed in the previous chapter (asymmetry, popularization, and commercialization) the truth is that those traits are not applicable in a homogeneous way to the whole web. There are certain areas within the web in which communication is clearly asymmetrical, in which users can be counted by the millions and in which there are obvious commercial interests. But there are also other areas in which those traits are not present and, therefore, in which it is difficult to sustain that the commodity they produce is the audience.

Chapter 5

1. When I talk of 'access platforms' here I am referring to the different technical devices that can be used to gain access to the content available in a communication medium.

2. In fact, one of the first results of Coalition for Advertising Supported Information and Entertainment (CASIE), the organization created by US advertisers and advertising agencies with the goal of turning the Internet into an advertising platform, was the proposal, together with the Internet Advertising Bureau (IAB), of a series of standard formats and definitions aimed at rationalizing and organizing the different forms of online advertising. We will examine this issue in further detail when we analyze the dynamics of the web audience measurement industry in the following section.

3. The first company to apply this model was Procter & Gamble (P&G). In the advertising contract signed in 1996 with Yahoo!, the price paid by P&G depended on the number of times users clicked on the banners inserted in Yahoo!'s pages (Meeker, 1997).

4. For a review of the research on the Internet and the World Wide Web within the field of communication, see Kim and Weaver (2002).

5. In the field of usability studies, Jakob Nielsen's (2000) work is perhaps the most popular and influential.

Chapter 6

1. Webcasts allow the web to function as a platform for the delivery of audiovisual content, that is audio and video files. It is possible that in the near future webcasts will become essential in the study of the web audience (Webb, 2004). In the present work, however, I will not carry out a specific and detailed analysis of their measurement. In fact, the strengths and weaknesses of the analysis of webcasts through the trace left in computers are similar to those of the methods analyzed here in greater detail, and, therefore, the goal of my endeavor will not be undermined by this omission. Regarding the analysis of the log-files generated by specific ISPs, this is based on the information generated by the computers of the ISP clients and collected in proxy servers. It is, therefore, not possible to estimate

the audience of any particular website (since the information comes only from the users of a specific ISP) nor to project the results to a larger universe (since the users of a specific ISP cannot be considered representative of any larger population). In addition, this type of analysis presents problems similar to the ones we will encounter when addressing the other methods analyzed here. The possible availability of demographic information about users does not compensate for these limitations, and, in fact, makes ISP log-files analysis a tool closer to direct-marketing research than to audience measurement and traditional advertising research.

2. The definition of 'website' is not at all obvious, since, due to the flexibility and complexity of the web, a website can in fact take many different forms and configurations.

3. 'Cache busting' techniques prevent the use of cache memory and force the requested pages to be served from the web server, not the hard drive or the proxy server.

4. For general industry guidelines regarding this process, see IAB (2004a, b).

5. For a detailed examination of the impact of 'spiders' and 'robots' in the passive methods measurement process, see IAB/ABCi (2002). In this document, the IAB and ABCi recommend not only the elimination of known 'robots' and 'spiders,' but also the identification of unknown ones through the use of pattern analysis.

6. For a case study in which all five procedures were applied and compared, see ABCi/IAB/MCR (2002).

7. For a detailed analysis of the different procedures and points at which the information used for the measurement of web advertising can be gathered, see Flint (2005), IAB (2004a, b), and PriceWaterhouseCoopers/IAB (2001).

8. In the field of audience measurement, measuring organizations are usually divided into three groups (Méndez & Lamas, 2003):

    a. *Own Service (OS)*: a particular company that carries out the measurement and sells the results to its clients.

    b. *Media Owners Contract (MOC)*: a media organization, or a group of them, carry out the measurement and put the results at the market's disposal with varying degrees of restrictions.

    c. *Joint Industry Committee (JIC)*: a body with representation from all the agents involved in the audience market carries out the measurement.

Chapter 7

1. There are other Internet tools that can be used for conducting surveys, e-mail being the most popular. Therefore, the web is not the only option when it comes to conducting online surveys. My goal here, however, is not to examine the Internet as a research tool, but to study the ways in which its audience is measured. I am not aware of any attempt to measure the Internet audience with online surveys that collect information through tools other than the web. I will focus here on the

use of the web for conducting online surveys to measure the web audience. For a comprehensive analysis of online surveys, see Best and Krueger (2004).

Chapter 8

1. In fact, some of the national panels created during the height of the Internet bubble have later been folded.

2. When these macro-panels are discussed, the name of Alexa is often mentioned. It is interesting to see how popular Alexa has become both in the academic and non-academic world. However, Alexa is not an audience measurement service—even though its global traffic ranking seems to point in that direction. Actually, Alexa does a much better job at collecting surfing patterns of web users than it does at measuring the web audience.

3. Panelists from outside the United States need to have a functional knowledge of English, and they, therefore, do not represent the non-US population. However, ComScore's goal is not so much to study the global audience in itself, but the global audience of American sites, who, it is assumed, will have a functional knowledge of English.

Conclusions to Section III

1. We will discuss this study in more detail in the next chapter when we examine the role of FAST within the web audience measurement industry. I would like to thank professor Kalyanam for sharing with me the results of the study.

2. For a description of the Dutch Webmeter system, see Molenaar et al. (2004).

3. Interestingly, and against many predictions, all of these initiatives are national in nature, rather than international or global.

4. As Gugel et al. (2005: 30) mention, "discussions have now shifted from why the two datasets are different to how one dataset might be used to enhance the other one."

5. Along these lines Gugel et al. (2005: 23) point out that,

> there definitely will be a need for the industry to integrate online ad server metrics with those of web panel measurement services. While a number of attempts have been made to do this in the past, industry participants have often agreed to disagree on precisely how this integration will take place. Although industry practitioners know that the numbers reported are different, they have not been able to agree on how one dataset might be used to enrich the other.

6. As Napoli (2003: 82) explains, "as long as all participants in the transaction treat the data as accurate, the inherent unreliability of the data has no significant effect on the exchange."

Chapter 9

1. These documents will be analyzed below.

2. In September 2005, Nielsen NetRatings initiated its accreditation process with MRC. Up to that moment, only the log-files analysis of CNN's website, carried out by CNN itself, had received MRC accreditation. Over the last year, several measuring services, most of them using passive methods, have been accredited by MRC.

3. The ARF, together with ESOMAR, is also responsible for the organization of the annual conferences on audience measurement (Week of Audience Measurement, WAM) which have served as basic source for the discussion of measurement methods in Section III of this book. These conferences also play a very relevant role in the configuration of the web audience measurement field.

4. Formerly known as the Internet Advertising Bureau.

Chapter 10

1. In fact, Euro-JIC follows the definitions provided by FAST.

2. Information about Euro-JICs can be found at http://www.ejic.org

3. In spite of this consolidation, new competitors have entered this market, such as Interactive Media Services, created in 2003.

4. RedSheriff was bought by Nielsen NetRatings in early 2004.

5. Some European JICs and auditors in charge of press circulation have also started to apply this method in recent years.

6. The resemblance to television audience measurement is also manifest in the expression "searching for the Nielsens of the Internet" (Flynn, 1995). This expression points to an interest in following the television model, with a respected source of measurement that uses the panel methodology, like Nielsen. However, the plural form "Nielsens" also points to the difficulties in finding such a single source of reference.

7. In fact, the best way of understanding the limitations of the different methods used to measure the web audience is by paying attention to what the different measuring organizations say about their rivals' methodologies. In the case of the material from the ARF/ESOMAR conferences analyzed in the previous section, the criticism of the different methods usually comes from organizations that use alternative methods: those who use passive methods criticize those who use active or mixed methods, and so on. In the case of the material from periodicals analyzed in this chapter, the criticism usually takes place among organizations that use the same method and compete in the same market—NetRatings criticizes Media Metrix, ComScore criticizes NetRatings, etc.

8. As Buzzard (2003) points out, Nielsen has followed the 'fast second' strategy, which has been rather successful in giving the company the lead in the field of electronic panels.

9. Currently, there are two main methods for inferring non-probabilistic Internet samples to general populations. One is "post-stratification weighting," which "attempts to obtain more accurate population estimates by weighting respondents by the incidence of known characteristics in the target population" (Best & Krueger, 2004: 18). The other is "propensity scoring," an approach that "estimates the likelihood of each participant being in a sample based on a set of covariates that would predict such recruitments and then weights the responses for each individual by their score" (Best & Krueger, 2004: 19).

10. Interestingly, the evolution of the web audience industry in recent years seems to point very clearly to the creation of national measurement operations, as opposed to the global ones that the medium seemed to demand and that were in full development at the turn of the century.

Conclusions

1. See *A Declaration of the Independence of Cyberspace* (Barlow, 1996), one of the most famous and interesting manifestations of that rhetoric.

2. Napoli (2003: 169) seems to share this opinion:

> Given the extent to which privacy concerns are becoming an increasingly prominent aspect of the new media environment, it seems unlikely that media-based systems of audience measurement ever will be able to replace completely the existing audience-based audience measurement systems.

3. In fact, developments such as the combination of methods and the use of data integration techniques seem to point in this direction.

4. In this sense, Napoli (2003: 13) speculates that:

> in the future alternative business models are likely to replace the traditional approach of inserting discrete advertising messages in media content and charging advertisers on the basis of presumed levels of audience exposure. Among the alternatives likely to become increasingly prominent are pricing structures based upon consumer behavior rather than exposure; business models that focus more aggressively on gathering and marketing the personal information of media consumers; and business models that increasingly rely upon audiences, not advertisers, to pay for media content.

5. It seems that the impact of audience measurement on the perception of the medium is often weaker among online users—who can experience its peculiarities, its richness, and its complexity—than among academics who study it. For example, Webster and Lin (2002) propose to think of the web as a mass medium, and they base their vision on an analysis of the results of the measurement carried out by Nielsen NetRatings. They show how most of the audience is concentrated on a small number of sites, but the truth is that the data they use refers only to two hundred websites. And even though they are aware of the fact that the web is made up of millions of sites, and that most of them do not show up in the

measurement conducted through panels, the measurement leads them to depict the web as if it were another mass medium. This example helps us understand the power measurement can have to influence our perception of a medium, and to lead us to forget those facets of the medium that are not present in the measurement results.

References

Abbate, J. (1999). *Inventing the Internet*. Cambridge, London: MIT Press.

ABCi (1998). *White Paper: How Interactive Ads Are Delivered and Measurement Implication*. Retrieved October 20, 2005, from http://www.abcinteractive audits.com/news/white_paper_2332.htm

ABCi/IAB/MCR (2002). *Comparative Analysis of Varying Methods of Computing Unique User Counts from Server Log Files*. Retrieved October 20, 2005, from http://www.abcinteractiveaudits.com/news/ABCi_Unique_User_041202.pdf

Adler, R. (1997). *The Future of Advertising: New Approaches to the Attention Economy*. Washington, DC: The Aspen Institute.

Aguado, G. (1996). *OJD y el Control de la Difusión de Prensa en España*. Barcelona: Ariel.

Agulló, J. (2000). Datos para el Medio Internet. In AEDEMO (Ed.), *7º Seminario de Medios* (pp. 27–41). Valencia: AEDEMO.

AIMC (2003). *Navegantes en la Red. Quinta Encuesta AIMC a Usuarios de Internet*. Retrieved March 24, 2003, from http://www.aimc.es/aimc.php

Allor, M. (1988). Relocating the Site of the Audience. *Critical Studies in Mass Communication, 5*, 217–233.

Almirón, N. (2001). *De Vannebar Bush a la WWW*. Barcelona: Edicions Tresiquatre.

Álvarez, P., & González-Quijano, J. E. (1998). Internet: Nuevos Medios, Nuevas Formas de Publicidad. In AEDEMO (Ed.), *6º Seminario sobre Audiencia de Medios* (pp. 403–420). Santander: AEDEMO.

Ang, I. (1991). *Desperately Seeking the Audience*. London: Routledge.

ARF (2001). *An ARF Methodological Review of ComScore Networks, Inc. NetScore*. Accessed February 21, 2003, at http://www.comscore.com/method/ arf_cs_review11502.pdf

——— (2003). *ARF Guidelines for Data Integration*. Accessed September 1, 2005, at http://www.thearf.org/downloads/DataIntegrationGuidelines.pdf

Armstrong, S. (2002). *Advertising on the Internet. How to Get Your Message Across on the World Wide Web*. London: Kogan Page.

Ballestero, F. (2002). *La Brecha Digital. El Riesgo de Exclusión en la Sociedad de la Información*. Madrid: Biblioteca Fundación Retevisión.

Barlow, J. P. (1996). *A Declaration of the Independence of Cyberspace*. Retrieved November 14, 2002, from http://www.eff.org/~barlow/Declaration-Final.html

Barnouw, E. (1967). *A Tower in Babel. A History of Broadcasting in the United States to 1933*. Oxford: Oxford University Press.

Beniger, J. (1986). *The Control Revolution. Technological and Economic Origins of the Information Society.* Cambridge: Harvard University Press.

Bennett, R. P., Hanson, S. J., Guenther, S. A., & Stone, M. (2002). Computing Unique User Counts from Server Log Files. Comparative Analysis of Varying Methods. In ESOMAR/ARF (Ed.), *WAM—Week of Audience Measurement—Online* (pp. 9–26). Cannes: ESOMAR.

Berners-Lee, T. (1999). *Weaving the Web: The Past, Present and Future of the World Wide Web by Its Inventor.* London: Orion Business Books.

Bertot, J. C., McClure, C. R., Moen, W. E., & Rubin, J. (1997). Web Usage Statistics: Measurement Issues and Analytical Techniques. *Government Information Quarterly, 14*(4), 373–395.

Best, S. J., & Krueger, B. S. (2004). *Internet Data Collection.* Thousand Oaks: Sage.

Beville, H. M. (1988). *Audience Ratings: Radio, Television, and Cable.* Hillsdale: Lawrence Erlbaum Associates.

Bhatia, M. (2004, 29th March). NetRatings Defends Its Research Methodology. *Advertising Age,* 22.

Blanch, M. (1999). *Cómo se Miden las Audiencias en Radio.* Barcelona: Editorial CIMS.

Bogart, L. (1988). Research As an Instrument of Power. *Gannett Center Journal,* 2(3), 2–16.

Burton, M. C., & Walther, J. B. (2001). The Value of Web Log Data in Use-Based Design and Testing. *Journal of Computer-Mediated Communication, 6*(3). Available at http://www.ascusc.org/jcmc/vol6/issue3/burton.html

Buzzard, K. (1990). *Chains of Gold: Marketing the Ratings and Rating the Markets.* Metuchen, NJ: The Scarecrow Press, Inc.

——— (2002). The People Meter Wars: A Case Study of Technological Innovation and Diffusion in the Ratings Industry. *Journal of Media Economics, 15*(4), 273–291.

——— (2003). Internet Ratings: Defining a New Medium by the Old, Measuring Internet Audiences. In A. Everett, & J. T. Caldwell (Eds.), *New Media: Theories and Practices of Digitextuality* (pp. 197–208). New York: Routledge.

Callejo, J. (2001). *Investigar las Audiencias. Un Análisis Cualitativo.* Barcelona: Paidós.

——— (2003). Audiencias Activas o Audiencias Cautivas. In J. J. Igartua, & Á. Badillo (Eds.), *Audiencias y Medios de Comunicación* (pp. 15–42). Salamanca: Ediciones Universidad de Salamanca.

Callius, P., Lithner, A., & Svanfeldt, S. (2005). Changing the Internet Audience Measurement Standard. In ESOMAR/ARF (Ed.), *WAM—Week of Audience Measurement—Online* (pp. 135–154). Montreal: ESOMAR.

Campbell, J. E., & Carlson, M. (2002). Panopticon.com: Online Surveillance and the Commodification of Privacy. *Journal of Broadcasting and Electronic Media, 46*(4), 586–606.

Carey, J. W. (1998). The Internet and the End of the National Communication System: Uncertain Predictions of an Uncertain Future. *Journalism and Mass Communication Quarterly, 75*(1), 28–34.

CASIE (1995). *Guiding Principles of Interactive Media Audience Measurement*. Retrieved March 20, 2002, from http://www.ciadvertising.org/studies/ student/96_fall/burnett/guide.html

Cassidy, J. (2003). *Dot.Con. The Real Story of Why the Internet Bubble Burst*. London: Penguin.

Castells, M. (2001). *Internet Galaxy: Reflections on the Internet, Business and Society*. Oxford: Oxford University Press.

Chaffee, S. H. (2000). George Gallup and Ralph Nafziger: Pioneers of Audience Research. *Mass Communication and Society, 2*(2&3), 317–327.

Clark, J. (2000). *Netscape Time. The Making of the Billion-Dollar Start-Up that Took on Microsoft*. New York: St. Martin's Griffin.

Clarke, D. (2000). The Active Pursuit of Active Viewers: Directions in Audience Research. *Canadian Journal of Communication, 25*, 39–59.

Cleland, K. (1995, 19th June). Hotwired Gets Gold Star from Nielsen. *Advertising Age*, 24.

——— (1998, 3rd August). Marketers Want Solid Data on Value of Internet Ad Buys: Demand Swells for Information that Compares Media Options. *Advertising Age*, S18.

Clemente, P. (1998). *The State of the Net. The New Frontier*. New York: McGraw-Hill.

Coffey, S. (2001). Internet Audience Measurement: A Practitioner's View. *Journal of Interactive Advertising, 1*(2). Available at http://jiad.org/vol1/no2/ coffey/index.html

Coffey, S., & Mazumdar, M. (2002). The Reach and Frequency Approach to Advertising Planning on the Internet. In ESOMAR/ARF (Ed.), *WAM—Week of Audience Measurement—Online* (pp. 141–153). Cannes: ESOMAR.

Collins, J. H., & Bhatia, M. (2001). Integrating Internet Site Audience Measurement into Media Planning and Buying. A Unified Method for Reach/Frequency. In ESOMAR/ARF (Ed.), *Worldwide Online Measurement Conference* (pp. 21–44). Athens: ESOMAR.

Cormier, L.-A., & Haering, H. (2003). The Quest for an Internet Currency. In ESOMAR/ARF (Ed.), *WAM—Worldwide Audience Measurement—Online and Out of Home/Ambient Media* (pp. 185–205). Los Angeles: ESOMAR.

Curran, J., & Seaton, J. (1997). *Power without Responsibility*. London: Routledge.

Cusumano, M., & Yoffie, D. (1998). *Competing on Internet Time. Lessons from Netscape and its Battle with Microsoft*. New York: Touchstone.

Davenport, T. H., & Beck, J. C. (2001). *The Attention Economy: Understanding the New Currency of Business*. Boston: Harvard Business School Press.

Dayan, D. (2001). The Peculiar Public of Television. *Media, Culture and Society, 23*(6), 743–765.

Demers, E., & Lev, B. (2001). A Rude Awakening: Internet Shakeout in 2000. *Review of Accounting Studies, 3*, 334–359.

Donaton, S. (1996, 4th November). Standards Required to Make Next Leap. *Advertising Age*, S30.

Donaton, S., & Sloan, P. (1995, 13th March). Control New Media. Artzt Spurs

Advertisers to Seek Greater Role in Programming. *Advertising Age*, 1.

Downes, D. M. (2000). The Medium Vanishes? The Resurrection of the Mass Audience in the New Media Economy. *M/C: A Journal of Media and Culture, 3*(1). Available at http://www.media-culture.org.au/0003/mass.html

Ejdys, P., Cisek, T., & Modzelewski, C. (2003). Real Profile: A New Approach to Online Media Planning. In ESOMAR/ARF (Ed.), *WAM—Worldwide Audience Measurement—Online and Out of Home/Ambient Media* (pp. 73–89). Los Angeles: ESOMAR.

Elliot, S. (1995, 3rd October). A Report Lies Down Guidelines for Any Attempt to Measure the Efficiency of Interactive Ads. The *New York Times*, 11.

———— (1997, 5th November). Internet Profiles to Acquire Rival. The *New York Times*, 11.

Elsworth, P. (1997, 24th February). Internet Advertising Growing Slowly. The *New York Times*, 5.

eTForecasts (2002). *World Wide PC Forecast 1990–2007*. Retrieved August 1, 2003, from http://www.etforecasts.com/products/ES_pcww.htm#1.0

Ettema, J. S., & Whitney, C. (1994). The Money Arrow: An Introduction to Audiencemaking. In J. S. Ettema, & C. Whitney (Eds.), *Audiencemaking: How the Media Create the Audience* (pp. 1–18). Thousand Oaks: Sage.

FAST/ARF (2000). *Principles of Online Media Audience Measurement*. Retrieved February 12, 2002, from http://www.fastinfo.org/measuremet/pages/index.cgi/audiencemeasurement

FitzGerald, J. (2002). Site-Centric Measurement. Can Traditional Panels Meet the New Standard? In ESOMAR/ARF (Ed.), *WAM—Week of Audience Measurement—Online* (pp. 43–56). Cannes: ESOMAR.

Fitzgerald, K. (2004, 15th March). Debate Grows Over Net Data: NetRatings, ComScore Numbers Diverge. *Advertising Age*, 4.

Fleishman, G. (1996). Web Logs Analysis: Who's Doing What, When? *Web Developer Magazine, 2*(2). Available at http://www.webdeveloper.com/management/management_log_analysis.html

Flint, A. (2005). Reducing Ad Server Discrepancies. Effective Global Standards for Local Markets. In ESOMAR/ARF (Ed.), *WAM—Week of Audience Measurement—Online* (pp. 49–70). Montreal: ESOMAR.

Flynn, L. (1995, 29th May). In Search of Nielsens for the Internet. The *New York Times*, 37.

Foan, R. (2001). Certainty in a Virtual World—Dream or Reality? The Drive for Global Accountability for the Web. In ESOMAR/ARF (Ed.), *World Wide Online Measurement Conference* (pp. 121–134). Athens: ESOMAR.

Fulgoni, G. M. (2003). Measuring Consumers' Internet Behavior. Unique Challenges Require New Solutions. In ESOMAR/ARF (Ed.), *WAM—Worldwide Audience Measurement—Online and Out of Home/Ambient Media* (pp. 47–72). Los Angeles: ESOMAR.

Fundación Auna (2002). *eEspaña 2002. Informe Anual sobre el Desarrollo de la Sociedad de la Información en España*. Madrid: Fundación Auna.

Gandy, O. H. (1990). Tracking the Audience. In J. Downing et al. (Eds.), *Questioning the Media* (pp. 166–179). Newbury Park, CA: Sage.

——— (1993). *The Panoptic Sort: A Political Economy of Personal Information.* Boulder: Westview Press.

Gillies, J., & Cailliau, R. (2000). *How the Web Was Born.* Oxford: Oxford University Press.

Goosey, R. W. (2003). Defining the Gold Standard for User Centric Global Online Audience Measurement. Developing Global Standards for Online Audience Measurement. In ESOMAR/ARF (Ed.), *WAM—Worldwide Audience Measurement—Online and Out of Home/Ambient Media* (pp. 141–170). Los Angeles: ESOMAR.

——— (2005). Advanced Techniques in Panel and Server Data. In ESOMAR/ARF (Ed.), *WAM—Week of Audience Measurement—Online* (pp. 33–48). Montreal: ESOMAR.

Gralla, P. (2004). *How the Internet Works* (7th Edition). Indianapolis: Que.

Green, L. (2001). Treating Internet Users as Audiences: Suggesting Some Research Directions. *Australian Journal of Communication, 28*(1), 23–32.

Greenstein, S. (2000). Commercialization of the Internet: The Interaction of Public Policy and Private Choices or Why Introducing the Market Worked So Well. *NBER Innovation Policy and the Economy, 1,* 151–186.

Guerrero, C. (2002). *Los Medios y sus Audiencias.* Sevilla: Mergablum Edición y Comunicación.

Gugel, C., Koegel, K., & Bruner, R. E. (2005). From Server to Panel. Data Integration via Frequency of Exposure. In ESOMAR/ARF (Ed.), *WAM— Worldwide Audience Measurement—Online and Out of Home/Ambient Media* (pp. 21–32). Montreal: ESOMAR.

Habermas, J. (1984). *The Theory of Communicative Action.* Boston: Beacon Press.

Haering, H. (2002). Monitoring Internet Audience Measurement Panels. Methodological Issues and Market Trends. In ESOMAR/ARF (Ed.), *WAM—Week of Audience Measurement—Online* (pp. 27–41). Cannes: ESOMAR.

Hafner, K., & Lyon, M. (1998). *Where Wizards Stay Up Late. The Origins of the Internet.* New York: Touchstone.

Hand, J. R. M. (2001). The Role of Book Income, Web Traffic, and Supply and Demand in the Pricing of US Internet Stocks. *European Financial Review, 5,* 295–317.

Hansell, S. (1998, 11th May). How New Media Are Racing to Become the Mass Media. The *New York Times*, 1.

——— (2002a, 27th May). As Jupiter Crumbles, Its Pieces May Help Build a New Order of Web Researchers. The *New York Times*, 7.

——— (2002b, 20th February). Internet Concerns Drop Plans to Merge on FTC's Opposition. The *New York Times*, 14.

Haylock, C. (2003). *Using Web Statistics.* Retrieved August 15, 2003, from http://www.hopkinsmedicine.org/ccp/conf2003/CamilleHaylock.pdf

Herman, E. S., & McChesney, R. W. (1997). *The Global Media.* London: Cassell.

Himanen, P. (2001). *The Hacker Ethic and the Spirit of the Information Age.* New

York: Random House.

Hine, C. (2001). Web Pages, Authors and Audiences. The Meaning of a Mouse Click. *Information, Communication and Society, 4*(2), 182–198.

Hoffman, D. L., & Novak, T. P. (2000). Advertising Pricing Models for the World Wide Web. In D. Hurley, B. Kahin, & H. Varian (Eds.), *Internet Publishing and Beyond: The Economics of Digital Information and Intellectual Property.* Cambridge: MIT Press.

Hong, J., & Leckenby, J. (1996). *Audience Measurement and Media Reach/Frequency Issues in Internet Advertising.* Retrieved August 2, 2003, from http://www.ciadvertising.org/studies/reports/measurement/AaapaperOptimize.pdf

Huertas, A. (1998). *Cómo se Miden las Audiencias en Televisión.* Barcelona: Editorial CIMS.

———— (2002). *La Audiencia Investigada.* Barcelona: Gedisa.

IAB (2002). *Interactive Audience Measurement and Advertising Campaign Reporting and Audit Guidelines.* Retrieved December 28, 2002, from http://www.iab.net/standards/measure_guide.pdf

———— (2004a). *Interactive Audience Measurement and Advertising Campaign Reporting and Audit Guidelines. Version 6.0.b United States Version.* Retrieved October 20, 2005, from http://www.iab.net/standards/pdf/2292%20IAB%20spreads.pdf

———— (2004b). *Interactive Audience Measurement and Advertising Campaign Reporting and Audit Guidelines. Version 6.0.b Global Version.* Retrieved October 20, 2005, from http://www.iab.net/standards/pdf/2292%20IAB%20global%20live.pdf

IAB/ABCi (2002). *Comparative Analysis of Varying Methods of Unique User Counts from Server Log Files.* Retrieved October 20, 2005, from http://www.abcinteractiveaudits.com/news/case040202.pdf

IFABC (1997). *IFABC Approves Global Reporting and Measurement Standards for Web Auditing.* Accessed May 23, 2002, at http://www.ifabc.org/news/news060997.html

I/PRO (2002). *A Standard for Auditing Web Site Traffic.* Accessed November 27, 2002, at http://www.ipro.com/downloads/ipro/ipro_audit_standard.pdf

Ivie, G., & Terlizzi, N. (2001). The MRC Minimum Standards. The US Case for Applying Consistent Auditing Standards Across Different Types of Media. In ESOMAR/ARF (Ed.), *Worldwide Online Measurement Conference* (pp. 135–143). Athens: ESOMAR.

Jauset, J. (2000). *La Investigación de Audiencias en Televisión: Fundamentos Estadísticos.* Barcelona: Paidós.

Jensen, K. B., & Rosengren, K. E. (1990). Five Traditions in Search of the Audience. *European Journal of Communication, 5,* 207–238.

Jhally, S., & Livant, B. (1986). Watching as Working: The Valorization of Audience Consciousness. *Journal of Communication, 36*(3), 124–143.

Jiménez-Blanco, D. (2003). Reflexiones sobre el papel de los mercados financieros. El desarrollo de las telecomunicaciones. *Telos (54).* Available at http://www.campusred.net/telos/home.asp?idRevistaAnt=54

Jones, S. (Ed.) (1995). *CyberSociety: Computer-Mediated Communication and Community.* Thousand Oaks: Sage.

———— (Ed.) (1998). *CyberSociety 2.0: Revisiting Computer-Mediated Communication and Community.* Thousand Oaks: Sage.

Kahn, R. E. (1994). The Role of Government in the Evolution of the Internet. *Communications of the ACM, 37*(8), 15–19.

Kalathil, S., & Boas, T. C. (2003). *Open Networks, Closed Regimes. The Impact of the Internet on Authoritarian Rule.* Washington, DC: Carnegie Endowment for International Peace.

Katz, E., Blumler, J., & Gurevitch, M. (1974). Utilization of Mass Communication by the Individual. In J. Blumler & E. Katz (Eds.), *The Use of Mass Communication* (pp. 19–32). London: Sage.

Kelly, J. (2001). *A Brief History of Spam.* Retrieved February 12, 2003, from http://www-106.ibm.com/developerworks/linux/library/l-spam/l-spam.html

Kelly, K. (1995, 17th July). MPA Joins Web Measurement Fray: Publishers Calling for Single Standard to Track Online Usage. *Advertising Age,* 13.

Kim, S. T., & Weaver, D. (2002). Communication Research about the Internet: A Thematic Meta-Analysis. *New Media and Society, 4*(4), 518–538.

Lamas, C. (1997). Las Encuestas en la Web. In AEDEMO (Ed.), *1er Seminario sobre el Impacto de las Nuevas Tecnologías en la Investigación, el Marketing y la Comunicación* (pp. 253–287). Gandía: AEDEMO.

———— (2000). Internet y el Reto de su Cuantificación. *Revista Fuentes Estadísticas (46).* Available at http://www.ine.es/fuentes/numero46/paginas/indice.htm

———— (2001). El Uso de la Tecnología en la Medición de las Audiencias. In AEDEMO (Ed.), *III Seminario sobre el Impacto de las Nuevas Tecnologías en la Investigación, el Marketing y la Comunicación* (pp. 7–30). Santiago de Compostela: AEDEMO.

———— (2002). La Investigación de Internet. *Telos (52).* Available at http://www.campusred.net/telos/home.asp?idRevistaAnt=52

Lanham, R. A. (1993). *The Electronic Word. Democracy, Technology and the Arts.* Chicago: The University of Chicago Press.

Lavilla, M. (2002). *La Actividad Publicitaria en Internet.* Madrid: Ra-Ma.

Lawrence, S. (2000, 14th February). Europe: Measuring Up. *The Industry Standard.*

Lessig, L. (2000). *Code and Other Laws of Cyberspace.* New York: Basic Books.

Licklider, J. C. R. (1960). Man–Computer Symbiosis. *IRE Transactions on Human Factors in Electronics, HFE-1,* 4–11. Available at http://memex.org/licklider.pdf

Licklider, J. C. R., & Taylor, R.W. (1968). The Computer as Communications Device. *Science and Technology, April,* 21–31. Available at http://memex.org/licklider.pdf

Livant, B. (1979). The Audience Commodity: On the 'Blindspot' Debate. *Canadian Journal of Political and Social Theory, 3*(1), 91–106.

Livingstone, S. (2003). The Changing Nature of Audiences: From the Mass Audience to the Interactive Media User. In A. N. Valdivia (Ed.), *A Companion to Media*

Studies (pp. 337–359). Malden: Blackwell Publisher.

Long, B., & Baecker, R. (1997). A Taxonomy of Internet Communication Tools. *Proceedings of WebNet 97*, AACE. Available at http://kmdi.utoronto.ca/rmb/papers/p20.pdf

Maddox, K. (1997, 3rd November). Web Counting Field Crowds Up with New Player: NetRatings Uses Profiling System to Track Users. *Advertising Age*, 56.

———— (1998a, 13th July). Stop Data Spin Doctors With Standardized Traffic Counts: DoubleClick Example Proves Need for Scrutiny. *Advertising Age*, 29.

———— (1998b, 19th October). Web Rivals' Plan to Merge Draws Cheers Media Metrix to Standardize Methodology. *Advertising Age*, 48.

———— (1999, 3rd May). P&G Interactive Marketer of the Year. *Advertising Age*, S1.

Maddox, K., & Riedman, P. (1997, 8th September). Research Firms Respond to Need for More Data. *Advertising Age*, 34.

Madinaveitia, E., & Agulló, J. (1998). Medios Digitales y Publicidad Interactiva ¿Qué Vamos a Medir? In AEDEMO (Ed.), *6º Seminario sobre Audiencia de Medios* (pp. 285–309). Santander: AEDEMO.

Maisel, R. (1973). The Decline of Mass Media. *Public Opinion Quarterly, 37*(2), 159–170.

Marx, W. (1996, 26th February). Light Years Ahead but Still Confusing, Web Measurement Takes Big Steps Forward. *Advertising Age*, S8.

Mattelart, A. (2000). *La Publicidad*. Barcelona: Paidós.

Mattelart, A., & Mattelart, M. (1995). Los Medios: ¿Hacia la Soberanía del Consumidor? In B. Díaz Nosty (Ed.), *Comunicación Social 1995/Tendencias* (pp. 207–214). Madrid: Fundesco.

McChesney, R. W. (1996). The Internet and US Communication Policy-Making in Historical and Critical Perspective. *Journal of Communication, 46*(1), 98–124.

———— (2000). So Much for the Magic of Technology and the Free Market. In A. Herman, & T. Swiss (Eds.), *The World Wide Web and Contemporary Cultural Theory* (pp. 5–35). London: Routledge.

McDunn, R. A. (2001). *Web Server Log File Analysis—Basics*. Retrieved April 15, 2002, from http://www-group.slac.stanford.edu/techpubs/logfiles/intro.html

McQuail, D. (1997). *Audience Analysis*. Thousand Oaks: Sage.

———— (2000). *McQuail's Mass Communication Theory*. London: Sage.

Mcchan, E. R. (1984). Ratings and the Institutional Approach: A Third Answer to the Commodity Question. *Critical Studies in Mass Communication, 1*(2), 216–225.

Meeker, M. (1997). *The Internet Advertising Report*. New York: Harper Collins.

Méndez, J. L., & Lamas, C. (2003). La Investigación de Audiencia de Medios Impresos. In J. J. Igartua, & Á. Badillo (Eds.), *Audiencias y Medios de Comunicación* (pp. 67–83). Salamanca: Ediciones de la Universidad de Salamanca.

Miller, P. (1994). Made-to-Order and Standardized Audiences: Forms of Reality in Audience Measurement. In J. Ettema & C. Whitney (Eds.), *Audiencemaking: How the Media Create the Audience*. Thousand Oaks: Sage.

Molenaar, R., Verhulst, E., & Appel, M. (2004). Webmeter. Internet Audience

Measurement for Media Planning. In ESOMAR/ARF (Ed.), *WAM—Week of Audience Measurement—Online* (pp. 9–20). Geneva: ESOMAR.

Morgan-Stanley (1996). *The Internet Report*. Retrieved May 2, 2003, from http://www.morganstanley.com/institutional/techresearch/pdfs/inet02.pdf

Morley, D. (1993). Active Audience Theory: Pendulums and Pitfalls. *Journal of Communication, 43*(4), 13–20.

Morris, M., & Ogan, C. (1996). The Internet as Mass Medium. *Journal of Communication, 46*(1), 39–50.

Mosco, V., & Kaye, L. (2000). Questioning the Concept of the Audience. In I. Hagen & J. Wasko (Eds.), *Consuming Audiences? Production and Reception in Media Research* (pp. 31–46). Cresskill: Hampton Press.

Napoli, P. M. (2003). *Audience Economics. Media Institutions and the Audience Marketplace*. New York: Columbia University Press.

Naughton, J. (2000). *A Brief History of the Future. The Origins of the Internet.* London: Phoenix.

Neuendorf, K. (2001). Viewing Alone? Recent Considerations of Media Audience Studies. *Journal of Broadcasting and Electronic Media, 45*(2), 345–354.

Neuman, W. R. (1991). *The Future of the Mass Audience*. Cambridge: Cambridge University Press.

Nielsen, J. (2000). *Designing Web Usability: The Practice of Simplicity.* Indianapolis: New Riders.

Noller, S., Pischke, O., & Sanhöfer, J. (2005). From Server to Panel. Data Integration via Frequency of Exposure. In ESOMAR/ARF (Ed.), *WAM—Worldwide Audience Measurement—Online and Out of Home/Ambient Media* (pp. 9–19). Montreal: ESOMAR.

O'Connell, F. (2002). User-Centric Internet Measurement and Its Role in Media Planning. In ESOMAR/ARF (Ed.), *WAM—Week of Audience Measurement—Online* (pp. 57–64). Cannes: ESOMAR.

Parker, P. (2001). *Jupiter Media Metrix Changes Its Tune on Pop-Ups*. Retrieved March 12, 2002, from http://www.internetnews.com/IAR/article.php/945671

Pérez Ruiz, M. A. (2002). Hacia un Nuevo Orden en el Estudio de las Audiencias: La Renovación de la Investigación de los Medios Publicitarios. *Telos (53)*. Available at http://www.campusred.net/telos/home.asp?idRevistaAnt=53

Perkins, A. B., & Perkins, M. C. (1999). *The Internet Bubble*. New York: Harper Business.

Porter, T. M. (1986). *The Rise of Statistical Thinking*. Princeton: Princeton University Press.

Power, P., Kubey, R., & Kiousis, S. (2002). Audience Activity and Passivity: An Historical Taxonomy. *Communication Yearbook, 26*, 116–159.

PriceWaterhouseCoopers/IAB (2001). *Online Ad Measurement Study*. Retrieved January 23, 2003, from http://www.iab.net/standards/pwc_report.pdf

Radway, J. (1988). Reception Study: Ethnography and the Problems of Dispersed Audiences and Nomadic Subjects. *Cultural Studies, 2*(3), 359–376.

Rajgopal, S., Kotha, S., & Venkatachalam, M. (2000). *The Relevance of Web Traffic for Internet Stock Prices.* Retrieved February 18, 2003, from http://gobi.stanford.edu/ResearchPapers/Library/rp1616.pdf

Rheingold, H. (1985). *Tools for Thought: The History and Future of Mind-Expanding Technology.* New York: Simon & Schuster.

———— (1993). *Virtual Community: Homesteading on the Electronic Frontier.* New York: Harper.

Riedman, P. (2002, 1st July). ComScore Takes on NetRatings. *Advertising Age,* 8.

Roscoe, T. (1999). The Construction of the World Wide Web Audience. *Media, Culture and Society, 21,* 673–684.

Ruddock, A. (2001). *Understanding Audiences: Theory and Method.* London: Sage.

Salgado, C. (1997). La Medición de Audiencia en Internet. In AEDEMO (Ed.), *1er Seminario sobre el Impacto de las Nuevas Tecnologías en la Investigación, el Marketing y la Comunicación* (pp. 165–187). Gandía: AEDEMO.

Schramm, W., & Roberts, D. F. (Eds.) (1971). *The Process and Effects of Mass Communication.* Urbana: University of Illinois Press.

Schudson, M. (1978). The Ideal of Conversation in the Study of Mass Media. *Communication Research, 5*(3), 320–329.

Shaw, S. (2003). Developing Unified Key Performance Indicators Based on the Integration of Site-Centric and Panel-Centric Online Data. In ESOMAR/ARF (Ed.), *WAM—Worldwide Audience Measurement—Online and Out of Home/Ambient Media* (pp. 111–138). Los Angeles: ESOMAR.

Smart, B. (2002). *Michel Foucault.* London: Routledge.

Smulyan, S. (1994). *Selling Radio: The Commercialization of American Broadcasting 1920–1934.* Washington, DC: Smithsonian Institution Press.

Smythe, D. W. (1977). Communications: Blindspot of Western Marxism. *Canadian Journal of Political and Social Theory, 1*(3), 1–27.

Terhanian, G., Smith, R., Bremer, J., & Thomas, R. K. (2001). Exploiting Analytical Advances. Minimizing the Biases Associated with Internet-Based Surveys of Non-random Samples. In ESOMAR/ARF (Ed.), *Worldwide Online Measurement Conference* (pp. 247–272). Athens: ESOMAR.

Thompson, J. B. (1995). *The Media and Modernity: A Social Theory of the Media.* Stanford: Stanford University Press.

Thompson, M. J. (2001, 28th March). Media Metrix Sues to Squash Rivals. *The Industry Standard.*

Thomson, J. (2000). *Privatization of the New Communication Channel: Computer Networks and the Internet.* Retrieved April 20, 2002, from http://www.sit.wisc.edu/%7Ejcthomsonjr/j561/

Trueman, B., Wong, F., & Zhang, X.-J. (2000). *The Eyeballs Have It: Searching for the Value of Internet Stocks.* Retrieved February 18, 2003, from http://faculty.haas.berkeley.edu/trueman/valuation59.pdf

Turow, J. (1997). *Breaking Up America. Advertisers and the New Media World.* Chicago: University of Chicago Press.

Webb, R. (2004). Online Measurement. Making Sense of Streaming Media. In ESOMAR/ARF (Ed.), *WAM—Week of Audience Measurement—Online* (pp. 43–

8). Geneva: ESOMAR.

Webb, R., Long, M., & Caldwell, J. (2003). A New Paradigm in Interactive Audience Measurement. In ESOMAR/ARF (Ed.), *WAM—Worldwide Audience Measurement—Online and Out of Home/Ambient Media* (pp. 91–110). Los Angeles: ESOMAR.

Webster, J. (1998). The Audience. *Journal of Broadcasting and Electronic Media, 42*(2), 190–207.

Webster, J. G., & Lin, S.-F. (2002). The Internet Audience: Web Use As Mass Behavior. *Journal of Broadcasting and Electronic Media, 46*(1), 1–12.

Webster, J. G., Phalen, P. F., & Lichty, L. W. (2000). *Ratings Analysis: The Theory and Practice of Audience Research*. Mahwah: Lawrence Earlbaum Associates.

Wentz, L. (1999, 7th June). P&G Effort to Set Online Ad Policies Moves to Europe. *Advertising Age*, 49.

Williams, R. (1992). *Television: Technology and Cultural Form*. Hanover: Wesleyan University Press.

Williamson, D. A. (1995, 8th May). This Modem Moves at High Speed. *Advertising Age*, 17.

——— (1996, 9th December). Groups Set to Unveil Web Ad Guidelines. *Advertising Age*, 1.

——— 1997, 16th June). Site Comparability Top Priority in IAB Guidelines. *Advertising Age*, 48.

Wimmer, R. D., & Dominick, J. R. (1987). *Mass Media Research: An Introduction*. Belmont: Wadsworth Publishing Company.

Zakon, R. (2005). *Hobbes' Internet Timeline v8.1*. Retrieved November 15, 2005, from http://www.zakon.org/robert/internet/timeline/

Zárraga, J. L. d. (1997). Investigación y Marketing en Internet. In AEDEMO (Ed.), *1er Seminario sobre el Impacto de las Nuevas Tecnologías en la Investigación, el Marketing y la Comunicación* (pp. 147–163). Gandía: AEDEMO.

O

P

R

X

Y

V

W